The Memoirs
of
Takashi Oka

Copyright © 2020 by Takashi Oka

All rights reserved.
Not for re-sale.

All articles from *The Christian Science Monitor* and *The New York Times* are reprinted here with permission.

Book design by Ben Williams

ISBN 978-0-578-76152-7
Library of Congress Number: TXu002218028

A Note on the Text

I first met Takashi Oka in 2013, shortly before he turned 89. He and his wife, Hiro, had just moved from Washington D.C. to New York City to be closer to their daughter, Mimi, and her family, and I helped them assemble some furniture and hang paintings in their new apartment. Takashi had a new iMac with a Bluetooth keyboard on which he typed easily and steadily, hunt-and-peck style, as if it were an old Remington. I knew that he was interested in writing a memoir, and I agreed to help. I soon discovered bits and pieces of texts that he had started and abandoned and then re-started somewhere else, many of which focused on the trauma of his experience in World War II. Takashi was bright and talkative and deeply knowledgeable about so many worlds, ancient and modern. But I also knew that memory was an issue.

Through the generosity of The Mary Baker Eddy Library, I was given access to the archives of *The Christian Science Monitor* and the articles he had written while employed there, which numbered over 3,000. I also had access to his writings for *The New York Times*. Using these resources, I could track his locations and dates, while giving myself a crash course in world history. As we talked about his past, his eyes would light up at various memories – visits to Hawaii as a young child, the portraits on the walls of his grandparents' house in Tokyo, the student riots in Paris in 1968 – and he would describe in precise detail experiences that, for whatever reason, he couldn't set to paper.

So we created a system: I would visit him two or three times a week, with a series of his old articles at the ready, and we would discuss whatever was on his mind. I would record the conversations on my iPhone and later transcribe the parts that pertained to the memoir. As I read the articles aloud to him, I noticed that several had an interestingly self-aware voice, as if he were not just a neutral observer-journalist, but also pre-emptively thinking about the act of composing a memoir. So the process evolved to place Takashi in conversation with his younger self. He and I then worked together to create a rough draft of a document, which he copyedited – a skill that, after a 60-year career, had remained hardwired within him. Hiro, Mimi, and Saya helped considerably with the task of filtering out elements that we couldn't independently verify.

The result is this text – a document that spans across family histories, collective memories, hard-nosed journalism, and the subtle shifts of tone in one man's perspective of over 90 years of life.

Ben Williams
August 2020

(Ben Williams is a theater artist in NYC who has worked exclusively on the creation and development of new plays and experimental performances.)

Foreword

If anything can be said of Takashi Oka, his was a life well lived.

A man of nearly innumerable talents, many cloaked by a gentle modesty, Tak spent six decades covering, and uncovering, some of the most consequential stories in Asia, the Middle East and Europe for *The Christian Science Monitor* and *The New York Times,* and later was instrumental in launching the Japanese-language edition of *Newsweek.* At ease in different cultures, he navigated rapidly changing, often dangerous situations, and then deftly explained them in a way that American readers could grasp their import.

This memoir recounts the life of a singular human being, a man who had been the youngest interpreter at the Tokyo War Crimes Trial, taught English to Americans at a Midwestern college, earned a Masters in Chinese studies from Harvard and, at age 84, completed his long-postponed Ph.D. – from Oxford.

Even for those people familiar with his career and writing, Tak's memoir provides a worthwhile bonus in the recounting of his family's journey during Japan's radical upheaval from feudalism to a rapidly industrializing, modern state. His maternal grandfather was born into a family of tenant farmers three years after the 1868 "restoration" of Emperor Meiji. Showing early promise, neighbors paid for a Western education – at a school founded by a former samurai who would later become his father-in-law. Leaving the paddy fields far behind, this son of poor farmers spent a career as a diplomat, reflecting a social mobility that would have been an unlikely event just a generation earlier. He also produced two globalist daughters.

One of them, Tak's mother, set him and his brother Akira on a highly unusual life trajectory for the times, raising them bilingually and as Christian Scientists. His account of the

Christian Science community provides a fascinating insight into this minority within the country's tiny Christian minority. And little surprise that a family with such a broad *weltanschauung* acquired eclectic tastes, like an uncle whose un-Japanese penchant for melted butter on his New Year mochi rice cakes was picked up by Akira. The rest of the family stuck to nori (seaweed) wrapped mochi dipped in soy sauce or sweetened soybean powder.

During the early days of the U.S. occupation, Tak had his first brush with foreign correspondents, and those encounters set him on a course that would interrupt his academic ambitions. The *Monitor's* Gordon Walker enlisted Tak as an interpreter on reporting trips. It was Walker who out-scooped rivals by filing a dispatch telling the world that Japan's pacifist postwar constitution had been dictated by a secret committee on Gen. MacArthur's staff.

History sort of repeated itself decades later when Tak, then the *Times* Tokyo bureau chief, hired me – a 21-year-old exchange student on summer break – to answer phones and run errands while the office manager was on maternity leave. I had been doing some freelance work for the *Japan Times* and The Associated Press, and always wanted to be a reporter but my school offered no journalism classes. Whether he knew it or not, Takashi Oka provided a crash course. I carefully watched how this master of the craft interviewed, in English and Japanese, and how he collected bits of information, then fashioned them into a polished dispatch. Eavesdropping as he built rapport with a source, I heard Tak repeatedly but casually say, "Really?" It was the equivalent of the Japanese word, *hon-toh*, which signaled to the interviewee that Tak was listening intently but without claiming agreement. It kept people talking.

Tak trusted me enough to share his frustrations with editors – a useful preparation for my own far-flung postings. One day, he showed me a cable from his foreign editor. It admonished

Tak for using "too many Japanese names." He had cited just three: the leader of the Japanese Socialist Party and the heads of two rival factions. It would have been impossible to have written the piece without the major players.

The summer stretched into fall, and I was being sent all over Japan, sometimes to take photographs or do spade work and set up interviews. The *Times* ran my photo of Leonard Bernstein and Seiji Ozawa cheering their respective orchestras as they played baseball. One night I was dispatched to watch Jane Fonda and Donald Sutherland perform an anti-war play near a U.S. base, and a half-dressed starlet angrily tossed me out of her dressing room after Sutherland pranked me by insisting Fonda was expecting me.

The *Times* Sunday Magazine had published a cover profile of the novelist Yukio Mishima, perennially speculated as a Nobel Prize choice. Mishima kept bugging the office, asking when his 50 copies were arriving. When they did, Tak sent me to a resort in Shimoda with the stack of magazines, and I ended up spending a long day with the disarmingly charming, seemingly cosmopolitan writer and his family, leaving me with a completely wrong impression of the gifted but fanatic nationalist.

In late November 1970, on the eve of my return to the University of Pittsburgh, I stopped at the *Times* bureau to say goodbye. Before I got a word out, Tak instructed: "Grab your camera, Barry, Mishima has taken over the *Jieitai* (Japanese Self-Defense Force) base in Ichigaya."

Perhaps it was adrenalin, but my Japanese comprehension soared and I grasped nearly everything within earshot, from shouts to whispered asides and rumors, and relayed what I heard by phone while Tak dictated the story on deadline to New York. He relates in this memoir that I kept jumping up to see over a frosted glass partition where Mishima held a general hostage. After his attempt to mount a coup was met by soldiers' jeers, the novelist performs the samurai's supreme self-sacrifice, disemboweling himself followed by decapitation by a follower, a final chapter perhaps more dramatic than any of his fiction.

Tak writes in this memoir of being grateful for not having to witness the gruesome scene. I myself had mentally buried much of the detail until reading his memoir. Clearly remembered, however, is my photographing Mishima's gray-uniformed, Shield Society student protégés at the moment they were told of his death. It made the Times front page. A week later I was an ordinary undergraduate again, but with a difference. The insights absorbed from Tak that extended summer could never have been gleaned in a classroom, nor his example as a gentlemanly, consummate journalist, which I have tried to emulate.

Barry Shlachter
August, 2020

(Barry Shlachter was a foreign correspondent in Asia and Africa for The Associated Press, returning on a Nieman Fellowship to Harvard, then became a reporter and editor for the Fort Worth Star-Telegram.)

Introduction

In writing this memoir, I want to revisit some of the more memorable events of my sixty-two-year career as a journalist. Having lived in Tokyo, Paris, Moscow, London, Saigon, Beijing, Hong Kong, Washington DC, and several other cities around the world, I've had the opportunity to write about a great variety of people: from the rice farmers of rural Vietnam to the generals who ordered the assassination of Ngo Dinh Diem; from the dissident writers in Soviet Russia to the student protestors on the streets of Seoul; from Margaret Thatcher to the British garbage men on strike; and from the *burakumin* caste of "untouchables" in Japan to Emperor Hirohito himself. In retrospect, I see that I was writing about events, both major and minor, of some historical value.

Another goal of this memoir is to place my own story within the story of Japan's joining the Western world. The latter could be said to have happened as early as 1868 or as late as 1945. As for the former, I was born in 1924 (or the 13th year of Taisho, according to the imperial calendar), so my parents – and their parents, and their parents' parents – experienced many of the extraordinary changes that Japan saw throughout the late 19th and early 20th century. Those changes, in turn, profoundly affected the environment into which I was born and in which I grew up.

For a Japanese person in the 1930s, I had a very unusual childhood. I grew up speaking English in a small, liberal-minded community in the suburbs of Tokyo. I attended the American School in Japan at the behest of my mother, who had lived in New York and Canada when her father was stationed there as a diplomat. Going back a generation further, his father-in-law – my great-grandfather – was a samurai who founded a school that promoted Westernized education in Japan.

Not only did I grow up speaking English in Japan, but I grew up a Christian Scientist. My mother had converted to Christian Science in between the World Wars. I went to the Christian Science Sunday School in Tokyo, and I'm still a member of the church today.

My mother didn't proselytize, but in the 1920s-30s, she was on a committee to promote *The Christian Science Monitor* to all sorts of people. She used to send marked copies of the paper to friends whenever she saw an article that mentioned a particular person or some subject that she thought might be of interest. Once in a while people would send her a letter of thanks.

Since we were living in Japan, there wasn't a lot to read in English outside the American School and my mother's religious literature. So from the time I first learned to read, I started devouring the *Monitor*. As a young kid, I became fascinated by what I read in the newspaper, which opened new doors to the world. As I would learn later, the newspaper had an excellent reputation for foreign news, at a time when American newspapers hardly covered the subject – for instance the *Monitor* was one of the few American newspapers to have a correspondent in Moscow during the Russian Revolution of 1917-18. I also read Japanese comics and young adult novels, but basically I became more fluent in English than in Japanese – which I came to regret, because it made me a minority in my own community.

I attended the American School until the fifth grade, when I had to switch to the traditional Japanese system. In order to do that, I had to have a certificate showing that I had graduated from a Japanese grade school – which I managed to get by finding a school that would take me for one week. That one week included a 10-day trip to the southern part of Japan, which I enjoyed very much. We were just a group of kids studying Japanese history, going to various historical places. We climbed

Kirishima, an extinct volcano in southern Kyushu. This is, we were told, where Ninigi, the grandchild of the Sun Goddess and the grandfather of the first Emperor of Japan, had descended from Heaven. Thus, went the history lesson, the Emperor descended directly from the Sun Goddess – and so are all Japanese, including me.

About two decades later, after the end of World War II, I moved to the United States. I eventually became a journalist, and it was only natural that the *Monitor* was the newspaper I wanted to join. Overall, I spent more than sixty years working for the newspaper, and it is thanks to this profession that I feel I have been able to contribute to what my mother drummed into me as my life purpose: being a bridge between Japan and the United States.

My story, imperfectly told as memories fade away and, at times, escape me now, will hopefully be a testament for all those who have lived with one leg in the East and another in the West. This balancing act is never easy, but is no longer an uncommon story.

Part I
JAPAN

Chapter 1

Antecedents

When I was born, my parents were living with my maternal grandparents, at 108 Sakura Shinmachi, which was then part of Komazawa-cho, Tokyo. Some years later the city of Tokyo expanded and Komazawa was folded into Setagaya-ku, but Sakura Shinmachi remains the name of the metro station, and the town is still known for its cherry blossoms, which line the principal avenue. Mr. Ihara, our neighbor who kept bees, said his honey smelled of cherry blossoms during this season.

My grandparents were from the city of Matsue. Chonosuke and Chiyo Yada, my mother's parents, came from the province of Izumo on the Japan Sea – a 25-hour train ride from Tokyo, in those days. You had to change trains either in Kyoto or Osaka to get to Matsue, the capital of Izumo and of Shimane Prefecture. Matsue faces the Japan Sea and is where Lake Nakaumi and Lake Shinji intersect. It is a city with many canals and is famous for its old castle and its *shijimi,* or little clams.

My mother's father was born in 1871. Grandfather Yada was the son of a tenant farmer on the Kando River near Matsue. Local legend says that at the age of 5 he was walking around in his village spouting passages from Mencius and Confucius. Impressed, the local landlord paid for Chonosuke to attend the nearest Western school, thinking that this promising boy would bring glory to the village. So the villagers banded together (the landlord paying the most) and sent him to one of the new primary schools that the Meiji government was establishing throughout the country. This was one of the ways in which bright young lads from the countryside achieved careers in government, diplomacy, or the justice system.

That's how my grandfather went to a school, which was founded by his future father-in-law, my great-grandfather Kan'ichi Watanabe.

Great-grandfather Watanabe was a samurai, the highest of the five classes into which Japanese society was divided. But his family was of the lowest rank, *ashigaru*, or foot-soldier. Still, in Meiji Japan, a samurai was socially superior to farmers and merchants. Being samurai, the men wore two swords – the longer one meant for battle, the shorter one to commit ritual suicide, known as *seppuku* or *hara-kiri*. I knew my Great-grandfather Watanabe only when he was well into his 80s, and remember him as a stern, distant figure. Although he no longer wore two swords, he was still a somewhat frightening figure to me as a child. I would come to know more about him through photographs and stories after he had passed.

Kan'ichi Watanabe was also from Matsue. Born in 1852, he was just two years old when Commodore Perry led a flotilla of four ships into Edo Bay and demanded that the Shogun open the country to foreign relations.

Until then, Japan had been a feudal society isolated from the rest of the world for 200 years. It had five classes: the samurai were at the top, followed by the farmers (from whom the samurai were recruited), the craftsmen, and the merchants. Below these four were the outcasts. In India they're called "untouchables." In Japan they're known as *burakumin*, roughly translated as "hamlet-dweller." Previously they had been called *Eta*, or filth. These people slaughtered animals, disposed of dead bodies, executed or guarded criminals, and performed various other functions that tended to be considered unclean.

In feudal Japan under the Tokugawa Shogunate, which had ruled Japan since 1603, even the nobility and vassal lords were not really free. They began to chafe under what became an all-powerful ruler, who imposed severe restrictions on the entire country. When Tokugawa Ieyasu (the first shogun) established his rule, he prohibited the local lords from owning more than one castle. If a lord had two or three, he had to destroy the other ones – this made it much more difficult for the local lords to unite and rebel. The Shogun also forbade the building of ocean-going ships. So the Japanese could not go out of their own country, and they also tried to keep foreigners from coming in, on pain of death. Once you left Japan, you could never come back. If you did, you were supposed to be executed.

Only a few Japanese ships were allowed by the government to go out into the rest of the world. In that sense, you might say that Japan was protected from the outside world, but it also lost out on the benefits of trade. This was the period when the British were conquering India, the French took over Indo-China, and the Dutch controlled Indonesia. Japan missed all these colonial acquisitions, because it had isolated itself.

Although Japan was closed to the outside world under Tokugawa rule, it was quite prosperous within. The country enjoyed 200 years of peace, during which the merchants were quite active, and, although heavily restricted, the merchants could deal with the Dutch, who were the only Westerners allowed to trade with the Japanese through the island Deshima in Nagasaki. As a result, people flocked there. If, for instance, you wanted to learn Western medicine (which became quite popular), you had to go to Nagasaki, because that was where the shogun allowed foreigners (Dutch, Koreans, Chinese, and those from the Ryukyu Kingdom) to live. Otherwise you learned the native herbal remedies.

In 1868, the Meiji Restoration changed the fortunes of many young men throughout Japan. Though called a "Restoration" – meaning that the Emperor, the historic ruler of Japan, was restored to power – in fact what happened was a revolution. Two of the most powerful feudal lordships formed an alliance and brought down the Tokugawa Shogunate. They were supported by thousands of young men from all over the country

– not only samurai but farmers and even merchants, intent on breaking the bonds of feudalism within their own provinces.

After 1868, the real power was in the hands of a few young and modernizing samurai. These were men who had traveled abroad and who had studied the West – its various systems of government, military structure, education – and the first big lesson they learned was from the Opium War.

China lost the Opium War in 1860. As a result, many of China's sea-going ports were divided up by the Western powers – Britain took Hong Kong, France took Kwangchow Bay, the Germans took Tsingtao, and so on. The samurai resolved that it must never happen to Japan. How could they avoid such a fate? In effect, by becoming part of the West – no Asian country had done that before.

In 1868, after a brief civil war, the Shogunate was overthrown and a new government came to power, intent on opening the country to Western institutions, civilization, and culture. The new leaders were youths who had participated in the Restoration – men from samurai, farmer, merchant, and other commoner backgrounds. Afterwards, enterprising young men (and young girls, in the case of the Iwakura mission) from Edo and the provinces left for San Francisco or London, seeking to acquire the new learning in the countries of its origin. As they began to trickle back to Japan, they brought ideas which were at the very least upsetting to the established feudal order, and which changed Japanese customs in everything from the structure of government to the style of dress. Legally, there was even a degree of female emancipation.

This was the atmosphere in which Kan'ichi Watanabe spent his teens and reached manhood.

FROM FATHER'S TIME TO MINE: PERSONAL HISTORIES OF A CHANGING WORLD

Japan — Feudalism's Echo

October, month of cloudless blue and golden rice stalks, is called "kannazuki" — month-without-gods — in most parts of Japan. According to ancient folklore, the patron deities of the island empire's 60-odd provinces are all absent from their homes during this month. All, that is, except one — Okuninushi, ruler of Idzumo. It is to Okuninushi's home the Great Shrine of Idzumo, that the other deities come, to hold their annual tenth-moon conference.

A tourist in bustling Tokyo, riding escalators in Ginza department stores or gaping at subways disgorging crowds of smartly dressed office girls, may wonder how persistent such superstitions may be. Yet it is still true that in all Japanese provinces except Idzumo, October is considered an unlucky time for marriages, while at the Great Shrine of Idzumo, it is the month of months for young couples to plight their troth.

I do not defend mythology, but Idzumo is my mother's native province, and I must confess that the story of an eastern Olympus stirs a kind of local pride. Besides, Okuninushi is supposed to have been a benevolent and laughter-loving ruler, who surrendered his lands without dispute to warlike Jimmu, the legendary first emperor of Japan.

Despite the improvements in communications that modern times have brought, it still takes a day and a night to go by train from Tokyo to Matsue, capital of Idzumo. This represents, of course, a fabulous speed-up since the rail-less days of the 1860's, when my Great-grandmother Watanabe spent a whole month traveling by rapid sedan chair from her home in Matsue to the Shogun's moated palace in Tokyo, then called Yedo.

As a child, I never tired of hearing Great-grandmother Watanabe tell of those faraway feudal days when top-knotted, two-sworded samurai strode through the narrow streets of Matsue below Lord Matsudaira's many-tiered keep. The castle, which still stands guard over the city, is now a public park, with paths where camellias perfume the air as winter yields to spring. No angry wars were fought underneath its walls, for it was built in a period when cannons imported from Portugal were already making stone battlements obsolete.

Great-grandmother was already a married woman when the Meiji Restoration of 1868 toppled the Shogun and the feudal system and catapulted Japan into the era of the steam engine and the gas light. But though she lived on almost into the threshold of the atomic age, she always folded her feet decorously together underneath her knees, even when traveling on Western-style trains, and she taught my mother that the tastiest way to boil rice was neither by gas nor electricity but in a heavy-lidded pot with a slow-burning wood fire.

Her speech was always gentle and well-mannered, but I do not like to contemplate what she would have said of the automatic rice-cookers that came into vogue some years ago and that even farm wives now demand.

Great-grandmother Watanabe loved the tea ceremony and the sweet-sour plum cakes peculiar to Idzumo that went with it. At the same time she was a marvelously efficient housewife who could lay her hands on a spool of thread or a ball of string at the very moment husband, children, or grandchildren needed a button sewed or a package wrapped.

And, of course, she was a wonderful storyteller, ranging from Idzumo folklore (how the impetuous prince, Okuninushi's father, slew a dragon and found therein a miraculous sword) to reminiscences about her own childhood days under the shadow of Matsue Castle.

Many of Great-grandmother Watanabe's stories had to do with Great-grandfather, whom I remember only in photographs. He began his career as a samurai and

Confucian scholar in the service of Lord Matsudaira of Matsue. Then came the Meiji Restoration, and changes from top to bottom in the nation's political, economic and social structure. The brightest young men from all the empire's feudal clans hastened to Tokyo and even to Europe and America, to acquire the new skills needed to lift their country from medieval feudalism into an industrialized Westernized state.

But Idzumo, that ancient land dreaming under the benevolent protection of Okuninushi's great shrine, was not in the forefront of this modernization movement. The Matsudairas of Matsue were one of the lesser of the feudal lords under the Tokugawa Shogunate, and their samurai sat on the fence during the upheaval that led to the Shogunate's demise. Thus they could claim no great rewards, nor did they incur any severe punishment, when the feudal system ended and a new military-civilian hierarchy took over.

Great-grandfather Watanabe was an eager student of the new Western learning, and would gladly have gone to Tokyo or abroad had he been given the opportunity. Whereas Great-grandmother Watanabe stuck to her sober kimonos, Great-grandfather did not scorn to wear the Western frock coat, particularly on formal occasions.

The end of the feudal system meant the end of the samurais as a knightly class and the first steps toward the inauguration of a universal educational system. Great-grandfather founded a modest private school in his home, where the young men of Matsue could learn English and mathematics as well as Confucian classics. One early student, Reijiro Wakatsuki, later became Prime Minister of Japan.

Lafcadio Hearn, the famous writer who became so enamored of Idzumo that he adopted one variant, Yakumo or Eight Clouds, as his nom de plume, was a friend of Great-grandfather's. But whereas Hearn had wandered over the face of the world, from Europe to America to the Far East, my grandfather never managed to cross a single ocean.

His life, however, exemplified the changes that Japan underwent as a nation from the placid days of the Shogunate to the stresses and strains of modern nationhood.

— Takashi Oka for *The Christian Science Monitor,* October 23, 1962. Tokyo.

During the civil wars of the 1860s, my great-grandfather was sent to Osaka as part of the Matsue lord's infantry force. He may even have seen fighting between the shogun's forces and the opposing soldiers from Satsuma and Choshu. At fourteen, Great-grandfather Watanabe had already become a drummer in the new revolutionary army.

Great-grandfather Watanabe's school was called the Shudokan, or "School to Learn the Way." Izumo was one of the more backward of the feudal provinces, but it was opening up to the new atmosphere. Universal education was very important to the modernizers – they could all agree on that, if not on democracy, which was still a mysterious word.

The youth of Matsue and the countryside flocked to this new school, until the newly-established prefectural government of Shimane opened Matsue Middle School and asked my great-grandfather Watanabe to close his own school. This was so that his school would not compete with the government school. In partial recompense, the government appointed my great-grandfather headmaster of a newly opened girls' high school in Hamada, capital of the neighboring province of Iwami.

Some time later, Watanabe also won the election to serve as a member of the prefectural assembly, or *ken-kai giin*. According to my great-aunt Hara, he did no electioneering at all – his students and former students did all the work – and he raised not a single *sen*, an impossible feat today. He retired after one or two terms but remained a local notable. When one of his students, Reijiro Wakatsuki, became Prime Minister in the 1920s and had a statue erected in his honor in Matsue, its inscription was by Grandfather Watanabe.

I remember him as a stern and taciturn patriarch. In contrast, his wife was cheerful and full of folktales. She told me the story of the rabbit and the crocodiles. The rabbit promises the crocodiles a reward if they line up in single file. So they line up, and the rabbit jumps from one crocodile to the next, skipping off with a gay farewell and leaving them gnashing their teeth. Later on, I learned that they ate the rabbit's tail, but I don't know if my great-grandmother took the story to that grim conclusion.

A Japanese Grandmother

Okuni-no-obasama — grandmother-in-the-country — my brother and I used to call her. That was to distinguish her from our grandmothers in the city, of whom we had two.

Actually, Grandmother Watanabe was my great-grandmother. She lived in Matsue on the Japan Sea, a sooty 25-hour train ride from Tokyo, and I had not seen her since I was four or five, when my mother had taken me back to her birthplace on a New Year's visit.

Every year, as New Year approached, a parcel would arrive for us from Grandmother Watanabe. In it there would always be homemade *mochi*, kneaded and pounded from a special glutinous rice. White and rather hard when raw, the *mochi* would soften and puff up to twice its normal size when toasted. Uncle Yada, who had been to London, liked to butter his *mochi*, and my brother Akira imitated him. Everyone else preferred the traditional flavorings: a crisp black seaweed wrapping, dipped in soy sauce, or freshly-ground golden soybean powder, mixed with sugar.

Besides the *mochi*, there would be pink and white ginger candy. And finally, Matsue's specialty, *menoha* or crinkly dried green seagrass, which when toasted and crumpled over hot rice gave off the most enticing smells of the sea, awakening memories even in midwinter of salt spray and long sandy beaches.

All this was carefully packed in various sized cardboard boxes and then assembled into one shipshape brown paper parcel, tied with twine, and addressed to our family in firm black Chinese brushstrokes.

"Grandmother Watanabe is the neatest person in the world," Mother would say as she painstakingly untied the knots, smoothed out the wrapping paper and opened the boxes one by one. "She had a proper place for everything."

Grandfather Watanabe, whose photograph hung in our family dining room, was a scholar. It was a prestigious but not a lucrative occupation, and since a scholar, like a samurai, is trained to disdain money, it was Grandmother who had to take care of all the practical details, feeding and clothing not only a family of three sons and three daughters but opening her home to several indigent students as well.

Later, it was Grandmother Watanabe who brought up my mother, her two sisters and two brothers. My mother's parents were diplomats, always being posted to exotic places like Tientsin, or Mexico, or Vancouver. "Better keep the children home until they're old enough to appreciate travel," Grandmother used to say. Which is why, until she was twelve, my mother never even saw Tokyo.

It must have been an idyllic childhood, at that. Matsue is a city laced with canals, bordered by Lake Shinji on one side and a long inlet from the sea on the other. The Watanabe home was at the edge of town, along one of the canals. My mother and her sisters used to go to school across rice fields, pausing now and then to try to scoop up mudfish in the glistening paddies with their white handkerchiefs.

Year after year the parcels from Grandmother Watanabe arrived, and year after year my brother and I wrote our thank-yous, promising that this time our parents hoped to take us back to Matsue for a visit. Almost before we knew it, we were in high school, and I was getting ready to graduate. We told ourselves we still remembered Grandmother-in-the-country, oh yes, we did, but as with Grandfather Watanabe, we couldn't be sure whether it was Grandmother herself who stayed in our memories, or only her photograph.

Just before the spring holidays, we suddenly decided, Akira and I, that there was no point in waiting any longer; we were old enough to go to Matsue by ourselves. Hurried letters went back and forth between Matsue and Tokyo. And there, finally, we were one evening, my brother and I, aboard the overnight express to Kyoto, and thence to Matsue. We would have to sit up all night on wooden seats in a third class carriage and spend most of the next day chugging through tunnel after tunnel down the wild, lonely Japan Sea coast. "Still," Mother said as she bade us goodbye, "the train is so much quicker than the palanquin Grandfather Watanabe traveled to Tokyo by — it was called Edo then — in the days before the Restoration. Even by fast palanquin, changing bearers at every stop, it took at least a month.

"Remember," she went on, "there are eighty tunnels, and after the last one you should be close to Yonago. That's still an hour from Matsue, but you'll start hearing the Matsue accent as people get on and off the train."

So it proved. There were indeed eighty tunnels, and our windowpanes were black with soot by the time we steamed into Yonago. A whole stream of local passengers came on at that important junction, and just as Mother had said, at least half of them were using the soft, slurred speech of Matsue.

Grandmother Watanabe was sitting on the wooden *engawa*, the garden side porch, shelling peas when Akira and I came into her smooth straw-matted living room through the front hall. "Here they are," called out Great-Aunt Hara, leading the way.

"Well, well," Grandmother Watanabe said in the soft Matsue dialect, "so you've come to see me at last." That was all she said, as she beckoned us to come closer so she could stroke us and see how we had grown. Tiny, round-shouldered, bright-eyed, in dark gray kimono and brown everyday sash, she could have been anyone's grandmother. But as I stooped down beside her, looking into her eyes and trying to remember whether I remembered her, I realized that it made no difference what photographic image I might or might not have retained. For it was as if her whole body, from her plump cheeks and neatly combed white hair to her still agile fingertips, was one concentrated smile. The sunshine of that smile filled the room and enfolded us in its warmth, assuring us that we had indeed come home to the land of our roots.

— Takashi Oka for *The Christian Science Monitor*, May 14, 1974. Paris.

As for Lafcadio Hearn, his presence made Matsue and Izumo well known in literary circles. A Greek-Irish journalist from New Orleans, Hearn came to Japan to teach English, and for a few years he taught at the same Matsue middle school that my grandfather Yada attended. My grandmother remembered him coming to her house and saying "Konnichiwa" in singsong Japanese. My only indirect connection to him was that for a couple of years I lived with my parents in the same house rented by Lafcadio Hearn's son. But I loved to read Hearn's *Kaidan,* or

Ghost Stories, as well as his lectures on Shakespeare at Tokyo Imperial University.

The Aoyagis, my great-grandmother's family, were of higher samurai rank than the Watanabes. They were direct retainers of the feudal lord (*daimyo*) and lived in the samurai area closest to the castle. But whereas great-grandfather Watanabe was steeped in Confucian learning and culture, my great-grandmother had the more practical, mundane task of keeping the house going. They had six children – the youngest boy died around age 7.

The oldest child, Chiyo, went to teachers' college, which was very unusual for women at that time. She got her certificate, became a teacher, and later married Chonosuke Yada. These were my mother's parents.

Grandfather Yada was born into a tenant farming family. But he went to the new Matsue Middle School (where his future father-in-law Watanabe was a teacher) and worked for his tuition, chopping wood and cleaning. He then went to Tokyo High School of Commerce, which later became Hitotsubashi University, one of the premier universities of Japan.

Apparently he had his heart set on becoming a diplomat and representing Japan overseas, especially in the United States. One day, as a prank, his Hitotsubashi classmates hung a sign on his back which read "Chonosuke Yada, Minister Extraordinary and Plenipotentiary," the full title of the ministers of those days. But my grandfather did indeed become a career diplomat. He joined the Foreign Service and became Consul-General – his first post was in China, in Hangkow and Tianjin. Later he served in Ottawa, New York, Honolulu, Mexico, and his final post was as Minister to Siam (now Thailand).

My mother told me many stories about her parents' life overseas. They were in China at the turn of the century – my Aunty Kiyo was born there during the Boxer Rebellion (the characters of her name are the same in Chinese as Qing, the dynasty in which she was born). The Yadas never really had a honeymoon because they had children right away, and then he was stationed abroad. Eventually they left the children with their parents in Matsue (my great-grandmother doing most of the work), and they finally had their honeymoon years later in Mexico, riding bicycles around the city. Porfirio Diaz was president then. A dictator really, he was the first *mestizo* to become president. But my grandfather told me Diaz was not terribly proud of the fact, and so he used to powder his face white. My grandfather himself didn't speak Spanish – the international diplomatic language at the time was French. His English (the language of commerce) was quite good, having studied it in high school and college, but it got much better in Canada, his second post.

My grandfather's career epitomized the changes brought about by the westernizing Meiji government after 1868. Despite being the son of tenant farmers, harvesting rice from less than half an acre, he passed the highly competitive foreign service examinations and became a diplomat. He told me with some glee that his rank at the Emperor's court was superior to that of Count Matsudaira, his former feudal lord. After his retirement from the diplomatic service, he accompanied the young Count as a personal adviser during a "grand tour" of Europe and America.

When I was a child and living in my grandparents' house, I used to love watching my grandfather get ready for formal dinners. He would put on his gold-braided uniform and green sash of the Order of the Siamese Crown, which he had received during his years in Bangkok. My grandmother was equally splendid, in shoulder-revealing decolleté, with an ostrich feather in her hair. Together they would entertain exotic visitors, such as princes and princesses from Siam.

A Time for Women – and Change

A woman of Japan's Meiji period could marry for love, have a career, and maintain her independence.

"My Grandmother Chiyo was a woman of Meiji," my mother used to say. For my generation, it's a term redolent with nostalgia, but it sounds like ancient history to the iPod-toting youngsters of today. Meiji connotes the springtime of modern Japan. He was the emperor who reigned from 1868 to 1912 and who presided over the transformation of his country from an isolated, feudal society dominated by the samurai, or warrior caste, into a 19th-century version of the modern world with railways, steel mills, and Parisian gowns.

I remember when I was a child, seeing Grandmother Chiyo weeding her garden and brushing caterpillars off her tea bushes at the crack of dawn. She wore a nondescript blue smock, but her large, dark eyes were intense and concentrated on the task at hand. Sometimes I would see her in the evening, with coiffed hair and wearing an elegant evening gown, preparing to go off to a party with Grandfather Yada.

Chiyo was born early in the Meiji era, when women began to be freed from their long years of subordination in a male-dominated society. The freedom was far from total, but compared to women's status during feudal times, it was revolutionary. Chiyo was one of the first women in her town to graduate from normal school (the equivalent of a teachers' college) and — even more extraordinary — to marry for love, not by arrangement.

Chonosuke, her husband by choice, was extraordinary in his own way. The school Chonosuke attended was run by Chiyo's father, a noted Confucian scholar, and eventually Chonosuke became Chiyo's sweetheart. After graduation, he went off to university in Tokyo and then, after passing the difficult foreign service examination, returned to the town of Matsue to ask for Chiyo's hand.

"Woman of Meiji" meant more than just being born during a particular emperor's reign. Usually it connoted old-fashioned virtues — women who were strict with their children, loyal to their husbands, and who maintained a certain decorum in their daily lives. But it also symbolized emancipation — women who could have careers or become flamboyant writers, or who, even as wives, carried about them a certain air of independence and individualism.

It was this second meaning that was more characteristic of my grandmother.

Chiyo's teaching career was short — Chonosuke whisked her off to his first overseas post, Tientsin (now Tianjin), in neighboring China, where he had been appointed vice consul. That was the year of the Boxer Rebellion in Beijing, and no sooner had the Yada family settled down in Tientsin than the fledgling diplomat had to send his wife and children back to Japan for their own safety. Meanwhile, Chonosuke accompanied an international rescue force that fought its way to Beijing and freed the foreign embassies that had been besieged by Boxer rebels in the capital city.

The next posting was Mexico. Chiyo's mother stepped in at this point and offered to take care of the Yada children until Chiyo and her husband had settled down comfortably in their new home. Later, the boys accompanied their parents to Vancouver. The girls joined them in Ottawa and New York.

It was in the latter two cities that Chiyo's native intelligence, wit, and grace really came into their own. She was an exceptional hostess at diplomatic functions, but also made her mark in neighborhood relations, volunteering recipes for sukiyaki or tempura, and mobilizing women in the small Japanese community to sew bandages for wounded soldiers during the First World War (Japan was an ally then).

When Chonosuke retired from the diplomatic service, he returned to his

> native village, where his spendthrift younger brother had just lost the family farm. Chonosuke had been inclined to repurchase the farm and lecture the prodigal by mail. But Chiyo insisted that the two of them should go back to the village and show that their years of glamorous diplomatic service had not deprived them of their capacity for hard manual labor.
>
> They spent the hot summer knee-deep in the muck of the paddy fields — hoeing, weeding, carrying fertilizer — Chonosuke grumbling at first, but gradually getting into the spirit of things. The brother, embarrassed, mended his ways for good.
>
> That, my mother said, was Grandmother Chiyo's crowning achievement as a woman of Meiji.
>
> — Takashi Oka for *The Christian Science Monitor*, June 23, 2006.

On my father's side, my grandfather Yoshikazu Oka was born in a village on the outskirts of Nagoya, of which his father, surnamed Okochi, was *nanushi,* or headman. Yoshikazu was apprenticed at a very young age to a Buddhist priest and accompanied him as an acolyte. This was in keeping with a promise my great-grandmother had made, following the custom of those days: that at least one son of a well-to-do farmer should become a Buddhist priest. So, at age 3, he was given to a priest of the Rinzai sect. This priest, my grandfather's adoptive father, traveled extensively throughout Japan from temple to temple, with my grandfather in tow. After many years, my grandfather also became an abbot of a temple in what is now Tomioka City on the seacoast of Fukushima prefecture.

But my grandfather was not really interested in being a Buddhist priest. Although he inherited his adoptive father's temple in Tomioka, he left the priesthood, got married, and became a coal merchant at a nearby coal mine, which supplied the newly opened railroad from Tokyo to Sendai. Like many get-rich-quick merchants, he overextended himself, went bankrupt, and moved to Tokyo, where his older brother had become a more prosperous coal merchant and owner of a mine in neighboring Chiba prefecture.

I never knew my grandfather Oka, who died before I was born. His bones – and those of all my father's family – are interred in the graveyard of the main Rinzai temple in Tokyo, called Seishoji, near Toranomon in Minato Ward. His widow, my grandmother, lived into her 90s, but I can't say that I know a great deal about her either, because we didn't live with her. They had seven children – five boys and two girls – and a house in Koenji, in western Tokyo, where we visited them every New Year.

The only things I remember about them from my childhood are these New Year's Day visits. My brother and I would always go to the oldest uncle and receive little red envelopes filled with coins. It was a big family, so we'd try to get them from as many of our relatives as we could. But since this was only once a year, we never managed to know them well.

My father was the youngest of the five sons. Masakazu Oka was born on March 2, 1892, in Fukushima prefecture. He was later baptized as William (his friends called him Bill), but his name was also Shogo. In Japanese, *go* is the number 5 – since he was the fifth son, he was named Shogo. It was a confusing thing: The Japanese pronunciation of the Chinese characters *Shogo* is Masakazu. Shogo was used less commonly because, in Japanese, anything that's given a Chinese-type pronunciation is considered more formal and elegant, the way a Greek or Latin word might be in English. So people just called him Masa. My mother always called him Masa, as did his friends, although a few other family members still called him Shogo.

My father was born to more modest circumstances than my mother's family. Like his father, he was apprenticed to a Buddhist priest in a nearby village. Also like his father, he hated the temple and kept running back home. Breaking with tradition and following his burgeoning entrepreneurial streak, he went out in the paddy fields to fish for loach (mudfish), the small fish that swam around during the growing season. The paddy fields were not public property, but people were allowed to fish in them. So as a boy of 14, my father would wade out and catch what he could, then take the fish to the market around 7 o'clock and sell them.

While still in his teens, my father wanted to learn English, thinking this was the language that would open the door to the world. He found an Anglican priest, the Rev. William Draper, in Yokohama, who would teach him English. As he studied with this minister, he was intrigued not only by English but by the Christian religion, and soon he was baptized.

After studying English and the Bible with Mr. Draper, my father went to work for him. Besides serving as a British missionary, Mr. Draper also started his own business as a trading agent. Draper then sold out to an American named Mr. Frazer, which is how my father came to the Anglo-American trading company Sale and Frazer. My father's first job with them was to sell railroad equipment to Japanese suburban railways linking Tokyo to various satellite towns. He sold the automatic locking devices for railway carriages, replacing the nineteenth-century pin-and-wheel devices. His salary was 42 yen per month, or about $24. By 1927, my father became the company's Tokyo manager. A few years later he held the same title for RCA Victor.

A father's international flair

"We had just finished breakfast, and my father, who usually left early for his Saturday game of golf, was in a rare talkative mood. "So," he said, motioning me to sit down, "you're nearly 14. Let me tell you what I was doing when I was your age."

"Every morning," he began, "I would get up at 4:30 and go off to the paddy fields to catch dojo — mudfish. They are small fish, as you know — not worth much. But people like to put them in a fish stew, and when I had a bucketful, I would take them to the market. I'd bring the money home, usually not even 1 yen (then worth about 50 cents), and give them to my mother. I know your mother gives you chores each morning — mop the floors and brush my shoes. Just don't forget what I was doing at your age."

Continuing his story, he recalled that he had been born in Tomioka, 200 miles north of Tokyo — a city I had never visited. His father was a Zen Buddhist priest without many parishioners. "So my mother had to scrimp and save to bring up her seven children, of whom I was the last. When I was 7, my parents sent me off to be an apprentice in a temple in the next town.

"But I was miserable, and soon came running home. The next day, my mother sent me back. Again, I ran home. After the third time, my mother said I could stay, but only if I helped out even a bit with the family income. That's what took me to the paddy fields to catch mudfish, even on cold winter mornings."

Later, my father's oldest brother, 18 years his senior, brought the whole family to Tokyo to live with him. He had joined the railroad at an early age and had worked his way up to become stationmaster of Shimbashi, a major station on the line to Yokohama, Nagoya, and Osaka. The job came with a gold-braided stationmaster's cap and an official residence, modest but adequate to house his parents, brothers, and sisters. My uncle also got my father his first real job with the railways, earning a couple of yen — less than a dollar — per month. He worked his way through night school, studied English with an American missionary in Yokohama, and was baptized William — much to the distress of my devoutly Buddhist grandmother. His teacher called him Bill, a name he proudly adopted.

Those were heady days for Japan. The country had emerged from 200 years of feudal isolation in 1854, when Commodore Perry and his Black Ships sailed into Tokyo Bay (then called Edo), and forced the Tokugawa Shogunate to open its door to foreign trade. Japan modernized, Westernized, and won two short wars in quick succession — with China in 1894-95 and with Russia in 1904-05. World War I sparked Japan's first big economic boom. While the Europeans fought each other, Japan exported an increasing range of goods, from textiles to cement and steel. And that boom enabled my father to meet my mother.

Bill Oka was handsome, athletic, and a born salesman with a winning smile. His English, though broken, got him a job with Sale and Frazer, an Anglo-American trading company in Yokohama — Mr. Frazer being American and Mr. Sale, British. His first coup was to sell a new coupling system to the railways, which had been nationalized early in the 20th century. That prompted Mr. Frazer and Mr. Sale to send their employee on a field trip to the United States and England, visiting the Baldwin locomotive works in Pittsburgh and the Victor Talking Machine Company in London.

En route, Bill's ship stopped in Honolulu, where he met my mother, whose father was Japanese consul general in the city. It was love at first sight. She was pretty and loved balls. He could be the life of the party when he dressed up as an American sailor with a black eye patch. He carried on a torrid correspondence with her, and, on the return voyage back across the Atlantic and Pacific oceans, proposed, and she accepted.

Even when his salary was modest, my father did things in style. My mother told me that when he walked down the Ginza in his *yukata*, his summer kimono, he would turn the eyes of all the women shopping at the fashionable stores on the street. With some of his fellow salesmen at Sale and Frazer, he bought a horse, of which he owned an eighth-share. "The tail was mine," he told me. Later he bought a Model T roadster, in the same way.

When the Victor Talking Machine Company (later RCA Victor), of which Sale and Frazer had been agent, began making records and record players in Japan, my father was made branch manager and also head of the artists' division.

In those days, if you were a Caruso or a Heifetz, your records had a red label; records for pop singers were given black labels. My father insisted that the great kabuki actors of Japan deserved a red label, and when the home office demurred, he created a white label especially for the stars of classical Japanese dance and singing.

As I grew older, he took me to the dressing rooms of famous kabuki actors like Kikugoro Onoe the Fifth and Uzaemon Ichimura the 15th, where I sat uncomfortably with my legs tucked under me. Meanwhile, my father chatted with his hosts as they were putting the last touches on their facial makeup, a task they never left to underlings.

The first million-record sale my father achieved was with a samisen-accompanied song called "Tokyo Ondo" (Rhythm of Tokyo) sung by the geisha performer Katsutaro. (A samisen is a three-stringed plucked instrument.) My father boasted that no matter how late he dined with his show business friends and clients, he always was in his office promptly by 9 o'clock. Breakfast around 7 was the one meal of the day he had with us — sometimes toast and cornflakes, sometimes rice and miso soup. Some evenings, if he had no other engagements, he would take us to his favorite sushi restaurant on the Ginza.

It was my mother who got him to play golf. She had dabbled with it in Honolulu, but she told him it would help him get to know fellow businessmen. Once he took it up in earnest, with a handicap in single digits, she became a golf widow. But later, when the children were grown, the nightmare of World War II had ended, and Japan was on a new trajectory of economic growth, she and he traveled together for his Rotary International gatherings in the US, Europe, and Mexico. It was a lifelong partnership that began in romantic Hawaii and that drew the two closer to each other as her friends became his friends and his friends hers.

— Takashi Oka for *The Christian Science Monitor*, April 30, 2009.

My mother, Fumi Yada, was born in 1900 in Matsue, when it was still a small city. When her family moved to Canada in 1914, she was baptized under the name Mary, and she spent her teens in Vancouver and Ottawa.

They had taken the Canadian Pacific from Yokohama, along the Great Circle route close to the Aleutian Islands – where she told me they saw whales – and then landed in Vancouver. She had memories of skating on the river, going to the opera, and attending Christmas parties in Canada. In 1916, she was in Ottawa and witnessed the great parliament fire. Around this time, her father and Mackenzie King were golfing pals and would go horseback riding together in the countryside. I think my grandfather knew then that Mackenzie King was a homosexual, but this was at a time when sexuality was a hidden subject. In any case, no one talked about it, and Mackenzie King would go on to become one of Canada's most famous prime ministers.

In 1917, my mother's family moved to New York City, where they lived in a seventh-floor apartment on the Upper West Side that faced Central Park. The virtuoso violinist Jascha Heifetz lived on the floor above, and they could hear him practicing. They might have socialized with him a bit, but I'm sure it was restricted by the fact that my grandmother hated Western music – she said it sounded like cats fighting. My grandmother played the *koto* (the Japanese harp), my Aunt Kiyo played the guitar, and my mother played the piano, the mandolin, and, after her father's next post, the ukulele.

In 1921, her father was the Japanese consul-general in Honolulu. It was at a consulate party in Hawaii, that my mother met my father. For my father, as soon as he met her, it was love at first sight. But he was on a business trip to inspect railway equipment makers in the United States and Britain – from Honolulu, he had to go on to San Francisco, Philadelphia, Pittsburg, Camden, New York, and London.

He wrote my mother every day of his voyage, and his

persistence paid off. After a year-long courtship, in which he practiced his written English in letters to her, he returned to Honolulu. She accepted his proposal, and the two married in Tokyo in 1922 at Josui Kaikan, my grandfather's alumni club.

Many years later, my mother told me the whole story, from her viewpoint. During her New York years, she said, she had had a lot of suitors, all sons of wealthy (and sometimes titled) businessmen. But when she compared them in her mind's eye with Masa, he won hands down. Whatever he had achieved up to then, he had achieved on his own – no rich relative had helped him. In Masa, she decided, she had found a husband worth having. So Masa it was.

I was born on October 21, 1924, at Akasaka Hospital in Tokyo (St. Luke's Hospital, where my parents would have otherwise gone, was still closed because of damage suffered in the Great Earthquake the year before). My brother Akira followed in 1927.

In 1936, my father left Victor to work for the old motion picture company Nikkatsu, and shortly after that he moved on to the Toho movie company. Toho became famous for producing and distributing *Godzilla, Rodan,* and many films of Akira Kurosawa, including *The Seven Samurai.* The company also owned several subsidiary businesses, which was where my father worked. By 1938, he became successively president of Tokyo Kaikan – a landmark Tokyo restaurant – and president of the Palace Hotel, a major international hotel. Although he was still working for Toho, his heart remained with Victor. He kept all the Victor shares he acquired during his career, which became the principal inheritance my brother and I received from our father.

My father was a serious, almost fanatic golfer, getting his handicap down from 22 to 8, out of sheer effort and application. It was the Tokyo Golf Club, which my father joined at Mama's instigation, that allowed him to hobnob with Prince Asaka (the son-in-law of Emperor Meiji), the Nabeshimas (former lords of

Saga in Kyushu), Ryozo Asano (President of Asano Cement and other Asano-related companies), and other big businessmen. I never learned to play golf, and my father didn't seem interested in teaching me. If I had really begged him, he might have, and I'm sorry I never did, because I missed a golden opportunity to become better acquainted with him. I regretted this all the more, because after I went to America, I could see him only occasionally, unlike my brother Akira, who became quite close to him. Incidentally, I remember Papa got a hole-in-one at Asaka Golf Club, and Prince Asaka and a friend gave him a silver cup to commemorate the occasion.

Meanwhile, my mother was too busy rearing two young sons, so she dropped the sport. Mrs. Benzo Mitsui was the champion woman golfer of Japan and our neighbor – she and my father golfed together so frequently that American friends suspected her of being his mistress. But my mother simply laughed at such insinuations. While it had its ups and downs, their marriage was rock solid.

However, World War II impinged on my parents' marriage. My mother was unabashedly pro-American, even during the darkest days of the war, whereas my father, a businessman, tended to go with the tide. After the war ended and American troops landed on Japanese soil for the first time in history, my father could see for himself how generally well-behaved the Americans were, and he quickly revised his opinions. As president of Tokyo Kaikan and the Palace Hotel, he threw himself whole-heartedly into tourist schemes to attract US troops who were on "R&R" leave in Japan.

As for my mother, she helped my father with his American contacts, especially with his friends in RCA Victor. She went with him on trips to the United States and elsewhere, and she was even made an honorary citizen of Texas – whatever that may have meant.

After only a few months of retirement, my father was asked

to head a small movie-processing company, Tokyo Genzosho, jointly owned by Toho and the German film company Agfa, a rival to Kodak. My father accepted the offer, and he remained president until his death, from lung cancer, in 1970. He was 78. Up until two months before his death, he still commuted every day from his home in Sakura Shinmachi to Chofu, where Tokyo Genzosho had its headquarters and laboratory. My father used to say he liked living in Shinmachi because the air was fresher there. My mother replied, "You never have a chance to breathe that air except late at night." He always left right after breakfast.

My mother was at his bedside every day as he was dying. She did not attend his cremation, sending me in her stead. When I brought home his ashes, she broke down, saying, "What shall I do? He was the light of my life." Four years later, in 1974, my mother died after a series of heart attacks.

Over the years, her sense of companionship with her husband deepened. She was a great hostess for my father, especially when he brought home his golfing pals and singer friends. In her early 70s, when my mother had jaundice but refused to see doctors because of her Christian Science faith, my father was nearly beside himself. He told me later that he prayed as best he knew how, and felt his prayers were answered when, after a serious heart attack, she told him she was willing to go to the hospital.

I was sorry that my parents did not have more time together, for they were beginning to enjoy each other's company in a much more profound and meaningful way than before. But I shall always be grateful for my parents' intertwined lives, which were, all in all, quite happy and fulfilling.

Chapter 2

Childhood

I grew up in a suburb west of Tokyo called Sakura Shinmachi, or Cherry-blossom New Town. Rows of cherry trees along the road lead from the tram stop to my Grandmother Yada's house. My grandparents bought the property after Grandfather Yada retired from his diplomatic career, and their spacious house was the first home I remember. My parents and my brother Akira and I lived there with them until 1937.

It was a large house with Western-style drawing rooms in front and a long, Japanese-style house behind, connected by a short corridor. The Western part of the house had a front hall with a balustraded mahogany staircase to the bedrooms upstairs. I don't know how my grandfather acquired this staircase, but he was quite proud of it. On the south side of the hall were two connected 10-mat drawing rooms – a parlor and a library with glass doors and bookshelves, atop which sat several heads of Buddha in the Siamese style, fluid and more elegant than the Kamakura Buddhas of Japan. Their library had Western books, most with uncut leaves. I inherited a set of these Latin and Greek classics – they are still uncut. On the walls of the drawing room hung photographs of the presidents and prime ministers of the countries in which my grandfather had served: Sir Wilfred Laurier of Canada, President Porfirio Diaz of Mexico, President Woodrow Wilson of the USA, and Rama VI, King of Thailand. Going past these portraits several times a day sparked my interest in biography and history.

The traditional Japanese part of the house had an *engawa*, or glassed-in corridor, with a floor made of cork, which my grandmother preferred because it made less noise than pine or cypress. Beyond were several tatami-matted rooms, which were used by my grandparents, the servants, and any guest who preferred sleeping on tatami. My parents, my brother, and I used the Western-style bedrooms upstairs. Family photographs adorned the walls of these bedrooms, but I was particularly fascinated by an oil painting that showed a wild-eyed woman in Roman dress, holding a snake to her bared breast. It must have been a portrait of Cleopatra committing suicide.

My earliest conscious memory is of walking with my grandmother to Fukazawa Oinari-san, the shrine of the Fox God. It was a long walk and I was thoroughly tired when we got home. No sooner was I in the door than Mama came in her kimono-nightie and asked me to mail a letter for her at the postbox, which was probably a three-minute walk from Baba's. I said that I was too tired, and she said she would go herself. So she did, taking time to change into a daytime dress. She looked so tired! A guilty conscience stayed with me for years.

Another early memory of the Yada house: I was in one of the upstairs bedrooms and banging on my plate with my fork to signal to Mama that I wanted more ice cream, or whatever else it was that I wanted. I don't remember whether she responded or not – just my banging on the plate with my fork.

Across the lane, barely wide enough for a motor-car to squeeze by, lived my friend Juntaro Yamamoto, whom I called Jun-chan. His family's property was huge – 3,000 tsubo (2.5 acres), whereas my grandmother's property was 400 tsubo (one-third of an acre) – with a pond, a bamboo grove, and a vegetable garden of tomatoes, cucumbers, and watermelons. I spent many happy hours with Jun-chan feeding the carp in the pond, digging in the garden for *takenoko*, or edible bamboo shoots, which Jun-chan's mother cooked with rice into a delicious stew, and pretending we were Momotaro the peach boy looking for buried treasure.

For two or three years my grandparents took care of children of a classmate of my grandfather's at University, a family called the Sendas. Mr. Senda was a trade merchant who lived in Tokyo and Calcutta, and he had also a place in the US – and he had a wife in every one of these towns. He didn't quite know what to do with the children. My grandparents very generously offered to take care of them, and they moved into the Sendas' house for two or three years to do so. I used to visit there a lot, which I enjoyed because, until then, I had only my brother to play with. The Sendas was a house full of people, and we played games, hide-and-seek, or cops and robbers.

Next to the Shinmachi trolley stop was a rickshaw stand that grandmother used only on rainy days. I would try to wheedle her into taking a rickshaw even in fair weather so that I could ride in her lap, but I rarely succeeded. To me, riding a rickshaw was like taking a Rolls Royce. The puller was elderly and slow-moving, and when I shouted at him to go faster my grandmother instantly scolded me.

I remember my mother's smile. I rarely saw her cross – the only serious disagreement I had with her and Aunty Kiyo happened when I was in my teens. I don't remember how it came about, but I told them that I would be happy just to be an English teacher in Matsue high school. My mother said, "Fine! Go ahead and do it!" To which I had no response. My nostalgia for Matsue grew from my dissatisfaction about not having my own *kokyo* or *inaka* (a hometown or ancestral village) where I grew up, and Matsue was the closest thing to that, even though actually I hardly spent any time there. Those few days in Matsue were exaggerated in my memory to make the city into my *inaka*, even though Shinmachi in Tokyo was the only childhood home I had.

Similarly, a seven-month stay in Hawaii when I was three years old inflated Hawaii into a kind of second *kokyo* or *inaka*. My mother had just had my brother Akira and wanted him to be in a warm climate for the first few months of his life. These were the days of coal stoves and drafty houses, though our house, being largely in Western style, was warmer than those of most of our neighbors. When mother's friend, whom I remember as Aunty Ikeda, invited her to spend half a year in Honolulu, my mother grabbed the opportunity and took us to Hawaii.

I vividly remember my trip to Honolulu. It was my first long voyage, on the Siberia Maru, a passenger ship belonging to N.Y.K., the Japanese shipping line. My mother was seasick the first night, but I scampered around the decks all day, without ever growing green around the gills. My three-month-old brother was still carried in a *kori,* or bamboo basket.

In Honolulu, I met my first girlfriend, Shirley. I'm not sure of the circumstances, but our neighbor Elizabeth Green, whom I called Aunty Elizabeth, was the intermediary. Shirley had curly blonde hair and was a lot of fun to be with. I also met the neighbors' children who all played on the street paved with sticky tar. The children taught me to roll the tar into cigarettes and pretend to smoke – in the process my teeth turned black. It took my mother two weeks to get my teeth white again.

I also made friends with the gardener's son and spoke with him in Japanese, even though my mother wanted me to speak only English in Hawaii. One day, he and I watched silently from his house as Shirley walked home from ours – she was crying because my mother had told her that I had gone outside to play, and that she didn't know where I was.

Aunty Elizabeth took me swimming at Waikiki, which was not the tourist monstrosity it became later. There were few houses along the beach and only a couple of hotels, the Royal Hawaiian and the Moana Loa. I played on the beach, building sand castles and watching them crumble with the incoming tide. Aunty Elizabeth put me on her back when she went swimming, pretending to be a big whale carrying me to the palace of the sea king Neptune. She also took me on an Easter egg hunt in her garden. I'm not sure whether this was the real Easter, or whether she had just selected another date. In either case, I had a great time looking for painted eggs under bushes or hidden behind the garden gate.

As a child I wished that I had been born in Honolulu. I treasured the books that Aunty Elizabeth's mother (who was related to the Hawaiian royal family) sent me from Honolulu. Sometimes I imagined myself being the son of a Hawaiian chief, and wearing plumes of exotic bird feathers. As a child, and even in my teens, I wished I had been born in Hawaii, which at that time was still just a US territory, not a state.

Instead I grew up Japanese in a somewhat Western environment. I was a Christian Scientist who spoke English taught by Americans, with the assumption from a very early age that I would go on to study in America, as would many of my friends. Only a few Christian Scientists lived in Tokyo - the Matsukatas, the Takakis, and my own family being the principal members of our little church.

Meanwhile, the whole of Japan was growing more nationalistic and militaristic. The invasion of Manchuria in 1931 was the opening shot of Japan's war in the Pacific. But, for at least a few more years, I was still just a kid.

* * * * *

Another special place of my childhood was our cottage in Karuizawa. My grandmother had bought a 1000-tsubo (almost 1 acre) piece of land there and then never really did anything with it - it was just a sleeping investment as far she was concerned. My mother had always wanted a summer place, and Karuizawa is quite cool compared to Tokyo, so in 1934, Mama took the initiative to build a summer cottage there in the Atago area.

My parents asked their friends the Raymonds to design the cottage. Antonin Raymond was a Czech architect and his wife Noemi was a designer from Switzerland. He came to Japan just after World War I with Frank Lloyd Wright, who designed the second Imperial Hotel after the first one burnt down. Raymond had also worked for Le Corbusier, and the houses he built looked like Le Corbusier's but with Japanese touches. The Raymonds had a son, Claude, who was a year behind me at the American School, and my father played golf with Mr. Raymond at the Tokyo Golf Club.

Our Karuizawa cottage was the first house my parents had owned. Most Japanese of my parents generation lived in rental housing until they were in their fifties, when they could expect a large lump-sum payment from their employers as a kind of once-in-a-lifetime bonus. The house had only a *totan* (galvanized tin) roof, and every time it rained the roof made so much noise that we had to cover it. Mrs. Raymond used the local larch pine, *karamatsu*, as a thatch, which unfortunately corroded over time from rain and volcanic ash. So the Raymonds substituted it with a slate roof like that of the New Karuizawa Golf Club (which the Raymonds also designed). The walls are a strong pine, which has a nice smell.

We kids loved the Karuizawa property. It had a field of grass and a forest of larch trees, where we romped around and chased the chipmunks and squirrels. There was a very good patch of tilled earth for corn, onions, spinach, eggplant, daikon, and so forth. In Tokyo, we got our produce from a farmer who would drive a truck into town, but in Karuizawa, a farmer carrying all his produce in a hamper on his back would come to our house. We also went horseback riding, even on the roads in town – which I enjoyed until one day when I fell and hit my head.

A few years after they built our cottage, the Raymonds built another house for us in Tokyo, and we moved out of my grandparents home. We lived in this new Tokyo house, atop a hill with a sloping lawn, for many years. My father hosted many spectacular garden parties there, and it was my home until I left Japan. Unfortunately, even though our Tokyo house survived the terrible fire-bombings of World War II, it did not survive the 1970s. The house was demolished and the property became a parking lot. I remember seeing the aftermath: one moment the house was standing, and the next thing I knew it was just stacks of cedar pillars laid out in rows on the bare ground, waiting to be sold as firewood. So much for our Raymond-designed house. Fortunately, we still have the cottage in Karuizawa.

* * * * *

The turbulent years between the First and Second World Wars in Japan were marked by wars and rumors of wars. Within Japan a cleavage opened up between the civilians like my family, who had been brought up in the Western learning promoted by the Meiji government, and the young army officers, who claimed to be following samurai traditions but who were actually treading in the footsteps of European fascism. Most ordinary Japanese and many members of the military preferred civilian rule but lacked the courage to stand up to the young officers.

A friend who was a lieutenant told me a story that illustrated the problem. A general was giving a lecture to a group of younger officers and was irritated by what he saw as lack of sufficient attention on the part of his audience. "Unless you listen harder," he snapped, "you'll never become generals." "Your Excellency," shot back a younger officer, "Our only aim is to die in battle for His Majesty the Emperor." Previously, junior officers would never have dared to say anything back to their superiors, but this time, my friend said, the general was forced to apologize to his students.

My mother was troubled by what she saw as a growing atmosphere of military arrogance and intolerance. Her ideals, nurtured in Canada and America, were liberalism and hard work, and she wanted me to study in the United States, which she saw as the epitome of these virtues. She instilled in me the idea that any student worth his salt should work his way through college. *Kugaku* – literally meaning "bitter learning" – was the norm for ambitious students without means of their own, and although my family had a comfortable middle-class income, my mother imparted that concept to me from an early age. Even in the home, there were always chores for me and my younger brother Akira to do – sweeping and mopping the floors, shining my father's shoes, bicycling to the bakery downtown to pick up fresh-baked bread and groceries.

The first step in my mother's education program was to enroll me in the American School in Japan. Of all my childhood experiences, the most important were the five years I spent at the American School in Japan (ASIJ), from 1929 to 1934. ASIJ is where I learned to read and write in English, and although this was later supplemented by my years at the Matsukatas' School (precursor to the Nishimachi School), the solid foundations were laid at ASIJ.

The school was founded by expatriate Americans, mostly missionaries and businessmen. At a certain point in the 1930s they adopted a system of textbooks devised by the Winnetka school system, and many of my teachers came from Chicago or that area. ASIJ was a small school, with about 160 students K-12. There were two classes to one teacher: first and second grade were together, third and fourth grade were also combined. So I had the same teacher two years in a row. The tuition was pretty steep, considering that Japanese public primary schools were free, but Grandmother helped out.

The campus was situated near the Naka-Meguro station on the Toyoko line, almost an hour away from Sakura Shinmachi. My mother took me there the first day. Among a group of yellow-painted wooden buildings, we met Mr. Mitchell, the principal. He was a tall, portly man who had taught at American schools in India. He walked me from his office to the first-grade classroom and introduced me to Miss Jeanette Brooks, my first teacher, who was half French, slender and petite, with brown, expressive eyes. The class was already in session when I came in. Miss Brooks was writing on the blackboard: "The wind said, 'Oooh'" – drawing out the "oooh". Then the class repeated in unison, "The wind said, 'Oooh.'"

I sat near the front, in the third or fourth row. In front of me was Jackie Gauntlett, a friendly half-English half-Japanese girl with long black hair and a bright smile. Although the school provided lunch, we had both brought our own *nigiri* (rice-ball) lunches, and at noon we sat on the lawn behind the school and ate. It was a beautiful autumn day, with a deep blue sky and no clouds. I don't remember our conversation, but Jackie was lively and friendly and I had a great time. She was not, however, the first girl I kissed. That honor went to Eleanor Lamott, my fourth-grade classmate. More on that later.

In those days, the campus measured about 12 acres, with a soccer field and a playground beside it with swings and exercise bars. The field was covered with clover, and on that first day Jackie and I spent some time after lunch looking for four-leaf clovers. Neither of us found any then, but a few weeks later Jackie proudly showed me one she had just picked. One year we all kept rabbits, which of course multiplied very fast. The teachers disposed of them without our knowing what had happened.

The American School had a multiracial student body, which was unusual in the Japan of the 1920s and 30s. I had classmates from America, Britain, France, Switzerland, Germany, Russia, Mexico, and China. I became such good friends with the Russian ambassador's son Mischa, who was in my class, that I was soon rolling my R's as he did, to my mother's great annoyance. I visited Mischa's house in Tokyo, where I remember encountering his big labrador, but we mainly played together in Karuizawa. At the time, his father was the Russian ambassador to Japan and later became ambassador to the United States. During the great Soviet purges of the late 1930s, he and his entire staff were repatriated to Moscow, and I was later told that they had been shot or imprisoned as German spies. I never found out what happened to Mischa.

In fourth grade, we were told to write a composition on the greatest contribution to the world that our countries had made. When I asked my parents for ideas, my mother suggested a vaccine to eradicate yellow fever discovered by Dr. Hideyo Noguchi in the early twentieth century. My father, however, said that joining the League of Nations in 1919 was Japan's major contribution to world peace – so that was what I wrote. Ironically, even as he spoke, Japan was in the process of leaving the League because of a resolution unanimously condemning Japan for the occupation of Manchuria.

It was around this time – October, as I recall – that I kissed Eleanor Lamott, my golden-haired classmate. The two of us were on the soccer field looking for four-leaf clovers, as I was wont to do. I found one, gave it to her, and on a sudden impulse, kissed her. She immediately ran into our classroom, screaming, "Takashi kissed me!" My classmates laughed, and I was so embarrassed I didn't know what to do. Eleanor and I are still good friends, all these years later, although I never repeated the kiss.

Jack Curtis was my best friend when I was growing up in Japan. His family was originally from Maine, but before they moved to the Kojimachi area of Tokyo, the Curtises had been in Harbin, the northeastern part of China almost entirely surrounded by Russia. In Tokyo, his father was the head of the National Citibank (what is now Citibank), but he would have furloughs to the US every 4 years or so, and he also traveled back and forth between Tokyo and Shanghai on business.

Shanghai was occupied by Japan then, but it still had an international settlement, and Jack's father was very fortunate to be able to avoid the fighting there in the late 1930s. Shanghai also had all sorts of goodies from the West, because, unlike the Japanese who were promoting Japanese-made goods, the Shanghai merchants were buying goods from all over, particularly from America and Europe. They had these fancy brands that were coveted by the Japanese. I remember that my father returned from a trip there with a stockpile of long-johns, which we all wore through the winter.

Jack's father also had a car, a Pierce Arrow, and a driver. So of course I wanted my father to have a car, but he was not interested – he was content with sharing ownership of a car with eight of his fellow salesmen.

My link to America, my best friend

Soon after the fall term had started at the American School in Tokyo, a new girl came into our fourth- grade classroom. Auburn-haired, with sparkling blue eyes, Barbara Curtis sat in the row next to mine and swept me off my feet. She told me she had lived most of her life in exotic Harbin, Manchuria, where her father was manager of an American bank. Harbin in those days had a large Russian population, and Barbara spoke Russian as fluently as English.

The next week, I was crushed when my new friend was promoted to fifth grade. But she had, in the meantime, introduced me to her younger brother Jack. For the next several years, until he went off to boarding school in Connecticut, he and I were best friends.

Blue-eyed like his sister and blond-haired, Jack was my living link to an America I knew only through magazines, books, and movies. To me, Jack's home epitomized the affluence and splendor of the American dream.

The Curtises lived in a handsome stucco mansion in a fashionable area of downtown Tokyo. The minute I stepped over the threshold, I knew I was in America. A Capehart record player stood in the entrance hall. These were the days of 78-r.p.m. records, and I never tired of asking Jack to put the machine on. As soon as one side of the record came to an end, a mechanical arm would reach out, turn the record over, and play the other side.

Every room in the house, including Jack's bedroom, seemed enormous. My creaky wooden house had a coal stove in the living room and a small stove, for charcoal briquettes, in the dining room. Otherwise, even in winter, we depended on the sun for heat. But Jack's house had central heating, and you could go from room to room and never feel the difference in temperature.

For Japanese in those days, "Western" or "American" meant grand, luxurious, substantial. Things Japanese could be delicate and exquisite, but were small, fragile, breakable. Western culture was said to be a culture of stone, while Japanese culture was one of wood and paper. Western things, whether houses or furniture or machinery, were built to last. In earthquake-prone Japan, most things were replaceable. The Grand Shrine of Ise, Japan's holiest temple, was a simple wooden structure, rebuilt every 20 years to look exactly the same as its immediate predecessor.

My own house, like that of many middle-class Japanese, was semi-Western, with both Western- and Japanese-style rooms. It was comfortable enough, but it could not compare in luxury and sense of permanence with Jack Curtis's house. Oh, to live in a country where every house was like Jack's!

Yet, at a deeper level, I was not envious of Jack. One part of me wanted to participate in the American dream. But another part of me was not uncomfortable with my Japanese background. Every Japanese is inured to the coexistence of things Japanese and things Western from an early age. My father wore Western clothes to work and a kimono at breakfast. Like almost all Japanese households, we had a set of tableware and cutlery for Western food, and another set for Japanese food. Art, music, dance, theater — almost everything we do or appreciate, we do in sets of two: Japanese and Western. We are not even conscious of making a differentiation, it is so instinctive.

Be that as it may, once our summer holidays arrived, the disparity between our modes of living ceased to matter. We and the Curtises and many other Japanese and Americans escaped the muggy heat of

Tokyo by moving to the mountain resort of Karuizawa. The resort sat on a plateau 3,000 feet above sea level. It took four hours by train, most of the last hour spent chugging up the mountains pushed by two electric locomotives.

What I loved about Karuizawa was that many of my American School friends, including Jack, spent their summers there, too. And unlike Tokyo, we could easily bicycle back and forth to each other's homes. For the duration of the summer, my American island in a Japanese sea was transported to Karuizawa.

Actually, we were a motley international crowd — not only Americans and English-speaking Japanese, but Argentines, Mexicans, Turks, French, Germans, Russians — a representative slice of the American School community. And, as in other countries, there was a differentiation between the summer residents and the locals, who were entirely Japanese and never seemed to tire of gaping at the outlandish antics of their visitors.

My house and Jack's were within five minutes of each other, and if we were not in one we were sure to be in the other. We went swimming in the ice-cold Andrews' pool, owned by a Canadian businessman and generously made available to the summer community. We joined a hiking club — our longest trek being an all-day excursion in the hills surrounding Karuizawa to a dairy with Jersey cows and kerosene lamps. We slept on the straw-matted floor and told each other ghost stories till we fell asleep.

The game of Monopoly was the rage in those days, and we would foolishly take a board up to my favorite perch in a huge fir tree. Inevitably, tokens and houses would drop and we would have to scramble down to find them. Still, we continued to use this perch.

Summer came to an end all too soon, and it would be time to head back to city life, which in the first few weeks always seemed so much more constricted than the carefree days in Karuizawa. Jack, too, eventually went off to boarding school in America. He came back once, for the summer, when we were in our teens. We had fun looking after a goat I had bought. But by then, Japan had been at war in China for three years, and though we did not know it, Pearl Harbor loomed on the horizon.

I shall skip over the painful war years. Brought up to become a bridge someday between Japan and America, I felt my whole life had become pointless. In Karuizawa, I would bicycle past Jack's empty house, wondering when and how the fighting would end and whether our friendship could ever be restored.

> When peace finally returned to Japan, I was a college student and working part time as a translator for the American military-occupation authorities. I'd heard nothing from the Curtises and had no idea what had happened to them.
>
> One day I was sitting at my desk working on a translation of a Japanese politician's diary, when my boss, a Nisei lieutenant, came to my desk and said, "There's someone asking for you." I looked up, and there, in a second-lieutenant's uniform, was Jack! He had studied Japanese in the Army, and been assigned to the very unit in which I was working. Neither of us will ever forget the exuberance of that moment. And our friendship, so dramatically renewed, has continued ever since
>
> —Takashi Oka for *The Christian Science Monitor*, October 2, 2000.

I lost touch with the Curtises during the war, but as soon as the fighting ended, Jack and I had our surprise reunion. Jack had learned proper Japanese and become a translator. At the time, Americans didn't fully trust the Japanese translators, but they didn't have enough of their own. So they used the Americans as supervisors of the Japanese, which added another layer of translation from Japanese to English. That's what Jack was doing. It was November 1945, and I was also employed as a translator at the International War Crimes Trial. The building in which I was working that day was two or three doors down from the Imperial Theater in Tokyo, where my mother and my aunt happened to be watching a musical. I took Jack over and surprised them, too.

His sister Barbara was very bright. She translated works from Russian to Japanese – a rare area of expertise. She eventually married a Japanese Nisei named Jim Adachi, and they were fixtures in the social scene in Tokyo for many years. She was always traveling back and forth to America.

Jack moved back to the US, went to college at Princeton, and became an architect in California. One year, he took a sabbatical to Japan to work for a Japanese firm, and we saw each other again. When I moved to the USA, I renewed contact, and we stayed in touch.

Jack loved the Japanese bath. The typical Japanese bath is made of cypress wood, and it looked like a round, deep keg. Being an architect, he had a bathtub made by the same craftsman who made bathtubs for the Emperor – that way he could tell his friends he was taking an imperial bath, even though he was 6'4" and could hardly fit in it. And it was in his bath that he died. Jack had a heart attack and that was it. But I think he would have been pleased to have departed in that particular way – in his Emperor's tub.

*****

From 1934 to 1937, I went to a private school that our friend Mrs. Miyo Matsukata ran in her home. In some ways, it was a bold decision on my mother's part to send me to the Matsukatas' school. She looked at the example set by her uncle (Chiyo's brother), who had graduated from Tokyo Imperial University and received a *gin dokei*, or silver watch, the mark of the top graduates at that time – after which, he didn't really do much of anything. To my mother, this proved that traditional accolades didn't necessarily guarantee a brilliant career.

Mrs. Matsukata was born in Greenwich, Connecticut, and she was an American citizen. She was the daughter of Ryoichiro

Arai, one of the first Japanese silk merchants in New York in the late 19th century. A community of well-off Japanese lived in New York then, and they were all members of the New York Japan Society. There was a Dr. Nitobe, who went to work for the League of Nations and became the Under-Secretary General; and Dr. Takamine, who invented a pill for stomach disorders (the enzyme he isolated was named after him, takadiastase) and became very wealthy because of it. Takamine had an American wife who was a Quaker, as was he.

While Mrs. Matsukata's father was selling silk, his very good friend Ichizaemon Morimura sold porcelain and chinaware, which quickly became very popular in the West. These were Japan's first great exports, silk and Noritake china, and during World War I, Japan became internationally prosperous for the first time. The Europeans were so busy fighting each other that the Japanese moved into the vacuum that was created.

My mother was part of this community in New York, and she knew the Matsukatas before she – and they – became Christian Scientists.

By 1922, Mrs. Matsukata had built her dream house in Tokyo – a large western-style mansion designed by the American architect Merrell Vories – and invited a woman named Florence Boynton to move in as a governess to the Matsukatas' six children. An extraordinary teacher, Miss Boynton also served as a Christian Science practitioner and Sunday School teacher, as well as a private tutor in their home. She had a major influence on my life and thinking.

I have vivid memories of Miss Boynton – her lovely face, with blue-grey eyes framed by curly brown hair, and her musical voice. She often said of herself that she was a born teacher. When she taught us the Psalms, she said they were poems meant to be sung, and she showed us how a Psalm was divided up into strophes. To illustrate the strophes, she marched up and down her room, pausing for emphasis. She had a great sense of humor but was also a strict teacher, both in Sunday School and in the English and history classes she taught there at the Matsukatas' house.

One of her subjects she called "Word Analysis." With certain key vocabulary words, she had us go to the dictionary to look up the Latin, Greek, or Anglo-Saxon root, to find synonyms and antonyms, to see how meanings had evolved over the centuries. She also drilled us thoroughly on the structure of a sentence – the basic subject, verb, object, and the various dependent clauses. She taught us to read poetry aloud, showed us the function of simile and metaphor, alliteration and allegory. Longfellow's "Evangeline," Whittier's "Snowbound" came alive for us, and we could see in our mind's eye the primeval forests or snowy farmhouses.

Miss Boynton had arrived in Japan soon after the end of the Russo-Japanese War, accompanying her friends the Allens and their four children. She taught English at two well-known high schools: Furitsu Itchu (First Prefectural High School) and Okura Commercial High School, the former being the premier high school in Japan, the latter for budding Japanese businessmen. For many years Miss Boynton was the only Christian Science practitioner in Tokyo.

Christian Science had become a presence in Japan around the turn of the century. Within the foreign community in Tokyo, there was a small circle of British and American Christian Scientists, including Baroness D'Annetain, who was herself English but whose husband was the Belgian Minister to Japan. Mrs. Matsukata joined the group around 1917, having been converted by Rear-Admiral Horn, the American naval attaché in Tokyo. Miss Boynton and Mrs. Matsukata had come to Christian Science separately, but their friendship soon blossomed, and in the early 1920s Mrs. Matsukata invited her to join her household. The two were essentially the first real Christian Scientists in Tokyo, and they were instrumental in founding the Christian

Science Society, Tokyo, in the late 1920s.

Miss Boynton had become a Christian Scientist in San Francisco, after being healed of cancer in the early 1900s. I relied on her to treat various childhood ailments. One in particular that I remember was of a nasty cold and fever I had caught when I was twelve, while seeing off friends at the Yokohama pier on a freezing winter's day. My father took me to the Matsukata home in a taxi, and as soon as I came in, Mari and Miye – the youngest two of the Matsukatas' daughters – relayed to Miss Boynton that I looked "as white as a sheet." She called me to her study and immediately gave me a Christian Science treatment. It was the first instantaneous healing I remember. One moment I felt feverish and sick. Within half an hour I was as bright and perky as normal.

Inside the Matsukata house, Miss Boynton's bedroom was upstairs, next to that of Mari and Miye. She also had the downstairs parlor as her study and office, where she received patients. I always knew when Mrs. Mitsui (the millionaire mother of Mrs. Takaki and of Mr. Takanaga Mitsui) had an appointment with Miss Boynton, because her elegant *zori*, or sandals, were neatly placed just inside the entrance hall.

Miss Boynton had a lively interest in current world affairs and had us read books by William Henry Chamberlin, who was then the *Monitor* correspondent in Japan and who had reported out of Moscow during the Russian Revolution. My interest in journalism and contemporary political affairs grew out of Miss Boynton's teaching and her ability to make current events, whether political or cultural, fascinating and alive.

Our curriculum somewhat resembled that of an American high school, with an emphasis on the humanities. Miss Boynton taught us Greek and Roman history; also the history of England in considerable detail. King John and the granting of Magna Carta was a highlight. She started us off in Latin, although we didn't go very far with it, and she gave us a pretty thorough grounding in French. Our textbook was the tear-jerker "Sans Famille," and she gave us a *dictée* every day around noon. Years later, when I was taking French at L'Athénée Francais in Kanda, my teacher wanted to know how I had managed to pick up an American accent in Japan – but he had no complaint over the working knowledge of the language that I had gained.

Miss Boynton also made us aware of the difference between right and wrong and the need to stand up and be counted if the time ever came. I must confess that when she was telling us about the Christian martyrs of Nero's day, I wondered whether I would ever have the courage to face the lions. She made us aware that we were living in the period of Hitler and his concentration camps, of Stalin and his purges. She loved Japan but had no sympathy for what the Japanese were doing in China. I do not remember specifically what she said about the Emperor or Japanese militarism, but her emphasis was always on the importance of absolute values, in contrast to the relativism of most Japanese. I was aware that the kind of education I was receiving was totally at odds with what the nationalists and fanatics wanted.

It is impossible to separate the purely secular aspect of what Miss Boynton taught from her work as a Christian teacher. She was a very loyal American, but what she taught was not a set of exclusively American values. I got more American history and associated folklore in my five years at the American School than I did with her. What she imparted was a sense of universal human values, emphasizing the worth of every individual before God.

Despite Miss Boynton's influence, I really didn't like it there, mostly because I only had two classmates, both of whom were girls. Mari and Miye Matsukata may have been my friends, but there's not too much you can do when you have such a small student body. The other four Matsukata children were in school elsewhere, and all six of them were older than me. I would eventually become close friends with Haru, the second daughter, but she was nine years older than me, which at that time was a big difference. There was only one boy among the sisters, Makoto, nicknamed Mako, who was four years older than me and who took a patronizing older-brother attitude toward both me and his sisters.

My mother tried to supplement my lack of male friends by signing me up with an English-speaking Boy Scouts troupe, founded by a missionary named Mr. Walzer. I remember the longest hike we took was to Kozu Bokujo, a dairy farm up in the mountains. It was there that I had my first oblique encounter with sex – I saw some bulls jumping on the cows, and I hadn't the faintest idea what they were doing. So I asked an older scout, who said, "Oh you're too young. I'll tell you in a couple of years." But by then I had left the Boy Scouts.

After the financial panic of the late 1920s, the Matsukatas had to retrench, and they rented out their house to a succession of diplomatic tenants – the Canadian Embassy, the Argentinian Embassy, and the Swedish Embassy. Today it is the Nishimachi International School, founded by their third daughter Tane Matsukata, and giving equal weight to English and Japanese in the curriculum.

A bond between cultures — Tane Matsukata's Students Learn to Forget Their Differences

The playground resounds with the shouts and laughter of children of many nationalities — blue-eyed, black-eyed, fair-haired, brown-haired, pale-skinned, dark-skinned.

It was recess time at Nishimachi International School, where 365 children from 30 nationalities, kindergarten through ninth grade, study, play, and learn to appreciate each other.

"What's so wonderful about children of this age," said the principal, Tane Matsukata, "is that they all learn to work together without intellectualizing, without stopping to think 'he's American' or 'I'm Indian or Japanese.' They learn what's fair play. They learn what's honesty. They learn, too, that there's more than one 'right' way of doing things. You do your things your way. I do my things my way. And you begin to see that the other kids' way of doing things may be just as valid as yours."

Nishimachi International School, founded in 1949, has a dual purpose, Miss Matsukata said. First, its original aim, to teach Japanese children to become world citizens. Second, to teach children of the international community in Tokyo to appreciate cultures and societies other than their own, especially that of Japan, the country in which they are living.

Small classes. Family-like atmosphere. Individual attention. These have been characteristic of the school from the start. It began with a student body of four in the home of Mrs. Yuri Murata, one of the school's founding parents. It continues to this day in the spacious Western-style mansion that used to be Miss Matsukata's parental home in a quiet, central residential area.

"To have a school here where Japanese can mingle with people of other nationalities and be accepted, not as Japanese, but as Toshi or Mari — this is a very needed choice in education. That's why I'm not interested in having the school too big."

Whatever their nationality, all pupils must learn both Japanese and English. Beginners receive private coaching until they reach the level of their age group. "It's important for an American child living here to learn Japanese," says Miss Matsukata, "because through this he finds out how feelings are expressed, what feelings are expressed, as well as something about art and history and the kind of country Japan is."

Her own background taught her to think in more than single-nation terms, Miss Matsukata says. She comes from a distinguished family. One grandfather, Masayoshi Matsukata, established the foundations of Japan's modern banking and financial system in the late 19th century. Conscious of Japan's need to learn from the West, he sent his sons to study in Britain, Germany, and the United States. Her other grandfather, Ryoichiro Arai, was one of Japan's first silk merchants in the United States, having established himself in New York in 1871 at the age of 17. Mr. Arai was a friend of one of Japan's pioneer educators, Yukichi Fukuzawa. "Go to America," Mr. Fukuzawa told him. "Make your headquarters there. Don't come back to Japan to live." Mr. Arai followed this advice. It was in America that his daughter Miyo met Prince Matsukata's son Shokuma, who was studying at Yale.

When the two were married and returned to Japan, Mrs. Matsukata felt the need of a more liberal, individual-centered education for her own children than the Japanese schools of the day provided.

Thus, her children, including Tane, were educated not only in private schools but also, for a period, in their own home along with the children of some family friends. The school became known informally as the Matsukata Academy, and it was the forebear of the Nishimachi School of today. The Matsukata Academy centered on Miss Florence Boynton, a remarkable American teacher whom Mrs. Matsukata persuaded to tutor her own children and those of some of her friends.

Miss Matsukata spent her last two years of high school and her entire college career in the US, at Principia College in Elsah, Ill. The Japanese attack on Pearl Harbor occurred while Miss Matsukata and her sisters were at Principia. As "enemy aliens" the girls were interned on the college campus.

Along with the sense of the worth of the individual inculcated during her years in the US, Miss Matsukata says she feels particularly grateful for the love that was expressed to her during her wartime internment.

"We were just accepted," she recalls. "No platitudes. Every time we went off campus we had to report to the FBI, but otherwise everything seemed perfectly natural. I didn't feel strange being there at all."

The war over, she returned to Japan with a master's degree in library science from Columbia University. But somewhere in the back of her mind there was a feeling that, if she ever got the chance, she would like to be able to pass on to others that same freeing sense of individual worth, that same accepting of people without first categorizing them as Japanese or Americans or whatever.

Miss Matsukata's first job in Tokyo was at the National Diet Library, modeled after the US Library of Congress. But she found it impossible to become enthusiastic over arguments as to whether the Dewey decimal system or the Japanese decimal system should prevail. Then, in 1949, a friend, Mrs. Yuri Murata, implored her to take over the education of her two young sons.

These were stirring times. A devastated, thoroughly disillusioned nation was beginning the painful process of economic and psychological recovery, of thinking through what went wrong in the years leading up to Pearl Harbor and Hiroshima, of taking the first, exuberant yet risk-filled steps on the road of democratic freedoms.

Mrs. Murata felt strongly that to prevent the tragedy of militarism and war ever overtaking Japan again, a new generation had to be brought up to think and feel in more than narrowly nationalistic terms. She did not see in the local schools of the period anywhere she wanted to place her children. Only someone like Miss Matsukata, who had herself experienced the wideness of the world outside, could, she thought, give a fresh impetus to education in Japan.

Miss Matsukata at first demurred. "I'm not a trained teacher," she said. "I don't know anything about children." But gradually Mrs. Murata's importunity persuaded her. This was in 1949, and the first classroom, for Mrs. Murata's children and two others, was a 9-by-9-foot room in Mrs. Murata's one-story home.

Since then, Nishimachi has grown steadily, from all-Japanese to international, from six-year primary school to kindergarten through ninth grade. Somehow Miss Matsukata and her devoted staff, now numbering 50, seem to have kept the family atmosphere and the careful attention to individual needs that characterized the early years.

Partly this is achieved by keeping the school on a small campus in the middle of

> the city, rather than transferring to the suburbs as many other private schools in Tokyo have done. The school's main building is still the gracious old Matsukata mansion with wood-paneled rooms and fire-places, and most of the parents want to keep it that way.
>
> — Takashi Oka for *The Christian Science Monitor,* November 4, 1982.

*****

The Matsukata school, being a private school, was not recognized by the Japanese education system, so in order to advance through high school - and eventually to an American college - I had to finish my requirements within the Japanese system.

My time in the Japanese school system began in the fifth grade, and I was still learning to read and write in Japanese, which I didn't like because of all the Chinese characters I had to study. There are over 100,000 characters, and students had to know at least 2,000. So, to me, studying Japanese was always associated with drudgery. By comparison, I thought English was fun.

One of my only regrets about leaving the American School was that I was just at the point where I could throw a decent baseball - that's when I had to quit. In Japanese schools, the compulsory athletic subjects were Judo and Kendo. You had to take one of the two, so I took Kendo. I was given a big wooden sword and a protective mask to cover my head and started learning the forms.

My brother Akira also went to the American School, but only through sixth grade. Just as he was about to graduate, the Mitsuis - who were sort of the Rothschilds of Japan - started a new school called Keimei, which was designed for Japanese children who had been educated overseas. It had a regular Japanese curriculum, but the English was much superior to that of a Japanese secondary school. I would have gone to Keimei myself except that I was too old – it was founded when I was in the second grade of high school. It was also modeled on a more British than American system, and I remember that Akira had to wear a uniform there – a blue shirt, tucked in. When the War began, the Mitsuis moved the school to one of their villas in the countryside, accessible by train from Tokyo. I think the students all lived in dormitories then because it was about an hour outside of Tokyo. My Aunt Kiyo used to teach English there, and she would make the three hour commute to get there and back every day. That school was started in 1940, and it has survived to this day.

Aunt Kiyo lived with us in my grandparents' house for several years. Before then, she had lived with her younger brother in Yokosuka, the naval port south of Tokyo, and later on she lived with the Matsukatas, where she was a Christian Science practitioner. She never married, and instead remained very close to the family. Aunty Kiyo was always around when I was growing up, which, for me, was a bit like having two mothers at the same time – both of whom were quite demanding.

Outside of school, I was one of the few kids in my neighborhood who spoke English. The Sawadas were one of the only other families I knew who did, having lived in San Francisco. My two uncles (my mother's brothers) had grown up in Vancouver and came back to Japan speaking English. However they soon stopped because they didn't want to stand out from their friends, none of whom spoke English. Once having learned to read and write the language, they never really forgot it, but it was dormant in them for years. Although all their relatives were Japanese, my mother and my aunt were more at home in the international atmosphere in which they had grown up.

As for me, I had started out playing with the neighborhood children in Japanese. But after I went to the American school, while my neighborhood friends went to the Japanese public school near Shinmachi, we didn't see each other so frequently. We exchanged stamps in our stamp collections, but the very close kind of running around together stopped, because I started having these other, English-speaking friends.

No one ever reproached me for speaking English. But I suppose I, like my uncles, consciously tried to avoid standing out. I only spoke English within my own family. That worked out all right – in fact, by the time of the War, when English had become an enemy language, I had joined what was called the English-Speaking Society. Most universities had them, and they featured speech contests and debates in English.

But all that was about to change.

Chapter 3

Pre-war Years

In 1937, as I wondered how the war would turn out, friends kept saying to me: "Well, you're 13 years old now, so don't worry. The war will be over before you're of age." But things got darker and darker, and my dream of going to America became more complicated. My mother was always telling me that I had to be a bridge between America and Japan, but that part was very frustrating because I had no idea how I was going to do it.

After 1937, I continued going to the Matsukatas' once a week or so, studying with Haru, who by that time was one of the only Matsukatas in Japan. All the other Matsukatas were at Principia – the Christian Science College in Illinois – or other glamorous (so I thought) places in America. Haru's brother Mako would go on to teach Japanese at Harvard, while Miye would attend the Boston Museum School of Art. Mari, the sister closest to me in age, left a few years later and would move on to grad school at Washington University in St. Louis, studying and then teaching dress design. The Takakis had also left Tokyo.

I felt isolated in Japan, while my friends were having a great time in America. From my point of view, they were all in a very fortunate position, away from the war, on an idyllic 2,000 acre campus in the village of Elsah, Illinois, where students could go get a hotdog whenever they wanted. Even the period of internment some of them experienced was, by comparison to what happened to other Japanese-Americans, almost luxurious. In any case, the reality was that once my friends reached the US, they were stuck there because of the war, just as Haru and I were stuck in Japan.

Despite the disparity in our ages, Haru treated me as if

she were an older sibling and not simply my English tutor, although she did carry on the teaching that Miss Boynton had begun. In March 1937, I went to middle school at Tamagawa Gakuen, and then I transferred to Rikkyo (St Paul's) High School in September 1940. Once a week, after finishing at Rikkyo at 3 p.m., I went to the Matsukata home in Azabu Nishimachi to read and discuss books with Haru – Walter Scott's *Ivanhoe* and *Lady of the Lake*, and John Greenleaf Whittier's *Snowbound*. I dipped my toe into Caesar's commentary on Gaul, although that was the extent of my involvement with Latin. No Virgil, no Cicero.

With Haru I didn't feel the constraint I sensed with the other Matsukatas. I always regarded her as an older sister, and I'm sure she, being nine years older, looked on me much like a younger brother. At the American School, Haru was a high school senior while I was still in second grade. That year the school play was about Hiawatha – the Longfellow poem based on that story, told in verse – and I remember that Haru played Old Nokomis, the grandmother, and I played the grandson, little Hiawatha.

Haru was the second daughter of Mr. and Mrs. Shokuma Matsukata. She had graduated from Principia in 1937, then returned to Japan to write a doctoral thesis about her grandfather, Prince Masayoshi Matsukata, who served twice as prime minister of Japan and who put the country on the gold standard during his lengthy term as finance minister.

I mention the Matsukatas as having a certain kind of reservedness, or hauteur, in my mind, because they were descended from a prince. When I was a child a group of us were chatting – one kid said that his father was an admiral, another said his father was a doctor, and so forth and so on, and then Mari said, "Well my grandfather was a *prince*." But it was the kind of title attained through merit, not from being born into the nobility. To be fair, I may have imagined this hauteur, seeing that my own father came from modest circumstances, being the son of a country Buddhist priest.

Koshaku, translated as prince, was the highest rank of nobility. It was given to leading court nobles and feudal lords, like Kujo and Takatsukasa or Shimazu, and also to statesmen and bureaucrats, like Hirobumi Ito. In 1868, the Meiji government abolished all feudal titles and, in compensation, gave the feudal lords titles of nobility, modeled on Bismarck's Germany – prince, marquis, count, viscount, and baron. Prince Matsukata was first made a count, then a marquis, and a couple years before he died, a prince. In 1945, even these hereditary titles were abolished with the new Constitution, but some of the prestige of those abolished titles continues.

We used to go to the Matsukatas' house for Thanksgiving dinner. Not many Japanese celebrated Thanksgiving, but there are two traditional Shinto harvest festivals in the fall, and since our families had spent time in the US, we just mixed up the three. We lived in the suburbs, and they lived in the middle of town, about an hour's train-ride away. It was quite an exclusive area of Tokyo, right in the center of town among many foreign embassies and wealthy, titled Japanese. The Mitsuis, who were our neighbors in Karuizawa, had their townhouse in this area.

Today I don't have any sense of the Matsukatas' social superiority, but in my teens it was a major problem for me. After all, the Mr. Matsukata we knew – Shokuma – was a son of the founder of modern Japan's financial and banking system. Mr. Matsukata himself had graduated from the agricultural faculty at Todai – called Tokyo Imperial University in those days, and plain Tokyo University today – and then became President of Tokyo Seito, which grew sugar cane in Taiwan and sugar beets in Hokkaido (He was always in hot Taiwan during the summer and in cold Hokkaido during the winter). But he was also an inveterate experimenter and a hands-on agriculturist, keeping earthworms in flowerpots in his house to aerate the soil. Their garden also had several large loquat trees, and I was sometimes commissioned to climb up and shake the fruit out of the branches.

Mr. Matsukata must have had his share of sad or unhappy moments, but whenever I saw him he was always in good humor. The February 26, 1936 rebellion of the Konoe Guards must have been a trying time for him. That day, our classes were dismissed after the morning session, and when I took the tram home, I saw soldiers with fixed bayonets at Shibuya Station. Several leading Japanese statesmen were killed during this brief but bloody rebellion. One of them, Korekiyo Takahashi, was the grandfather of a classmate at Tamagawa Gakuen High School. Even then, Mr. Matsukata never showed a gloomy face, at least as far as we children could discern.

I think that Mr. and Mrs. Matsukata had a rather unusual marriage, in that they were both compatible with each other, and therefore happy with each other. In most Japanese marriages, the husband just sort of barked his orders and the wife obeyed. Even today, marriage in Japan is basically between families: behind the husband and the wife a hierarchy can become an enormous weight. But Haru's parents were more like an American family. For a Japanese man, Mr. Matsukata was not stern. I remember we went to an amusement park one time, and Mari got stuck on a rope dangling between two poles. She was frightened and couldn't go forward or backward. So her father told her to jump, and he caught her in his arms.

As for my own father, I don't remember him saying much to me about the political situation in those early years. One of the first and most blunt lessons I learned about how national feelings could cut across individual and family relations, was when I wanted to see my American friends the Meads (who were cousins of the famous Margaret Mead). They were Protestant missionaries who lived in Beijing, and they frequently visited us on their way back and forth between China and the United States. We received a letter that said, in effect, that we were not welcome, because the Meads' Chinese friends were deeply angered by the Japanese occupation of their homeland.

My mother was much more openly pro-American than my father, even though he worked for an American company. But anti-American sentiment was spreading quickly. It was a strange time – I remember a friend's mother saying, "Don't you want to wash your hands every time you shake hands with an American?" She was astonished that some Americans had so much body hair, even on their hands.

Because my father worked for RCA Victor, we would get records every month, and we had a combination record player/radio. However, my father had the shortwave band on the radio disconnected because it was not allowed in Japan in those years. Akira was very handy with all things mechanical, and he had a hobby of making primitive crystal radio sets, which he would break up before anyone could catch him. In those days, the BBC was broadcasting to the Far East with powerful signals out of New Delhi, and Akira and I would stay up at night and secretly listen in. The Tokyo house, like our Karuizawa cottage, had thin sliding doors covered by paper, so it was very difficult to keep anything secret, and of course our father knew what we were up to. All he said was: *"Tampa kiite inai daro ne"* (You aren't listening to short-wave radio, are you?) We assured him we were not. I suppose he trusted us enough to not get caught. Anyway, that was how we got more information on the war.

In June 1940, my cousins Seitaro and Yasuko Yada returned to Japan from Bombay with their mother, whom I called Aunt Teruko. She was married to Makoto Yada, whom we called Uncle Makochan, and who had been with the Yokohama Specie Bank (today the Bank of Tokyo) since graduating from Kyoto Imperial University in the late 1920s. He was short and sturdily built and did his mandatory military service with the Konoye Imperial Guards. I remember that when I was six or seven, I went to Kudan with my grandmother to greet Uncle Makochan when he was discharged. After working in Bombay, my uncle's next post was London in June 1940, at the height of the German blitz. He went by ship around the Cape of Good Hope and arrived safely, but sent his family home from Bombay to Japan. Akira and I were delighted to have new playmates. Seitaro was an unusual child, bright and friendly, and I was fascinated that he and his sister Yasuko spoke Hindi, having come from Bombay. In fact, Yasuko spoke nothing but Hindi then. We all went to Karuizawa for the summer.

At Grandmother Yada's house – a ten-minute walk from our house – I was eagerly learning to play contract bridge, since my mother and aunt only knew auction bridge from their girlhood in New York. Both my grandparents loved card games, including Japanese *hanafuda* (flower cards). But contract bridge was a new language, and Uncle Makochan initiated me into its mysteries, starting with how to bid small slams and grand slams. He was a great teacher, patient and humorous.

As we gained these new friends, we continued to feel the absence of others. In August 1940, Miss Boynton returned to the United States, permanently, as it turned out, on the Asama Maru – one of the last Japanese passenger ships to make the trans-Pacific crossing. She took Mari Matsukata with her. That fall, Mari enrolled as a senior at Principia Upper School (high school), and she went on to Principia College the following autumn.

In November 1940, I experienced the first deaths in my family. Grandfather Yada had a stroke as he was walking home with Grandmother from Shinmachi Station. They had just been to a diplomatic reception with some of their closest friends, when he suddenly fell. I found out the next morning, when Mama and Aunt Kiyo went to the Yada house.

A month later, Seitaro, Uncle Makochan's son, died at the age of 7. He had been staying at our house for a week or so, and then he suddenly went into convulsions. I called Mrs. Matsukata in a panic and she told me he had probably just eaten something bad. This didn't reassure me at all. I also called Seitaro's mother, Aunt Teruko. Seitaro was taken to Keio University Hospital and died about a week later. Uncle Makochan was away in London, so I had to write him a telegram giving the doctor's report. I had to look up "encephalitis" in the dictionary to find out how to spell the name of the disease, which most people then knew as "sleeping sickness."

I also wrote a long letter to Miss Boynton, telling her that these were the first deaths that had personally touched me. About a month later I received her response. It was short, and made no reference to the events about which I had sought her comfort and guidance. "Never lose your joy." Essentially, that was all she said. I was furious and full of self-pity. I had written Miss Boynton seeking comfort and reassurance, and what did I get: a short sermon on joy!

As the weeks passed, and as I read her letter over and over, I began to recognize what she was trying to tell me. Only joy can erase sorrow, can nothing-ize it, as a Christian Scientist might say. Miss Boynton had done what she had always done. She had acted as the practitioner in my case. Well then, if I was the patient, I had to follow the practitioner's instructions. I became determined to express joy in all my thoughts and actions. But the following four years would prove very trying.

On December 8, 1941, I woke up to hear on the radio that Japanese ships – half a world away, half a day away – had attacked Pearl Harbor. Japan, the country of my birth, was at war with the United States, the land to which I longed to go.

My memories of Haru became more meaningful during World War II. There was an unspoken bond between us – a sense that we were both stuck in Japan, separated from our friends and family, with no idea what would happen next. These 3 families – mine, the Matsukatas, and the Takakis – were all very close, and the children all went to Principia, so I expected that's what I would do, too. It was a plan that I'd been following my whole life.

But after Japan attacked Pearl Harbor, my dreams of studying in America seemed permanently shattered.

During these years, Haru, like me, became consumed by the details of life during the war. She essentially became a farmer, carrying buckets of night soil to her vegetable patch. She never completed her dissertation about her grandfather, even though she continued to work on it almost every day with Wakita Sensei, a specialist in Japanese history. It wasn't until 1956, when Haru married Edwin Oldfather Reischauer, a major Japan scholar, that her academic work moved forward. Ed helped her prepare a doctoral thesis at Harvard, which she then turned into two separate projects: her own autobiography, which was published in English and Japanese under the title *Samurai and Silk* (and became a best-seller in Japan), and a scholarly biography of Prince Matsukata, which she was unable to complete before she died.

Meanwhile, I lost interest in my studies. Tamagawa Gakuen, where I had enrolled in 1937, was a permissive school that allowed students to study at their own pace – so I hardly studied at all. If you had the discipline, it was not a bad place to be, and I had a classmate who did quite well. But I spent much too much time playing around and ended up with terrible grades. My parents were both concerned, but my father had more or less left my education in the hands of my mother, as most Japanese fathers tended to do. He only got involved when he saw that I was getting grades in the single digits – out of 100. He gave me a dressing down, and I promised to mend my ways, but it was very late.

By September 1940, my mother decided that I needed a more rigorous school. So she consulted with a friend who was a Rikkyo (St. Paul's) graduate, who said he could arrange for me to transfer to Rikkyo, a school that was not so easy to get into. Of course you had to pass exams, but you also had to bring gifts to the principal, and even then you might not get in. That was the culture then, so that's what we did – and I got in.

If you graduated with a B average, you could advance from Rikkyo High School to Rikkyo College without an exam. I didn't have the required B average. Instead, I thought I could study really hard in my final year in order to pass the entrance exam of some other more prestigious university. Rikkyo High School had a reasonable reputation then, but Rikkyo University definitely was considered second-rate in those days (not true today). The pinnacle of the education system was Tokyo Imperial University, probably the only Japanese school that could compete with Harvard or Yale. So I told myself that I would cram enough to make it into someplace better, but then I didn't really study. Instead I spent that year with my classmates Yoshikawa and Yokoyama playing billiards. There were several billiards parlors around the university, and they were basically the only available amusements. If you were under 20, as I was then, you couldn't drink alcohol, and you couldn't smoke until you finished high school. I had no interest in smoking, but I was quite interested in drinking beer and sake, but mostly I went to coffee houses and drank coffee. Then after a year of fooling around, it was time to take the test.

At the Rikkyo college exam, part of the test involved a composition titled simply: "Ah! The Nine!" We weren't given any other information about this title, but I knew that it referenced an early episode in the war in which five Japanese mini-submarines had participated in the attack on Pearl Harbor. All but one were sunk, and one of the crew of that sub was captured and sent to a POW camp. Knowing that there were two men per submarine, I recognized that the composition should have been titled "Ah! The Ten!" – because there were ten people in total on these mini-submarines. But since only nine were killed, they expected us to write an essay on the patriotism of these young men, who were the same age as we were, and how they had sacrificed themselves. So I wrote something in that vein, but I know that some of my friends were completely mystified. They didn't really follow current events, and they had no idea what this essay was supposed to be about. So they just wrote fanciful essays on whatever they thought would be appropriate. Anyway, I got into Rikkyo University, but just barely. That was in 1942.

The war had begun, but it didn't really affect our normal lives as students until closer to the end. At Rikkyo, my whole class was conscripted – not immediately to the army, but to various companies making munitions. And so, yet again, I wasn't doing any real studying. We went for about six months to such a place, and then we had another six months back in school. Before the war got so severe, we would go off for a month or so to work in a factory or on a farm, sometimes during the summer holidays. But as the war grew more intense, the time we spent working in factories and farms stretched longer and longer.

Of course, we shouldn't have had to get drafted to work like that, but we were, and all students were – so there was nothing particularly unique about my case. Even before the war, all young men were required to take physical exams for the army at age 20, with a mandatory two-year service beginning at age 21. Japan was a type of society in which people did everything together, from kindergarten to university. You couldn't freely do whatever you wanted. Although the war might have somewhat altered that order, I couldn't just run off somewhere.

As I think of it now, these years – particularly high school – were really very empty years. My only interest was in going to college in America, and if I couldn't do that, then I didn't particularly care where I went. That was my attitude. I had the impression that I was turning into a *furyo*, a boy who had gone wrong. For years I had been able to ignore the constant sabre-rattling, but as the war stretched on, I felt that the main purpose in my life had been deflected.

I would come to rely on my Christian Science faith as never before to get me through the next several years.

Chapter 4

WAR

The three great duties of Japanese citizens – or so I was told in middle school – were to go to school, to vote, and to serve in the military. The physical examination, *shintai kensa*, which every boy received, signaled our entry into manhood. At age 20, the event – for both boys and girls – is accompanied by various ceremonies. The new adults go to a Shinto shrine at midnight, and in Tokyo, as in other cities and villages, you will hear the gong of the local temple utter a deep roar, as if the gong itself were a body coming alive.

* * * * *

Even before the War, Japan had a somewhat complex relationship with America. On one hand, Abraham Lincoln and George Washington were popular figures, and the history of America was told in generally positive terms in Japanese high schools. Many Japanese wanted to study in America and did so. On the other hand, many people thought that Americans were too interested in making money, which went contrary to the samurai ideal. Of course, Japanese merchants made money, but the merchants were a lower class than the samurai and even the farmers. That system, though abolished, had existed for hundreds of years and still influenced thinking. Nonetheless, when Japan entered the modern world, America was viewed as an inspiration. More American missionaries and businessmen came to Japan than from any single European country.

But Japan also looked to Britain, an island nation that ruled the seas, and accordingly laid great emphasis on its navy. When Japan went to war with China in 1895, they beat the Chinese, and ten years later they beat the Russians. In between, in 1902, Japan formed an alliance with Britain – it was the first non-European country to do so. This was also the first mark of becoming an equal of the West. The British, seeing that Japan was becoming the dominant power in Asia, wanted a partnership. For the Japanese, the alliance with Britain provided an entrée into the club of world powers.

In World War I, Japan quickly occupied the German colony of Tsingtao, after which it hardly did any fighting – in fact Japan prospered because, for the first time, Japanese goods could enter the world market. At the end of the war, Japan sided with the victorious Allies, and the 1920s ushered in Japan's democratic period, when there were two political parties alternating with each other for power. The military, at that time, was not so dominant.

However, Japan's late entry into the modern world caught up with it. Japan became an imperialist power when imperialism was going out of fashion – or at least when the British and the French (and the Americans in the Philippines) were taking steps towards freeing their colonies, rather than conquering new ones. The Japanese were beginning to consider Manchuria as a colony. In 1931, they invaded and installed a puppet regime – arriving a hundred years late to the colonial game. The British, having occupied India and elsewhere around the globe, were quite ready to accommodate Japan's colonial ambitions – so long as it was only at the expense of China, and so long as Japan observed international law.

To the Chinese, Japan's invasion of Manchuria represented more than political greed or ambition – I think China resented the fact that Japan considered itself a Western power. Before World War II, the five major powers of the world were Britain, Germany, France, the US, and Japan. China was not included. Rather than joining with China to resist the European onslaught, Japan tried to join the Europeans. By the end of 1937, Japan had bloodied its hands in as terrible a fashion as any colonial predecessor, with the Nanking Massacre. At the same time, Stalin was doing terrible things in the Soviet Union that distracted the world's attention from Japan's activities north of the Great Wall.

China's anger eventually found voice in a complaint to the League of Nations that Japan was violating the League covenant. The League sent a commission, headed by Lord Lytton, that traveled all around Manchuria and Beijing, and concluded that the Chinese were right – that Japan was the guilty party, and that Japan was in the process of invading further into Northern China. Japan was ostracized by its former allies, and it withdrew from the League of Nations.

Dr. Nitobe, whom my family had known in New York and who was the Under-Secretary General for the League of Nations, got embroiled in the controversy. Nitobe apparently felt that Japan's actions were no different from the British colonization of India or France's of Indochina. The colonialists' justification was that they were going to uplift the natives. So he went to America and lectured to that effect, and was summarily ostracized as a propagandist for the Japanese.

About the same time, Hitler walked into the Rhineland and thereby annulled the major results of World War I. Thus there were two countries who had defied the League of Nations – one country defying the West in Europe, and one defying the West in Asia. Germany and Japan, having originally become modern nations within three years of each other, signed a treaty against the Communist International in 1936, and then formed an alliance in 1940. By that time World War II had already started, so the alliance didn't specifically bring Japan into the War, but it brought the Japanese closer to Germany.

*****

For Japanese citizens, the war years were difficult and

long – although the US bombing raids that destroyed most Japanese cities, including Tokyo, did not begin until March 10, 1945. During most of the war, mental confusion weighed down my thoughts like a heavy, wet blanket. Still, as I reflected on my correspondence with Miss Boynton, I recognized that she had written to me as a practitioner answering a patient's call. If I was her patient, I had to obey her instructions. So, during all the fraught years that followed, I tried to become more consistent in expressing joy, however difficult or trying the circumstances.

After Pearl Harbor, Uncle Makochan was interned in the British countryside for a few months – I don't remember the name of the town – then repatriated to Japan in August 1942. He returned on the Kamakura Maru, the newest and most elegant Japanese passenger ship. He told us how the Kempeitai, the feared military police, boarded the ship as it approached Japanese waters and interrogated all the passengers to test their loyalty to Japan. One of the tests was to remember the name of the year according to the Japanese calendar – in which 1942 was the 17th year of Showa. Some of Uncle Makochan's fellow-repatriates failed the test and were harshly scolded by the gendarme.

Also traveling on the same ship was Sadakazu Takaki, whom we knew as Sada, and who carried with him a succinct three-page letter from Naka Matsukata, the oldest Matsukata daughter. She told us of Miss Boynton's passing. After many years of remission, her cancer had re-erupted. Naka had been with her at the end, and she wrote that as she stood at her teacher's bedside, she saw her struggling to say something. Instinctively Naka said, "I know what you want to say, Benchin," using the Matsukata children's name for her. "You are saying, 'God is my Life.'" Miss Boynton nodded, gave a radiant smile, and passed on.

I didn't think I would, but I wept privately after hearing of Miss Boynton's passing. She had been my practitioner, my Sunday school teacher, and my high school teacher. But Naka's letter also told briefly about other Christian Scientist friends who were doing well, like the Bells in Yokohama, and Miss Elizabeth Duer, a Christian Scientist of British and Japanese descent. Miss Duer was a student of Atomi Sensei, who was one of the leading Japanese-style painters of her day. Miye Matsukata began painting lessons with Miss Duer, as did I. But whereas my drawing skills were primitive, Miye had shown sufficient promise for Atomi Sensei to accept her as a *deshi*, or close disciple.

In 1942, the Matsukatas moved out of their Nishimachi home to an equally comfortable Western-style residence in Kamakura, right above the beach at Zaimokuza. Haru's cousin, Shigeharu Matsumoto, lived in the neighborhood. He was a source of secret information, since he worked for Domei News Agency and had been Domei bureau chief in Shanghai in the 1930s. Another cousin, Saburo Matsukata, also brought secret information to us. An avid mountain-climber, he also ran the Japanese-owned Manchurian News Agency in Hsinking, or Changchun, capital of Manchukuo. It's one of the odd quirks of the postwar US occupation policy that neither Shigeharu Matsumoto nor Saburo Matsukata was ever purged, despite their high-profile wartime positions at Domei.

One day when I was about seventeen, I jumped on my bicycle and on an impulse rode all the way to Kamakura – about thirty miles south of Tokyo – to visit Haru. I hadn't intended such a long ride, and when I got there I had to call my mother to tell her where I was. At Haru's house I met Shigeharu, who had just visited Vietnam. It was the first time I had heard any details about the country with which I would subsequently become intimately involved during the long years of the Vietnam War. I was fascinated by his descriptions of the country. I spent that night at the Matsukatas' house and bicycled home the next day.

Haru and I never discussed Christian Science, to the best of my remembrance, but I sensed that she had her private doubts about the religion in which she had been brought up. But we did discuss current events and how the war with America was going.

I think she received most of her information from her cousin Shigeharu, which she then passed on to me. In any case, she was my source for what was going on in elevated political circles during the war.

Some time after my trip to Kamakura, Mr. Matsukata bought or leased a 500-tsubo (about half an acre) lot in Kita Kamakura, where I helped him and Haru plant large sweet potatoes. They had been developed by Mr. Matsukata according to the Maruyama formula and were full of starch and grew fast, but were not at all tasty. In wartime Japan, the point was not necessarily to have delicious food, but to have enough to eat. As I mentioned, Mr. Matsukata also cultivated earthworms as a way to aerate and enrich the soil – on the ledge of the large upstairs room that had been our classroom, he had flowerpots full of earthworms wriggling just below the surface. Every effort helped.

Here I must interject an episode involving the Matsukatas and their neighbor, the Swedish Minister to Japan, Mr. Widar Bagge.

In the late 1920s, the Matsukatas moved out of their large Tokyo home into a smaller but almost equally comfortable house next door at 22 Nishimachi. Once the war began, they were unable to receive any literature from the Christian Science Church in Boston. The normal international postal system had been suspended, and the Japanese authorities censored everything except the diplomatic mail. Mr. Bagge, who was not a Christian Scientist, had a friend in Sweden named Mrs. Gadelius, who was – in fact, she had been an original tenant of the Matsukatas. At the time, there was no such thing as a copy machine, so Mrs. Gadelius transcribed – by hand – the weekly lesson-sermon sent out by the Christian Science Publishing Society in Boston, and mailed it to Mr. Bagge through the diplomatic post, expecting him to pass it on to Mrs. Matsukata.

As the police were very suspicious of any Japanese trying to meet with foreigners, Mr. Bagge created a perfect ruse. He kept a flock of beautiful, long-plumed bantam chickens that were free to roam through his two-acre garden. The chickens were not supposed to venture next door into the Matsukatas' garden, with its lush vegetable patch, but how were the chickens to know? Only a wire fence separated the Matsukata property from the Swedish Legation. Inevitably, Mr. Bagge's colorful chickens would wander into the Matsukatas' vegetable patch, and the minister had to depend on Mrs. Matsukata to shoo them back. That became the occasion for Mr. Bagge to personally hand over the letters from Mrs. Gadelius, with their copied-out Christian Science lessons. Thus my family and other Christian Scientists in Japan became beneficiaries of these letters, via the diplomatic pouch from Sweden. Having successfully evaded censorship, the only obstacle was Mrs. Gadelius's European handwriting, which was very difficult to decipher. This covert operation, with the chickens serving as intermediaries, continued until Japan's surrender in August 1945.

*****

One of the most frightening experiences my family had during the war was an encounter with the Kempeitai. The Kempeitai, much feared by citizens at large, was the Japanese equivalent of the Gestapo, and it targeted not only suspected Communists, but also liberals whom it accused of being secret Communists.

In August of 1942 or '43 (the exact year eludes my memory), my mother, Akira, and I went to visit our family friends, the Yamanos, who had a peach orchard near Shizuura. The Yamanos invited us to spend the weekend there on the beach and pick peaches in their orchard, which we did with great delight. I had to leave Sunday afternoon because of a summer class, but my mother and brother stayed on an additional two days, coming home either Tuesday or Wednesday. I think Akira's school was on holiday, so they hadn't really set a firm time, because they had no plans.

On Tuesday evening, my mother called me in Tokyo. I answered the phone, expecting she would tell us that she'd be back the following morning. Instead she said that she had been arrested by the Kempeitai. She had been called in for questioning, and didn't know when she could return to Tokyo. She couldn't say much over the phone, but she was obviously in considerable distress. They had detained her at an inn in Mishima, the next train-stop from Shizuura, and she was told to stay there at the inn with Akira, then to report the next morning for further interrogations.

My father was very upset. Despite the late hour, he immediately contacted a friend he knew in the army, a major-general with whom he sometimes went horseback riding. The general said he would try to get her out and promised to call back the following morning.

Being in the active service, my father's friend understood the internal power mechanisms of the Kempeitai. The officers at the actual district level were all captains – not the highest rank, but still very powerful. Sometimes they had jurisdictional disputes with the civilian police, who were also very powerful. Our friend knew that these gendarmes would get pretty upset if they thought that a superior authority was demanding things of them, so he called around and looked for another captain or anyone equivalent in rank to these particular officers, someone who could then talk to them.

We spent a sleepless night. It took our friend about a day, but he called back late the next night, saying he had found the right person. The wheels were in motion, and he assured us that my mother and brother would be back the following day, which is indeed what happened. They were back with us late the next afternoon.

Through further inquiries, my father found out that an

elderly woman about to board the train for Tokyo had noticed my brother on the platform. He was jotting down in a notebook the numbers of locomotives in the train yard. This was his hobby, and because Numazu was an important transfer point, he was having a field day, finding locomotives he had never seen before. The woman thought that this fourteen-year-old was engaged in suspicious activity and told a Kempeitai officer she saw on the train, who then detained my mother and brother. My mother had also been reading an English publication, one of Mrs. Gadelius's Christian Science copies. She thought the Kempeitai might grill her as to how she had obtained English-language material in Japan when it was at war with the United States. Our friend, the general, had feared the same, and he had explained to his colleague that this was just a law-abiding citizen, who did read English books because she was brought up in Canada and New York. In fact, however, the Kempeitai officer merely chided my mother for reading an enemy-language book. He never asked her how she had obtained it.

For me it was a very scary time, because we had just heard about an English Reuters correspondent named Cox who was arrested in 1940, and who died in custody. He tried to escape, and they killed him. So what happened to us isn't very much when compared to the fate of those who actually went to jail. But it was an indelible experience all the same.

*****

In October 1944, I turned 20, the age for mandatory military service. But during the war, the age had been lowered to 19, so both the new cadre of 19-year-olds and the 20-year-olds had their physicals the same year. The army had a hard time absorbing such a large number of recruits at once, so their actual entry into the army was staggered, and for many there was a long wait. I was not actually called up until July 2, 1945.

Thus I remained a student for most of the war, although we spent little time in the classroom. We were sent wherever the army discerned a need – to a factory, smelting brass to make cartridge casings, or to a village that needed help with harvesting rice. With all these military and other extra-curricular duties, my university career was a joke, in terms of any kind of academic learning, but I did end up with a degree in economics. Perhaps as a rejection of the militarism of the war years, the prevailing philosophy in the universities of those days was Marxism, and the most popular professor at Rikkyo University was Dr. Minoru Miyagawa, a Marxist economist who would later be jailed as a Communist. But, again, I probably spent more time in billiards parlors than in the classroom.

To many Japanese, it was very exciting that our country had captured Singapore and was occupying much of Southeast Asia. If you read the *Kido Diaries* – the diary of Marquis Koichi Kido, who was close to the Emperor – you see that the Emperor, who had been opposed to the war in the beginning (mostly because he thought Japan couldn't win), became quite exultant when Japan occupied Singapore in February 1942. Singapore had been a British stronghold for so many years, and now, at last, it was the cornerstone of Japan's new Asian empire. But the euphoria didn't last long. In April, the Americans orchestrated the Doolittle Raid, basically as a way to reestablish morale after Pearl Harbor. It shocked the Japanese. Even though the raid was a single attack early in the war, it proved that Tokyo was vulnerable. Then in July, the Japanese navy suffered a defeat with far-reaching consequences at Midway.

As for me, I was not at all in sympathy with what the Japanese were trying to do, which was to take over Asia. The government was saying, of course, that they were liberating Asia from the Western grip, but I still felt the Japanese attitude was full of a certain hypocrisy.

The Japanese moved their headquarters for all of Southeast

Asia to Saigon, where they preserved the French colonial authorities – because they were the Vichy French, who were collaborating with the Germans, and therefore with the Japanese. Everywhere else, particularly in Indonesia, the Japanese eliminated the colonial power and either ruled directly or installed people like Sukarno as local puppet leaders. But in Vietnam they did neither.

I remember asking a Japanese colleague who was with the Japanese Expeditionary Forces, why, when they had gotten rid of the colonial administrations in other parts of Southeast Asia, why only in French Indo-China they didn't install a new kind of local regime. His answer was that the priority of the Japanese Expeditionary Forces was to maintain the supply chain, particularly food that the JEF needed. To that end, they preferred to keep the colonial structure in Vietnam, and not allow local revolutionaries take over. So even though much of Southeast Asia was occupied by the Japanese, the fight was still a matter of the indigenous people freeing themselves from colonial overlords. The Japanese were seen as "liberators" from the Dutch or the French, but their rule was effectively colonialism through a filter. The Japanese army was trying to use whomever seemed to them to be the major force in a given particular area.

I never got to go to Southeast Asia then, though I wanted very much to see Singapore and Vietnam. I had been studying French, since English was an enemy language, and you could see French movies in Tokyo. I remember one movie about the Paris opera and the ballet – I thought it was much superior to anything that was in Japan at the time.

The liberation of India, too, was an exciting thing. The figure who interested me the most was Subhas Chandra Bose, who fought for Indian independence. I liked him because he was a fiery orator who spoke beautiful, Oxonian English. Listening to him inspired an almost romantic support for Asian liberation. Whereas Gandhi believed in nonviolent struggle, Bose felt he had to fight the British any way he could. At one point he fled to Nazi Germany, and from there he made wartime broadcasts to the Indian people, in Bengali. I remember meeting a group of young Indians right after World War II – when I, like them, was in my twenties – who were fans of Bose's Free India Radio broadcasts. They said that they listened to him all the time.

Bose had to cooperate with the Japanese, because they controlled all of Southeast Asia. When Japan surrendered on the 15th of August, he tried to get to the Soviet Union, thinking the Russians would support him. He got as far as Taiwan, where his plane crashed. His death spawned rumors of a huge treasure that he had been carrying onboard, and conspiracy theories that he had not actually died.

I saw Bose give a speech in Tokyo in 1944. There was a summit of leaders of countries occupied by Japan, including Sukarno of Indonesia, Laurel of the Philippines, and Bose from India. He spoke at Hibiya Hall – Tokyo's equivalent of Carnegie Hall – and I went just like I would to any concert there. There was a big crowd, and I was very impressed by him. He was tall, bald-headed, with a big, good-looking face, and he was wearing the austere uniform of the Indian National Congress. He was fiery, and so emphatic that he was going to win.

Throughout the war, government propaganda told us that if and when American forces landed, the Japanese would fight back, even if only with bamboo spears. We would win because of our superior moral might. We did not fear death, whereas our American foe lacked the kamikaze spirit. Few of us believed this propaganda, but we had essentially no other sources of information. The Allied bombings that began towards the end of '44 – and particularly the ones in Tokyo – disillusioned many Japanese and disrupted most of our communications.

In the summer of 1944, the Americans occupied Saipan and Tenian islands in the Marianas, only a couple of flight hours from Japan's home islands. By October they were bombing Tokyo,

Osaka and other major cities, sparing only Kyoto, the former Imperial capital. The largest air raid, on the night of March 9, leveled most of eastern Tokyo, killing nearly 100,000 citizens – almost comparable to the Hiroshima death toll – and turned most of eastern Tokyo into a landscape of ashes and dust.

This was a new experience for most Japanese, including myself, who lived in the home islands. For much of the war, American air raids on Japanese cities were few and far between. But during the last six months, even small and middle-sized cities were systematically reduced to ashes, mostly by napalm bombs dropped from planes, and some by bombardment from U.S. navy ships. Because most houses in Japan were built of wood, it took little to wipe out an entire city. The last city to be destroyed, on August 15, 1945, was Kumagaya, about 40 miles northwest of Tokyo. It was a city I frequently passed on my holiday trips to Karuizawa.

For me and my family, April 17 was the day our immediate neighborhood was targeted. I was on the roof of our house all night, singing hymns and pouring buckets of water on the roof to keep the house from burning down. I realized for the first time how a fire creates a wind. I felt the hot breath of the wind and saw the cinders and pieces of wood flying over. I was stamping on them and dousing them with water. My father, mother, and aunt were all trying to put out flaming debris that fell in the garden. We only had one well – an ornamental well with no pump, but fortunately it had real water in it. We only had a bucket on a drawstring, but that well saved our house.

In the middle of all the chaos, we saw an American plane get shot down, perhaps a mile away, by anti-aircraft fire. As the plane went down, my Aunt Kiyo exclaimed, "I hope the pilots are safe!" In that moment, I was incensed because those were the same people who were trying to kill us. Later, I felt ashamed for having none of the compassion that she did.

When morning dawned, we could see that most of the

houses near us had also survived. We were living in the suburbs, with gardens surrounding most houses, so there was no mass conflagration – only the houses that were directly hit by napalm bombs burned down. It was springtime and the cherry blossoms had just come out. There was one in our yard, and the whole avenue was covered, like a tunnel of cherry blossoms. I saw a long gash in our garden, and when I dug into it I found a large piece of the propellor and engine from an American plane. I walked out into the street, and I could see napalm still burning right in the street, in liquid puddles of fire.

The March 10 air raid, which leveled eastern Tokyo and took the lives of my friend Yoshikawa's family, was the most dramatic. Yoshikawa and I were on air-raid warden duty at the university – sleeping on the tables where we studied by day – in the western part of Tokyo. We watched the eastern sky light up with flames. Yoshikawa said quietly, "My house is probably burning right now." We spent a sleepless night in the Senda house on the outskirts of town in Sugamo. My friend Tonao Senda had a large Japanese-style house, tatami-matted except for the Western-style parlor, which had an upright piano and an ornamental female doll, typical of many bourgeois Japanese homes in those days. Although there were no houses burning in our immediate vicinity, we knew Yoshikawa's home was in the lumber district of Kiba, east of the Sumida River, where all we could see was fire.

At dawn, we saw that Tonao's neighborhood had escaped damage, but we were certain that eastern Tokyo had been reduced to ashes. Both the Yamate line and the Tamagawa line were still running, and I got home using public transportation all the way. Yoshikawa told me later he had bicycled back to where his home had been, and found only ashes. His mother and infant brother perished in the flames, and one uncle had survived by jumping into the canal and staying under water for as long as he could, surfacing for quick bursts of air. All he suffered was a singed nose.

A month later I saw Yoshikawa off at Tokyo Station, when he took the train to his regiment in the Osaka region. Since then, we have managed to see each other at least once a year, even after I moved to the United States. Yoshikawa took up Spanish after the war and was a tour guide in Spain and Latin America for many years until becoming an acupuncture specialist, first in Tokyo, and more recently in the seaside resort of Fujisawa near Kamakura. His favorite poet was Lorca, whom he read in Spanish.

On May 26, there was another large air raid on Tokyo, this one aimed at the western section, where we lived. The Imperial Palace, though not targeted, caught fire from cinders that landed on its roof and burned to the ground (The Emperor was safe in an underground bunker, and his family was at Nasu in the mountains north of Tokyo). Large, heavily residential parts of western Tokyo went up in flames. That day I went to the university on my trusty bicycle – by then the only reliable form of transportation – passing smoldering ruin after ruin.

American friends like Robert Peel, who came to Japan immediately after the war, told me they were shocked by the contrast between Europe's major cities – where some buildings collapsed, but others did not – and Japanese cities, which were vast, flat wastelands, with only an occasional chimney or bank vault poking up from the rubble.

* * * * *

Meanwhile, American troops landed on Okinawa and, after hard-fought battles on its main island, occupied most of it. Newspapers told us that high-school students, boys and girls alike, retreated to seaside caves and continued fighting desperately until many were killed or jumped off the cliffs into the sea. There was no mass surrender.

It's hard to fathom, but that was the atmosphere of those days. In origin, I suppose, it goes back to the samurai, but this particular phase really appeared in the 1930s, when the army became powerful enough to think of itself as the guardians of morality. It dictated what citizens could or could not do. You couldn't go to dance halls. Up until high school, boys had to have their hair cropped – only after you went to college could you grow your hair. For 1,000 years, before Japan modernized, the samurai had been like the knights in medieval Europe – warriors who adhered to a code of honor. By the 1930s, that code had been radicalized. A group of young militarist officers, strongly influenced by the Nazis, led a purification movement that seized on the old ideals of samurai honor. Samurai cut open their stomachs – the act of *seppuku* or *hara-kiri* – to avoid defeat. If they were defeated, it was considered dishonorable to continue to live. In extreme circumstances, if a samurai had no weapon with which to kill himself, he bit his tongue and bled to death. They were taught that to surrender was to live in shame for the rest of one's life. That became part of the samurai ideal – it was not necessarily the merchants' or the farmers' ideal, but the samurai way of thinking permeated society as a whole. People thought it was a more honorable way to live – even though the samurai, since they lived by the sword, didn't have much to do in peacetime.

Hiroshi, one of my cousins, became a kamikaze pilot and perished in the Philippines. Another cousin married her brother's best friend, also a kamikaze. Within a month of the wedding she was a widow.

* * * * *

As it turned out, I spent only two and a half months in the army. I was called up for military service on July 2, 1945. I was to enter Infantry Regiment No. 63 in Kofu, about 50 miles due west of Tokyo on a plateau ringed with mountains, a countryside previously dominated by vineyards and orchards. Our neighbors gave me three *banzai* (cheers), and my father accompanied me by train to Kofu. I entered the barracks with a *furoshiki* – a square, decorated piece of cloth universally used as a bag – to carry my student uniform after I had exchanged it for a clean (but worn) army uniform with a second-class private's single star. My army shoes were old and mismatched – the left shoe was larger than the right. I could not have looked spick and span when I appeared before my father in my faded uniform and mismatched shoes. He just smiled at me, took my student clothes, and left. I hardly remember what we said to each other – probably *"Genki de ne."* Stay in good health.

Thus began my brief enlistment in the Imperial Japanese Army. The training was much like the reserve officer training I had received in university, and not particularly arduous. We had no real weapons, just short swords and wooden sticks the size of bayonets, which we practiced thrusting at our adversaries. The training included suicide attacks against oncoming enemy tanks. We were given sticks ending in a cloth-covered contraption made to look like a ball, and told to lie flat on the grassy ground while other trainees rolled a mock tank, made of wood, towards us. As the "tank" passed us, we stuck our cloth-covered balls right under its tread. It all seemed quite ridiculous, both to me and my fellow-trainees. After our third try, our trainer, an elderly corporal, said, more in resignation than in anger, "You think you're just sticking a wooden ball under a tank, but once you're in a real battle situation, that ball is going to explode, and ninety-nine times out of a hundred, your guts will explode with it." Meanwhile, the sky was blue, a lark was singing, and try as we might, we could not get into a proper kamikaze mood.

Two weeks into our training, a night raid by American B-29 bombers leveled Kofu city to the ground. The whole city was engulfed in flames, and when day dawned we could see that only smoking ruins remained. Ironically, my regiment, which was at the western edge of the city, remained intact.

That was the end of my basic training. We recruits were sent to guard a municipal storehouse with piles of rice – the rice was burned on the outside but edible within. Later, I became an orderly at the municipal hospital, attending to soldiers from my regiment who had been severely burned during the air raid. Civilian victims were also at the hospital, and I shall never forget the screams I heard all night from a girl whose legs had to be amputated, without anesthetics. I was told she was only 15 years old.

Nurses were in short supply, and my first specific duty was to help take care of an older soldier who had served seven years in China and whose face was swathed in bandages. I helped him with his bathroom visits and with changing his bandages, sometimes extracting maggots. After three days, I could see new skin growing across his forehead and temples. I recalled what our housekeeper told us of her experiences as a Red Cross nurse during the Russo-Japanese War – how she preferred patients in surgery to those with internal illnesses, because she could always see the healing process take place.

*****

In mid-July I was sent to Tokyo to take part in a two-week anti-gas training course. We learned to don gas masks expeditiously and make believe we were scouring the ground to remove traces of poison gas. During one such exercise the air-raid siren sounded and we could see B-29 bombers zooming overhead. Instead of bombs, clouds of pamphlets rained down on us. We picked up all that we could, but within half an hour, officers went through our barracks and confiscated everything they could find. The pamphlets were cleverly written, in good Japanese, warning of air-raids and landings by US troops to come, and urging us to surrender. One soldier showed me a pamphlet he had stuffed into his trouser pocket. He told me that when the Americans landed – as they surely would – he would run towards them waving his piece of paper and offering to surrender. I said nothing, but I knew I would probably do the same.

As for myself, if Tokyo was ever invaded, I wasn't sure what I would do. I had no desire to die fighting in a war in which I did not believe. Sometimes, in fanciful moments, I would rehearse walking up to the American lines with a white handkerchief and surrendering, but I had no idea how the American soldiers would react. If I was shot, that would be the end of my story.

One Sunday during this short stay in Tokyo, my mother and aunt came to see me, with a bento box filled with rice balls and a slice of salted salmon. I was of course overjoyed to see them and ate with gusto. I told them a bit about the kind of life I was leading and told them not to worry. What else could I say?

On August 9, I took the train back to my regiment in Kofu. Reading that day's newspapers on the train, I saw banner headlines that the Soviet Union had declared war on Japan and invaded Manchuria and Karafuto, the Japanese southern half of Sakhalin Island. There was another headline that intrigued me: "New-type bombs dropped on Hiroshima!" The word "nuclear" was not used but most of us could guess that the U.S. had developed a workable atom bomb. It did not surprise me because, while still in university, the colonel heading our military training program had told us that Japan would win the war because it was developing atomic weapons. He did not mention what America might be doing.

Under a smaller, separate headline, were obituaries of prominent people killed, including an Imperial prince who had been at Fifth Army headquarters in Hiroshima. It is rare for an Imperial prince to be put in harm's way, and my immediate reaction was that this "new-type bomb" must have been lethal over a wide area. We did not see any of the ghastly pictures of the Hiroshima victims until many weeks later.

Since Japan's surrender, few Japanese have talked about the atomic weapons their own country was trying to develop. Compared to Germany's V-2 rockets, there does not seem to have been anything in Japan's arsenal that could possibly have changed the course of the war. But while most Japanese blame the U.S. for dropping the atom bomb over Hiroshima and Nagasaki, they tend to glide over Japan's own wartime efforts to create an atomic warhead.

* * * * *

Then came the fateful day when, for the first time in our lives, we heard the voice of Emperor Hirohito.

On August 15, 1945, I was billeted in an empty primary school in a western suburb of Kofu. Green farms and paddy fields surrounded the school, and we slept in the classrooms. As part of the transfer, I was given a brand-new uniform and, for the first time, shoes that fit. I was awaiting the regiment's transfer to the beaches of Chiba, in order to prepare for the expected American landing.

That morning, I was brushing my teeth in the school's washroom next to my classroom, when I heard the NHK radio news begin. The first item was brief and surprising: "At 12 noon the Emperor will give a radio address." There was no further explanation, but my heart was racing. The Emperor had never made a public address before, except for state-of-the-nation addresses written by the Prime Minister and usually carried by newspapers the next day. What would he say? Would he announce Japan's surrender? Or would he tell his people to keep fighting to the end?

My thoughts raced to a conversation I had had with Haru's father earlier that year in April. Mr. Matsukata had come into Haru's study, where I was having my lesson. The conversation turned to the fighting in Okinawa, which had been going on for nearly two months. "The fighting in Okinawa is almost over," he said. "The next American landing will be on Honshu." Mr. Matsukata sighed. "I'm afraid we are going to have to ask the Emperor to become directly involved." He didn't say he was asking the Emperor to announce Japan's surrender, but that was the implication. "In any case," he said, "wherever you are, be careful. Don't do anything rash."

But what would the army do? It had vowed to defend Japan to the death, even if the people had nothing but bamboo spears. Other countries could follow the Chinese saying: *"Kuni horobite sanga ari"* ("Though the country be defeated, the mountains and rivers will remain"). But Japan, in 2,000 years of history, had never been defeated. If the descendants of the Sun God were defeated, nothing would remain. That is what our military instructors had told us, and that is what they themselves believed.

I thought also of what one of my classmates, Hino, had told me the year before, when we were helping farmers build irrigation ditches in Okegawa, a farming village thirty miles northwest of Tokyo. We were out in the fields, eating riceballs during our lunch break. "Oka," he said, "what would you do if we were suddenly told the war is over? I would rub my stomach and shout for joy!" I don't remember what I replied, but I believe I was too cautious to say much.

By this time, all our classmates who were a year older – the so-called 1923 class – had been drafted into the army or navy. A few who were well off would have farewell parties in a restaurant – a rare treat for most of us. We also saw off classmates from out of town at Tokyo or Shinjuku stations, boisterously shouting "Banzai!", singing the ribald *"Fuji no shirayuki"* about what happens to the white snow of Mt. Fuji when it melts and flows down into the red light district of

Mishima, cheering and waving the *hinomaru*, the Japanese flag, as the train pulled out.

Some farewells were more heartfelt, as when my classmate and best friend Yoshikawa was called up less than a month after the great air raid on Tokyo. Both Yoshikawa and I had taken up figure skating when sports were made a compulsory part of the academic program. A year later, we had to shift to speed skating when the military authorities declared that only girls could continue with figure skating. Neither of us was good at carving out figures of eight, but we enjoyed it a good deal more than bayonet practice, which was also compulsory.

All these memories were with me as I spent the rest of that morning, on August 15, trying to digest what the announcer had said. None of my comrades seemed particularly excited or disturbed. I was ordered to join a work party of six men to pull a cart to regiment headquarters in what was left of Kofu city to receive our vegetable rations for the day. By that time in the war everyone was hungry, and we mixed rice with bran, potato peelings, and any other semi-edible substance, until finally our food tasted like straw. We were headed by a lance-corporal in his early forties who, in civilian life, was a librarian at Tokyo Imperial University. The seven of us assembled and set out.

It was a beautiful day – blue sky, a few summer clouds, a frog croaking in the paddy field. We rolled a wagon into the city, loaded it up, and were on our way back to the regiment when, at about 11:45, our leader decided to take a short break by the roadside and allow us to munch on some of the tomatoes and cucumbers we were taking back to our billet. Since none of us had a radio, I asked the corporal if I could take fifteen minutes to go to my father's friend's house nearby to listen to the Emperor's broadcast. I visited there each Sunday afternoon, and it was where I kept my Bible and a few other treasured articles. "Fine," he answered. "And you can tell us what the Emperor said." His tone was casual – obviously he was not expecting more than the usual invocation to fight to the death. So off I went to my father's friend's house.

When I arrived, I found him and his wife and her sister in formal attire, sitting Japanese-style in their tatami-matted reception room. "Come in," he said, "The broadcast is just about to begin." He was in black frock-coat and tie. She was in blue *suso-moyo*. They sat stiffly in the *o-setsu-ma*, the drawing room, but I had my boots and gaiters on, so I remained standing awkwardly in the entry hall, waiting for the speech to begin.

Promptly at noon, the NHK announcer came on the line. Immediately after the introduction, we heard the high-pitched, reedy voice of the Emperor. He read from a prepared manuscript in the archaic style of an Imperial address, filled with classical language difficult for ordinary Japanese to understand. But I distinctly remember the following passages: "We have ordered Our Government to communicate to the Governments of the United States, Great Britain, China, and the Soviet Union that Our Empire accepts the provisions of their Joint Declaration." Then later, at the end: "Unite your total strength, and devote yourselves to construction for the future. Cultivate the ways of rectitude, foster nobility of spirit, and work with resolution, so that you may enhance the innate glory of the Imperial State and keep pace with the progress of the world."

Nowhere did he use the word "surrender." Indeed, some of my friends who were in the army in other parts of the country thought that the Emperor was telling them to fight on. But to me the meaning was clear, since the Potsdam Declaration, announced a few days earlier, had called for Japan's unconditional surrender.

I was overjoyed. A flood of emotions swept over me. The war was over – it was over! We could resume our normal lives! And eventually, I could go to America.

My heart was singing. But I kept my emotions to myself, since I had no idea how my father's friend and his family would react. It was an intense moment. The women were weeping. The face of my father's friend contorted with rage. He took a few steps towards me and shouted, "Do you know what this means? Korea is lost! Taiwan is lost! Karafuto (southern Sakhalin) is lost! Manchuria (he said in Japanese: "*Manshu*") – lost! All the gains of the Meiji era lost! We have become a *yonto-koku* – a fourth-rate power!"

Then he turned to me and in a quieter tone said, "Now, Takashi, be very careful. No one knows what will happen next." He was probably referring to the expected reaction of the army. "Keep your head down. Take care of yourself, of what you do and say." I excused myself, saying I had to get back to my work party, closed the sliding door, and ran back to my comrades.

They were still sitting along a roadside fence, nonchalantly munching tomatoes and cucumbers. "Did you hear what the Emperor said?" the corporal asked me. "We didn't bring a radio with us."

Cautiously I replied, "Well, the reception was bad, so I wasn't sure exactly what he said. But I thought the Emperor said we would accept the Potsdam Declaration."

Immediately, the usually mild-mannered corporal's face became as contorted as that of my father's friend. But the corporal's reaction was more personal. "So what did we fight this war for?" he shouted. "First we were bombed out of our home in Tokyo. Then we were bombed out of our home in Tochigi (his native province). Now we have nothing. My wife and children are in a Buddhist temple deep in the countryside, where they have been living as refugees. We have no idea how to rebuild our lives. So what was the point? We've lost everything!"

He calmed down and gave me the same admonition as my father's friend. "We must all be careful what we do or say. No one knows what is going to happen – what the army may do."

Our little group walked back in silence, each lost in his own thoughts, to our billets in the country schoolhouse. Here, too, the mood was funereal. It was a hot day, and I watched a sergeant sitting in one of the classroom chairs, fanning himself. The radio newscast was talking about the aftermath of the Emperor's broadcast. There had been some disturbances. Nothing was as yet very clear. The sergeant continued fanning as the broadcast went on, but at a slower and slower pace. Finally he put his fan down and buried his face in his arms.

* * * * *

Once the war was over, novice soldiers like me had little to do while awaiting discharge. The Japanese military was still seeking some means of preserving even a portion of the army, and we were soon told that we would be part of a small force to help the Americans police Japan. The army leadership seemed to fear that prostitutes would proliferate, and that Japanese women from good families might be proffered to American soldiers to keep them from running wild across the country. Perhaps the officers remembered how their own troops had raped and murdered civilians after capturing Chinese cities and towns.

Be that as it may, we were transferred from the regular army to the Kempeitai, which had struck terror amongst the citizens of the Asian countries Japan had occupied. This new Kempeitai was to be called *Tokubetsu Kempeitai*, or Special Gendarmerie. Instead of being a lowly second-class private, I and all my comrades were given the three stars of a superior class private, since that was the lowest rank anyone in the Kempeitai could have.

But as I might have told our generals, the Americans would not stand for the survival of the Imperial army in any shape or form. On September 16, I was formally discharged and returned to civilian life. The major in charge of our battalion gave a belligerent final address: "American troops have landed in Japan and will soon occupy all the principal cities. They will pamper the women and allow them to have their hair permed and tinted. Remember what you learned in the army, and do not forget who you are. Our country will rise again. Be patient, and willing to endure. Japan will rise again!"

When the American troops finally arrived, I gave my three-star patch to the first American GI I saw – a guy from Tulsa, Oklahoma.

* * * * *

After sixty years, August 15, 1945 still remains the most important milestone in my life. I felt that was when I really started living, when life in the present tense had immediate, real meaning for me. My first feeling as I listened to the Emperor's tense, high-pitched voice was that this moment was the true beginning of my life, that everything up to then had been merely preparation. I was no longer Japanese – the moment had transcended any sense of nationality or collective identity. I was simply a person.

I would go on to write about that day many more times over the course of my career. In 1981, I wrote an article for the *Monitor* called *Taro's War: Memoir of a Japanese torn between two worlds*, in which I told my war story in the third-person – knowing it was going to be published, but trying to communicate my experience faithfully. Every time I write about that day, I remember something different. But to me, every telling is just as valid. Because the me that remembers it now is different from the me of forty years ago, even though we're remembering the same thing.

Chapter 5

Post-War Annus Mirabilis

From the day of the Emperor's announcement to my discharge from the army on September 16, I was in a flurry of excitement and anticipation. September 2 saw the signing of the Japanese surrender on the *USS Missouri*. Within a week, the first American troops landed in Japan, and the Supreme Allied Commander, Gen. Douglas A. MacArthur, established his headquarters in the Daiichi Seimei Building. I felt in limbo, because I was still in the army yet unable to act on any of these new events.

I was stationed in what had been the Toshima Teachers College (*shihan gakko*) where my unit worked in the kitchen. We cooked rice in huge pots, exactly like the *goemon-buro* in which we had taken baths. So, once the rice was cooked and distributed and the rice-pots cleaned, we jumped in them and took baths. Then we rinsed them out and cooked the next day's rice. The sergeant leading our group told us to sweep the floors to pick up any stray grains of rice which might have spilled from their containers. We did so and used them for the next day's breakfast – and promptly got an avalanche of complaints about broken bits of glass and other debris interspersed with the rice. For a while I was assigned to cook tastier items for the officers. They had a live pig, which they told us to kill and cook – but none of us had ever killed a pig before. So we clumsily wielded our knives, and there was a lot of squealing before we got the pig in the stew pot.

After my army service ended, I resumed my status as a student at Rikkyo University. But I was dissatisfied. During the war, I had viewed my time at Rikkyo as temporary – I felt that my education would not really begin until I got to Principia. I attended some classes, especially with Miyagawa Sensei, the Marxist economics professor who been imprisoned during the war. When he returned to campus he was greeted as a hero by the students, including me. He was an excellent lecturer, conversational in style, and his classes were always crowded.

But war had given us a variety of experiences. We were not simple students any more. Some, like my classmate Tanabe, had been in the *tokkotai* in the Navy, where their version of being kamikaze suicide pilots had been to ride torpedoes and guide them straight into an American ship – the larger the better. It was Tanabe who told me that, as a junior officer in this suicide group, he had heard the Imperial broadcast of August 15 on a beach in the picturesque Inland Sea. The reception was so poor that he thought this was just another military pep talk, and he gave his men a stirring exhortation to be ready to fight and die for the Emperor. "I was so embarrassed," he told me, "when I found out what he really said." Others, like Kamijo, who had been in the *bajutsu bu,* the equestrian club, at Rikkyo, were in the Army Supply Corps, which used horse-drawn wagons. Some of these men left the service with a large amount of military materiel and horses, and went into business in the transportation field.

I came out of the army without even a bayonet – which, admittedly, would not have been very useful in civilian life. I did have a new uniform and new shoes, and on September 16, I was finally discharged as a superior class private – *jotohei*. My battalion was billeted at the Toshima Normal School in Ikebukuro, so it was easy for me to take the Yamate line to Shibuya, then ride the Tamagawa tram to Sakura Shinmachi.

The cherry blossoms had long since faded and caterpillars munched on the green leaves. I got home and found only our housekeeper, Kashiwagi, who told me that my father was away on a business trip and my mother, aunt, and brother

Akira had moved temporarily to our summer home in Karuizawa. I telephoned my mother and found that two Christian Scientists, who had arrived in Japan a couple of weeks after Japan's surrender, were also on their way to Karuizawa by train from Tokyo. So I took the first available train and was soon reunited with my mother, brother, and aunt, to our unbounded joy.

I saw Mrs. Matsukata, who had come from her village in Gumma to meet these two Christian Scientists. The Matsukatas had been living in the *o-kura* – the storehouse of their mother's ancestral home – which looked as solid as a Japanese castle. I had visited them there a couple of times, after their Kamakura house was requisitioned by the Japanese Navy. One of their Tokyo houses was destroyed, and they were still renting the other to the Swedish Embassy. Now they were about to move back to Kamakura. But since their own *besso*, or villa, in Karuizawa had been rented out, Mrs. Matsukuata would stay with us.

The Christian Scientists she was to meet were Robert Peel and Gordon Walker. They had just left the Philippines, where they were helping Filipinos to rebuild their lives after the brutal Japanese occupation, and also helping to rebuild the Christian Science church, which had been totally destroyed during the bitter clashes between Americans and Filipino guerrillas fighting for independence.

Robert Peel was a former professor at Principia College – where he knew the Takaki and Matsukata children – who had been drafted into the U.S. Army, and he was to stay at our home. Gordon Walker was *The Christian Science Monitor's* chief war correspondent in the Pacific theater, and he would stay at the Mampei Hotel, where the Nazi representative in Japan was also staying. Gordon spoke German and wanted to ferret out all available intelligence about the Nazi presence in Japan. I did not know it then, but I found out later that Mr. Peel was a special agent of the CIC, the Counter-Intelligence Corps, whose main duty was to find and arrest top Japanese leaders like General Tojo and Prince Konoe. Their other purpose was to meet Mrs. Matsukata and deliver letters from her children in the United States. Walker and Peel were to arrive by train from Tokyo that very day.

So, after my first lunch with my family since leaving the military, I walked back to the station to meet the train. As a crowd of Japanese disgorged themselves from the train, I quickly saw two Americans, a good head and shoulders above the crowd, in Eisenhower jackets. I rushed forward and introduced myself and welcomed them to Karuizawa.

Because gasoline was in short supply and the few charcoal-burning taxis at the station had all been booked, we walked back to my mother's cottage – both Gordon and Bob (as he told us to call him) delighting in the mountain coolness, while I delighted in showing them my Karuizawa. Majestic Mount Asama, an active volcano 9,000 feet high, loomed in the western sky as we passed the residences of various prominent Japanese – Prince Konoe, the former Prime Minister; his close friend Mrs. Saki Mitsui, our neighbor in Tokyo and the ladies' golf champion of Japan (from one of the eleven millionaire Mitsui families); also Saburo Kurusu, Ambassador to the U.S. at the time of Pearl Harbor (Mr. Kurusu had a self-deprecating sense of humor – he told me that, during his internment in the U.S., Americans would say they had been "double-Kurusued" by Japan). My new American friends, however, were more interested in the silver birch trees, goldenrod, and bluebells, which reminded them of the fields and forests of New England.

A Meeting That Set The Course of My Life

> ... the first soldier introduced himself as Lt. Robert Peel. The second was a war correspondent, Gordon Walker of *The Christian Science Monitor*. We were soon

on a first-name basis, and Gordon explained that he had decided to come with Bob because, on their first train ride in newly occupied Japan, two would be better than one. Also, he was looking for an interview with a German Embassy official who was, he had been told, the head of the Gestapo in Japan.

My mother had been able to wheedle a good cut of beef from our butcher, and she prepared a succulent sukiyaki dish for our guests. We sat by the fireplace and talked far into the night. Bob had been teaching at the college where our friend's children had stayed throughout the war. His field was English literature — the very subject I had been hoping to study. In the Army, however, Bob had been assigned to the Counter-intelligence Corps and was about to participate in a series of arrests of high-ranking Japanese war criminals.

Gordon had spent the war in the Pacific, island-hopping with General MacArthur's troops as they steadily moved closer to Japan. Bob and Gordon were both lean six-footers. Bob seemed serene and spoke melodiously with an accent betraying his English ancestry. Gordon had the tense energy of a coiled spring. I learned that, on the train ride, Gordon had carried a pistol, not sure of what might happen, while Bob was unarmed. He never carried a weapon except when ordered to, he said.

Then a college student, I met often with Bob after he'd returned to Tokyo. He had been given leave to live in Japanese surroundings and took advantage of the contacts he developed through our friend's family to meet widely with Japanese intellectuals, politicians, even with members of the imperial family. (He gave Princess Takamatsu, the Emperor's sister-in-law, her first solo jeep ride, an event chronicled in the pages of this newspaper.)

Bob, the teacher, read Shakespeare with me. We went through "Romeo and Juliet," Bob explaining that the words Romeo and Juliet exchange during their first dance are a sonnet: "If I profane with my unworthiest hand /This holy shrine, the gentle fine is this:" and so forth.

He was also an instructor in democracy, to me and to other Japanese he encountered. Freed from long years of repression, Japanese men and women were marching in the streets, waving red banners and demanding rice and employment. The long-hated police, now deprived of their swords, handled these demonstrations gingerly, whereas Bob would tell me of Oliver Wendell Holmes saying that freedom of speech did not mean you could shout "Fire!" in a crowded theater.

Bob was delighted to find Christians who had kept their faith, especially followers of a fiery preacher, Kanzo Uchimura, who refused to bow before the Emperor's photograph. One of these Christians, Prof. Yasaka Takaki, told Bob that Japan had rushed into the modern age without experiencing either the Renaissance or the Reformation, and was now paying the price. It was a comment I have since thought of often, not only in connection with Japan, but with other non-Western countries striving to modernize as well.

Six months after his arrival, Bob was demobilized and returned to the US, where he went on to a distinguished career with this newspaper and as a scholar. I had many occasions to see him after I emigrated to America in 1948. But those early days after the war with Bob remain a glowing light in my memory. Gordon was an influence of a totally different kind. A journalist through and through, he would never rest until he got to the bottom of things.

In March 1946, a committee of Japanese preparing a new constitution for their country came up with a totally different draft from the extremely conservative versions that had been leaked to the press up to that time. Gordon immediately recognized that the US had had a hand in the drafting of it. Gordon scooped his journalist colleagues by bringing to light the fact that the constitution had been written by a small group of

Americans headed by Col. Charles Kades and working in total secrecy.

Years later a friend who had been a member of this team told me of her astonishment when the article appeared. "Who did he talk to?" she asked. But like all good journalists, Gordon never revealed his sources. Gordon Walker inspired me to become a journalist. Bob Peel was my guide in a deeper sense — both intellectual and spiritual. I will always be grateful for having known these two men.

— Takashi Oka for *The Christian Science Monitor*, September 25, 2003.

That first evening with them, after my mother had cooked supper, we told our new friends how we had survived the war years. Then I walked Gordon to his hotel, the Mampei, and returned home to find Mrs. Matsukata and Bob engaged in earnest discussions about the little Christian Science community in Japan. Bob told us that he had found out about us by calling Mrs. Takaki, lady-in-waiting to Empress Nagako, at the Imperial Palace in Tokyo. He had no number – he just asked the operator, in English, if she had the telephone number of the Imperial Palace. By calling the Imperial Palace, he got through to Mrs. Takaki, and found where we, the Matsukatas, and other members of the church were living. I listened, and participated in the conversation by the crackling fire, until about 10 that night, and probably fell asleep there.

Gordon Walker was a journalist with a lean, hungry look, who started his reporting career under the legendary Charles Gratke, longtime foreign editor of *The Christian Science Monitor*.

Gratke was killed in an airplane crash in Indonesia in 1949, so I never had the privilege of meeting him. But he nurtured and profoundly influenced a whole generation of *Monitor* journalists, from Peel and Walker to Hank Hayward and Harry Ellis.

Robert Peel looked every inch the Harvard scholar. He was a Christian Scientist and an intellectual – and the two are not necessarily the same. He and his sister, Doris, strained against their mother's British-rooted churchly vision of Christian Science, but remained devout Christian Scientists themselves. He had grown up in Canada, and after his father died, moved to Boston, where he attended the Boston Latin School and then Harvard. Peel later wrote a definitive three-volume biography of Mary Baker Eddy, the founder of the Christian Science movement and its church, the First Church of Christ, Scientist, in Boston.

I learned a great deal – in different ways – from these two early postwar friends. Bob was like my Sunday School teacher and college professor combined into one, and my relationship with him, which lasted from the time I met him in Japan (1945) until his passing in Boston (1993), was one of student to teacher or beloved older brother. With Gordon Walker, it was much more one of cub reporter and veteran journalist. Gordon gave me the professional training I needed to become a foreign correspondent while I was working at the *Monitor* headquarters in Boston. He was assistant overseas editor, while I was first a copy boy, then a clerk in the overseas news department.

Gordon, like many journalists, started out at the *Monitor* as a copyboy himself, running errands for the writers. Then as a junior reporter turned war correspondent, he covered the steady American advance from New Guinea to the Philippines and Okinawa. He had a flat Boston accent, and he rarely gave the accolade: "I wish I had written that myself!" – but I did receive it once, when I wrote an article on then Crown Prince Akihito. The Crown Prince was passing through Boston on his way home from the coronation of Queen Elizabeth II in Westminster Abbey. I don't remember how many revisions I had to write before Gordon was satisfied with it.

My mind was set on majoring in English literature, a goal which Bob encouraged. He set time aside from his busy schedule as a U.S. military intelligence officer to read Shakespeare and Walt Whitman with me. We also discussed the differences between Nazi Germany – which Bob had visited in the 1930s – and the militarism of pre-war Japan. For Americans like Bob, who came to Japan as members of the U.S. Occupation Forces, it was natural to compare Japan with Nazi Germany. In doing so, he felt a subtle, recognizable difference between the two. Germany came from within the heart of Western history and culture, whereas Japan was an almost unknown, unfamiliar civilization. In American eyes, the German sin had been committed within the family of Western culture, while, to Bob, the Japanese awoke memories of a totally alien culture with no points of reference to which Americans could relate.

Bob had been drafted into the Army, and maybe because of his background he became an undercover agent of the military police. One of the first tasks of the military police was to arrest the people that they considered to be war criminals. In Germany it would have been Goering, Hess and the like, but in Japan there was no real equivalent of the Nazi party, because Japan's militarism didn't start as an ideology with a political party.

Bob was looking for some point of reference which would bring Japan into a more familiar context for him. I believe he found it in Harry Reeves' *The Anatomy of Peace.* Bob enthusiastically circulated the book among his acquaintances, including me. He saw that a copy reached Emperor Hirohito, through his brothers Prince Chichibu and Prince Takamatsu. He also formed a lifelong friendship with another recipient of the book, Haru's cousin Shigeharu Matsumoto, who became a leading Japanese intellectual and who served for many years as director of the Rockefeller-supported International House, Tokyo.

Had Peel chosen journalism as a career, he would undoubtedly have been outstandingly successful. Instead, he focused his life's work on religious scholarship, more particularly by establishing a bridge between the Christian Science Church and the scholarly community in general. He was my friend and mentor throughout his long, distinguished religious and academic career.

He also had a wicked sense of humor, as may be testified by those who saw his reenactment of the elaborate Buddhist tea ceremony, which he had witnessed at the home of a friend in Kamakura. Accompanied by his friend Ed Rotsinger, Bob kept a straight face throughout the proceedings, pouring the powdered green tea into priceless imaginary tea bowls, passing the invisible bowls from guest to guest, watching them make the required two-and-a-half slurps of tea, then cleaning up. We had to observe in total silence – we were allowed to burst into laughter only after the two tea masters had finished their self-appointed tasks.

After the war, Haru became a journalist, working first for *The Christian Science Monitor* and then for the *Saturday Evening Post*. She had moved into the tatami-matted servants quarters of their Gumma house in the fall of 1945, while the Swedish Legation still occupied their Nishimachi house (later she built her own house near the one in Gumma). Bob, who remained in Japan until May 1946, rented a large Western-style house at the top of Sendaizaka, a ways down the street from the Matsukata house. When Haru started working for the *Monitor*, her room in the servants quarters became the *Monitor* office. Bob walked to it daily from his room down the street, the Counter-Intelligence Corps (CIC) having authorized him to live and work off-campus as long as he showed up regularly at the CIC headquarters to file his reports.

Around this time, Haru fell in love with Bob, but he remained just a platonic friend. So she gravitated to a left-wing journalist, Hugh Deane, who worked for a British paper or agency, and with whom she had an on-again, off-again relationship until she re-connected with Ed Reischauer. I remember Mrs. Matsukata was mad when she found one of Hugh's shoes in Haru's Nishimachi apartment.

Later, Haru joined the *Saturday Evening Post*, and she continued to be prominent in the journalistic community in Japan. She was one of the founding members of the Foreign Correspondents Club of Japan. Over the years, she introduced many prominent journalists from the United States and other countries to the intricacies of Japanese politics and journalism.

* * * * *

In October 1945, I was looking for a part-time job and pestering Haru to find me something with the American Occupation forces. Several of my English-speaking friends had found work with the Americans, including Masayoshi Yoshikawa, who became a clerk in the U.S. Red Cross library in one of the few buildings in downtown Tokyo that had withstood the bombs. One of the perks of his job was an unlimited supply of hot coffee and American cookies.

Haru helped me find a position at the International Military Tribunal for the Far East (IMTFE), the counterpart of the Nuremberg war crimes trials in Germany. We had a mutual friend there, Yale Maxon, who had been teaching English in Kanazawa (at Fourth Higher School) before the war, and who then joined the Navy, carrying out sensitive assignments, such as interpreting for the U.S. lawyer who was interrogating former Prime Minister Hideki Tojo. Haru and I knew Yale Maxon because his family used to spend their summers in Karuizawa. He was the one who found me a job with the International Prosecution Section of the IMTFE, and from that I moved to the court. In January 1946, I passed the examination and became a court interpreter at the trial of Tojo and other so-called "A-class" war criminals.

The trial began in April and ended with the sentencing of seven, including Tojo, to the gallows. I was with the court until I left for America in 1948, and my work there was by far the most interesting thing I had ever done up to that point.

The IMTFE held its sessions at the former War Ministry in Ichigaya. The main building, where the trials were held, had a central clock tower, with an auditorium which had space for the international press and a spectators' gallery. Every day for two years, I took the commuter train from Shinmachi to Ichigaya via Shibuya and Yoyogi or Shinjuku, then walked up the driveway from Ichigaya Station on the Chuo line to the IMTFE courtroom. Cherry blossom trees lined the driveway, and I watched them bloom two years in a row.

I sat in the interpreters' booth on the stage, overlooking the defendants to the left and the black-robed judges, headed by Chief Justice Sir William Webb, to the right. Every morning at 9 o'clock I was at my seat before the judges, prosecutors, and defendants filed in, and the chief marshal would proclaim in a stentorian voice, "The International Military Tribunal for the Far East is in session."

All the 28 defendants – including Tojo – had been prominent generals, admirals, bureaucrats or politicians. Tojo's eyes were hawklike, inspiring fear and awe, not friendship. His uniform was always freshly pressed, its top button open at the neck – I remembered how he used to wear this open-necked shirt when touring Japanese-occupied Southeast Asia during the war. Tojo's shiny bald pate and keen eyes behind nondescript glasses are indelibly etched in my memories of those days.

It was not a normal, straightforward type of interpreting session. The Americans, who were holding the trials, were suspicious of the Japanese interpreters. They were afraid that the Japanese would select any element that could be more favorable to Japan and distort the testimony. So the Americans used *nisei* to check on the interpreting done by Japanese nationals. The *nisei* were all American citizens by birth, and many had spent the war interpreting at POW trials. This extra level of superintending the interpreters was not altogether necessary, because the differences of nuance would have evened out in the end. But these *nisei* interpreters had created their own position themselves, and they were very protective of it. They insisted that Japanese was a very difficult language to translate and that it required multiple levels of checking.

I only interpreted in the courtroom three days a week. The other days I translated documents elsewhere in the building, and later I only worked about half the time. The idea was that interpreting was so strenuous that you could only do it for half an hour at a time, and I was translating both from English into Japanese and from Japanese to English. I had a session in the morning and another in the afternoon, but I think only three hours altogether interpreting in a given day.

I was 22 when I started, and it so happened that I was the youngest interpreter by many years. My bilingual upbringing made a difference, particularly with the judges – none of whom spoke Japanese. They preferred to have interpreters who spoke good idiomatic English. Some interpreters were quite good but had a heavy accent, and so the judges preferred other people, like my very friend Henry Toshiro Shimanouchi, who had learned flawless English at Occidental College. He went on to make a career out of interpreting.

We interpreters came from various backgrounds. One was a customs inspector, some were from the Foreign Ministry, but the difference between us was that some were considered technical people, while others were the kind of career diplomats who could go on to become ambassadors. Either way, there was a sense within our group that we were serving an elite function, at a moment of historical importance. But many of us also thought that our new jobs, though new and exciting, were a one-time experience that no one expected to be doing forever.

As for the civilian defendants and their lawyers, very few seemed brilliant or outstanding. Seeing them, I felt a profound sense of let-down. Were these shilly-shallying, ineffective and mostly senile men Japan's leaders throughout the war and the years before? Perhaps since the Manchurian Incident of September 18, 1932? When I saw their faces in the newspapers of the day, they looked distinguished, larger than life. But in the courtroom they seemed so ordinary, like any strap-hanger on his way to work on a commuter train. The professional diplomats and bureaucrats were equally disappointing.

There were a few leaders whom I actually admired. One was Admiral Keisuke Okada, Prime Minister from 1934-36, whose testimony was clear and dispassionate. A political moderate, he was targeted during the abortive February 26 military rebellion of 1936, in which he disguised himself as a kimono-clad civilian to evade his would-be assassins. His brother-in-law, shouting "I am Okada!" was sabered down in his stead. Admiral Okada was close to Emperor Hirohito, and he had opposed the war with America from the beginning.

* * * * *

In 1946, I also met Jim and Ellen Watt, Christian Science practitioners sent to Japan by the Church in Boston. MacArthur, who had grandiose ideas about converting Japan to Christianity, invited churches in the U.S. to send representatives to his headquarters in Tokyo. The Christian Science church, which does not normally send missionaries abroad, responded by sending the Watts, who had been practitioners in Chicago and New York. The Watts also had overseas experience – in the 1920s they had been in Kharkov in the Ukraine. James Watt was an engineer who had been recruited by Herbert Hoover to help with famine relief there.

The Watts returned to the United States in the early 1930's and lived in a woodsy Chicago suburb called Downer's Grove. When World War II ended, Jim became the U.S. Army chaplain for U.S. troops serving at Yokohama Port, and he commuted to Tokyo to help re-organize the pre-war Christian Science church in Tokyo. Bob Peel and fellow Americans in the Occupation Forces also did much to help reorganize the Tokyo church which had been forced to shut down in 1940, when the Japanese government passed a new law recognizing only three Christian churches: Roman Catholic, Greek Orthodox, and Protestant. The Episcopalians split, some joining the general Protestant church, others remaining independent. Those who did not join the general Protestant church were persecuted by the Japanese government, which imprisoned some of their bishops.

Also in 1946, I went on a reporting trip with Gordon Walker to an area in Ibaragi, northeast of Tokyo, where he wanted me to interpret for him. My permanent engagement by that time was already to the IMTFE, but this trip was only for ten days or so. Mark Gayn had already written a book, *Japan Diary*, on the nests of rightists there, but then Gordon wrote a series for the *Monitor* on the same subject, unearthing nationalist extremists not covered by Gayn. After the war, the rightists in Japan had to go underground, and they had a certain amount of popularity among the people in that area. I interviewed some of them. I didn't feel any great hostility towards me – I think they were not so concerned with me as they were with Gordon. In any case, it was my first foray into the work of journalists.

* * * * *

I continued my job as court interpreter for the IMTFE until the trial ended in the summer of 1948. The sentences were pronounced in October. Seven people, including Tojo, were sentenced to death, and those sentences were carried out in

December. But when the courtroom sessions ended, I left. The court had closed to let the judges write their verdicts, so there was no need for me anymore.

I had applied to Principia College as early as 1946, and I was accepted in 1947, but at the time travel was still banned for non-official Japanese. Normal civilian travel would not resume until the spring of 1948. That's when I finally got on a freighter, the *Flying Scud*, and left for America on May 15, 1948. When the Tojo verdict was announced, I read about it in the United States.

The Yada family, with Great-grandfather seated left.
The children are (left to right): my Aunt Kiyo, my mother, my Uncle Mako.

My Great-grandfather Watanabe.

Left: Grandmother Yada

Right: Grandfather Yada, in all his regalia.

Left: With my parents.

Above: With my brother Akira and in Karuizawa.

Left: With my mother on our way to Hawaii.

Right: With my father on one of his visits to the U.S.

Left: At the main entrance to the International Military Tribunal for the Far East.

Below: Behind the scenes at the IMTFE, with fellow translators. I am standing second from left.

Clockwise from top left: Hiro in New York, before we were married; Hiro and I in Hong Kong (photo by Inger McCabe Elliott); Mimi and Saya in Hawaii – a photo that I always kept on my desk; Hiro and I in Tibet, in front of the Potala Palace.

My brother and I with our families at the house in Karuizawa. (left to right) Hiro, me (holding Saya), Mimi, Midori, Nobue (holding Kim), Jun, and Akira.

Top: Shaking hands with Deng Xiaoping, with Earl Foell looking on.
Bottom: (l to r) Charlotte Saikowski, Me, John Hughes, Geoffrey Godsell, and John Allan May.

Top: In Egypt with: (standing) Kumi, Jun, Mimi, Ben, Kiko, Hiro, me, Saya, Luc, and (front) Morio, Taro, Takuma, Miyé, and Kazuma.
Bottom: Receiving my DPhil at Oxford in 2008.

Part II

JOURNALIST

Chapter 6

Arrival in America

A golden bridge between worlds

Lafcadio Hearn, who popularized Japan for Western readers around the turn of the last century, tells of a young Japanese returning to his country from his studies in Europe. As his boat approaches Yokohama, the student rushes to the deck and strains for a glimpse of Mount Fuji. But however hard he tries, the sacred mountain is nowhere to be seen.

"Higher, look higher, young man," an older passenger advises him. He does so, and there, majestic above the clouds, he finds the familiar, perfect cone.

I had a similar experience when I first arrived in the United States from Japan, half a century ago. I tingled with excitement, for finally I was about to fulfill my dream. I was going to America!

For most civilians, travel across the Pacific in those days was still by sea. I took the train from Tokyo to Yokohama, and there boarded a freighter, the California Bear.[1] I was one of just eight

---

[1] At the time of this article, I misremembered the name of the ship, perhaps unconsciously conflating its destination with a symbol that sounded more American.

passengers. My father, who had made his own round-the-world voyage 20 years earlier, saw me off.

Twelve days later, we were off the California coast. John, the generous-hearted steward, woke me that morning humming "California, Here I Come." Our ship was going to pass directly under the Golden Gate Bridge, and like Lafcadio Hearn's student, I ran outside to see the bridge. But morning mists swirled around and I could see nothing. "You're looking too low," said John. "Lift your eyes higher."

Even so, at first I could not penetrate the fog. But as I kept raising my gaze in accordance with John's instructions, suddenly I caught my breath. There, floating ethereally above the mist, was the great orange suspension bridge that had greeted so many Asian immigrants and so many thousands of US servicemen returning from the far side of the Pacific Ocean in war and in peace.

Since then, I have traveled more times than I can count between Japan and America, but always by air. Once, the pilot invited me to the cockpit as our plane was passing near snow-clad Mt. McKinley in Alaska. That was certainly a thrilling experience. But it cannot compare with my first view of the Golden Gate Bridge, which has merged in memory with everything that was fresh, lovely, and exhilarating about a land that I now call my own. There are so many firsts when one comes to a new country. My first artichoke, which I had no idea how to eat. My first waffles. My first porterhouse steak. Images of food seem to dominate, perhaps because of having gone through a long period of wartime deprivation. But there are other images as well, beginning with several firsts experienced aboard that eye-opening voyage to America.

For instance, my first refrigerator raid (another food image!). I was introduced to this practice by my cabin-mate, Ken. He was a Nisei (the second generation of Japanese to call America home) from San Francisco and had been looking into business opportunities in Japan. John, the steward, stocked a refrigerator in the pantry with a wide variety of soft drinks plus bread and all the ingredients for a Dagwood sandwich. After dinner, there was often a movie. After the movie, Ken would wink at me and then head straight for the refrigerator, with me in tow. He would fix us some fanciful combination of turkey, salami, lettuce, and cheese. Today, I wonder how I ever managed to gulp it all down. But in those days, the sensation was Sybaritic and heavenly.

A more exotic first was the first wedding I attended. This was a new experience, not only for me, but also for the captain and his whole crew. How often does a workhorse freighter become the venue for the exchange of marriage vows? Two of our passengers were Americans who had fallen in love with each other while working in Japan. Their contracts completed, they were about to leave Japan when they had a brilliant idea. Why not a romantic shipboard wedding?

They came aboard with a wedding cake and all the other trimmings. Ships' captains are authorized to conduct weddings. But our captain, a stout and genial officer who had commanded only freighters for his entire career, had never presided over such an event. He was understandably nervous. The crew was delighted over this break in their humdrum daily routine.

The morning of the wedding dawned bright and clear. But there was a stiff breeze. The ship, lacking the stabilizers that a passenger liner would have, bucked the waves like a horse at a slow gallop. The bride had not acquired her sea legs, and the rumor spread that the great event might have to be postponed. Then the captain changed the ship's course — at least for the duration of the ceremony — so that the waves would be less of a problem.

Amid the cheers of the crew, the bride appeared, somewhat pale, in a pearl-white wedding dress. A creaky portable Victrola was cranked up and played Wagner's "Wedding March." The couple exchanged rings, and the captain — resplendent in his dress uniform — duly pronounced them husband and wife. The crew cheered again, and we applauded. But just as we did so, the bride clapped her hand to her mouth and went rushing back to her room.

Within a day or so, however, the new couple could be seen walking up and down all over the ship, exclaiming with the rest of us over the sightings of flying fish and whales, and quite obviously enjoying each other's company.

And so a voyage that had begun with the auspicious coming together of a man and a woman ended with the injunction to "look higher," and the Golden Gate's soaring symbolism of the coming together of nations.

— Takashi Oka for *The Christian Science Monitor*, October 23, 2002

I wasn't alone on my voyage across the Pacific. Mrs. Matsukata came with me on the *Flying Scud*, and we were to meet my mother and Aunt Kiyo, who were traveling on a different ship, when we arrived in the US. Then we would travel on to Boston for a Christian Science conference. Fred Foote, who had succeeded Jim and Ellen Watt as the official Christian Science Church representative at the MacArthur headquarters, found passage for Mama and Aunt Kiyo to the US on a US Navy transport used for Occupation personnel. My recollection is that there was no civilian transport in those days, and that Japanese were not allowed to use US Army transport by air. Sea transport was regulated to a lesser extent, so that's how we went – though on separate boats. Fred also helped me to get authorized to attend Principia College as an International scholarship student. My first passport was a Japanese passport issued by the American occupying authority.

Mama and Aunt Kiyo arrived before me, in Seattle, where they encountered some confusion. Apparently a church member was supposed to greet them, but he missed the US official who was in charge of that particular crossing. So my mother and aunt were put into an immigration detention center, because nobody knew what to do with them. Then the Church's Committee on Publication for Washington State (it's called a committee, but it was just one person) sorted it out, and they were released. They took a train down to San Francisco, where I met them.

They and Mrs. Matsukata stayed with the Allens, who were old family friends of the Matsukatas. Mr. Allen was a retired railway engineer who had built tunnels and bridges throughout Japan, and who had also known Miss Boynton. Meanwhile, I was met in San Francisco by George Ikeda, a Nisei businessman who took me to his house in Alameda near Berkeley. I remember that after dinner Uncle George stacked the dishes in the dishwasher and told me to let the dishwasher do the work – yet another first for me.

After a couple of days, Mama, Aunty Kiyo, Mrs. Matsukata, and I boarded a Union Pacific train for New York via Chicago. I was astounded that it took a whole day just to cross Wyoming, and from morning to nightfall I didn't see a single person – just herds of cattle and horses. The train ride was quite bumpy, and I had difficulty writing letters until we pulled into a station. Compared to that, Japan's Shinkansen is smooth as silk.

When we got to Chicago, we were met by Papa's former secretary from his management days at the Tokyo Club. She was a striking Italian beauty, and she and her mother invited us to dinner at her home, taking us there by car. It turned out to be an apartment in a nondescript building, with a floor strewn with newspapers. From the bedroom came the sound of snoring. Our friend's husband, a truck driver, worked the night shift and slept during the day. In Japan, Occupation Force Americans were privileged people, with special trains and accommodations – but here we finally saw Americans as ordinary people.

Our friends served us a scrumptious Italian lunch, with spaghetti carbonara and a fantastic homemade chocolate cake for dessert. We were impressed by the great care they had taken, in this modest kitchen setting, to serve us a meal that could have come straight from the Waldorf Astoria. After a long, leisurely meal, they drove us to the LaSalle Street Station in the Loop, to catch the train to New York. We had little sense of time and got to the station with just a few minutes to spare.

In New York, we were met by the Yajimas at Penn Station and went to their home in Port Washington on Long Island – a very comfortable two-story house on affluent Sunset Hill.

Yuri Yajima was the daughter of Japanese silk merchants who were contemporaries of the Morimuras, founders of Noritake and Nihon Toki ceramics. She was an only child, and since her parents had no sons, her husband Kiichi took on her family's surname when they married (a common practice in Japan). Mr. Yajima – "Call me Kiichi," he said – was from a modest family in Shikoku and ran a textile company. He had an office on Fifth Avenue in midtown Manhattan, and I would often ride with him on the Long Island Railroad into Penn Station, where I began to explore New York.

The Yajimas were very generous and hospitable. They had been in America for a long time and organized a small relief effort from their spacious basement, sending care-packages back to Japan. In the early days of 1945-46, when the country was still very poor, these care-packages of food and clothes meant a lot to a family. On subsequent visits, I used their in-home shipping facilities to mail my own packages overseas. Their house was always full of visitors from Japan, from students like myself, to businessmen like Mr. Hattori – of the famous watch company – to artists like Kenzo Okada. Mr. Okada and I had discussions there on current affairs and even played a few card games.

The Yajimas had wonderful meals for their frequent guests, both American and Japanese. When the meal was Japanese, they shut the curtains so no one could see in from the street – that was because they always ended a meal with *ochazuke* (green tea poured over rice), which of course we all loved. Despite the many years they had spent in the U.S., the Yajimas were afraid that if their neighbors saw them shoving the *ochazuke* into their mouths with big slurping noises, they would think they were Oriental barbarians.

I sometimes talked with Mrs. Yajima, Yuri's mother, who had attended Nihon Joshidai (Japan Women's University) when very few Japanese women went beyond high school. Mrs. Yajima knew English, but didn't speak it much herself. She told me that, in her day, the high school boys wore black uniforms, while the girls wore kimonos tucked into pleated *hakama*.

The Yajimas were also members of the Christian Science Church. I believe Mrs. Yajima said it was her maid who converted them, sometime during World War I. They were married in Christ Church, an Anglican church in Karuizawa, and my family was invited to their wedding reception at the Mampei Hotel. It was the first formal dinner I had ever attended, with so many knives and forks at each place setting that I didn't know where to begin. I just tried to imitate whoever was sitting next to me.

Kiichi joked a lot and did magic tricks. For instance, he would take a coin and say he was going to tell it a sad story. Every so often he would take the coin to his ear to see whether he could hear it crying. Finally, lo and behold, he squeezed out a tear from the coin. (He had wet cotton behind his ear). Kiichi was a great person, and later he was the best man at my wedding.

* * * * *

The purpose of our trip across the country was to attend the annual meeting of the Christian Science Church in Boston, held on June 7. This particular meeting was the first of its kind since the end of the war, so a lot of international members who hadn't been able to attend for many years showed up. It was a rather special atmosphere.

Later in July, I had two weeks of Christian Science class instruction in Chicago. I stayed with Mama and Aunt Kiyo at the Allerton – my first long hotel stay. I also saw the Watts again, whom I had recently met in Japan. They had come back to Chicago and had set themselves up as Christian Science practitioners. They were students of Mary Sands Lee, who would be my teacher as well, and they introduced me to her.

The Christian Science religion has no ministers because the pastor of the church is actually two books, the Bible and Mary Baker Eddy's *Science and Health with Key to the Scriptures*. Instead, it has lecturers, teachers, and practitioners. The lecturers speak about Christian Science to a general audience, and the teachers conduct the two-week course that people take when they are interested in deepening their study of Christian Science. This course is called class instruction, and it is what one takes in order to become a Christian Science practitioner, although not everyone who takes the course ends up making a career as a practitioner. The practitioners are full-time spiritual healers, who charge a fee for their services. They provide spiritual prayer treatment to people seeking healing through Christian Science and not through medical practice.

I took class instruction from Mary Sands Lee, who lived in the northern part of Chicago. Mrs. Lee was born in 1869 – when I met her in 1948, she was about to turn 80 – and she would live to be nearly 100. She was a well-educated woman who had deep insights into human character. Whenever I had to make an important decision in those years, I always consulted Mrs. Lee.

Because Principia was relatively close to Chicago, I stayed in contact with her while I was in college. From time to time we would meet for dinner. She had very long legs and a short upper body, so when we went to restaurants she always asked for a couple of telephone books to sit on.

Mrs. Lee became a Christian Science teacher around 1922, and she taught for the rest of her life. A wonderful intellectual, she was also interested in subjects other than religion. She had gone to Radcliffe not long after its founding, and she took courses from George Santayana and George Lyman Kittridge. Because her eyesight was too poor for reading, Mrs. Lee could only audit the classes. Therefore, she didn't become a formal student. But she paid the tuition, enrolled in classes, and she had people read the texts to her – so she essentially had a 4-year liberal arts education. She was also a Christian Science practitioner, and many of those who came to her had remarkable experiences.

I learned a great deal from Mrs. Lee, and I also had a lot of fun with her. I remember she told me about having gone to the Chicago World's Fair in 1893. She also frequently went to Europe, where she enjoyed the cultural riches of Paris, Berlin, and other great cities. She told me about traveling the Rhineland, and she said that one of the things that she missed about becoming such a devout Christian Scientist was the glass of beer she used to enjoy on the boats that went down the Rhine.

* * * * *

That summer of 1948, I wrote my first article for *The Christian Science Monitor*. I did it largely because Bob Peel and his sister Doris were nagging me to write something for them. At that time, Doris was the *Monitor's* book editor, but she was also a poet who published her first novel when she was 19. She and Bob wanted me to write an article about intellectual trends in Japan, and, after much persuading, I finally sat down at a typewriter. It took me all night to write it. But they said my work was okay, and so it went into the *Monitor*. That was my first article, published before I started classes at Principia.

Letter From Tokyo: Postwar Trends

Postwar trends of the Japanese reading public indicate that while a large section of the nation is going all out for American movies, American sports, American jazz, and even American slang, a good portion of this same group still turns mainly to French and Russian authors for intellectual enjoyment.

A few weeks ago, while riding on one of Tokyo's crowded streetcars, I heard two high school girls discussing books they had recently read. "What do you think of *Crime and Punishment*?" one was saying. "My, that was a sad story. I wept all the way through it." "Really?" the other replied. "Wait until you read *The Brothers Karamazov*." One of them turned her head, and I was quite surprised to find I had seen her before. It was at a dance sponsored by the Students' Society for the Study of American Culture, where she had been an eager member of a class in the jitterbug — explained by the instructor as an outdoor dance popular in Washington's day.

Since Japan's surrender and its subsequent occupation by Allied troops, the vogue of studying American culture has practically swept the nation. English has never been so popular as it is today. Outworn copies of *Life, Good Housekeeping,* and the *Saturday Evening Post* are sold at fantastic prices, while the Japanese edition of *Reader's Digest* — now in its second year of publication — causes a regular stampede the day it is put on sale. Yet if any college student should be asked, "Who is your favorite author?" nine times out of ten he would reply, "Tolstoi," or "Dostoievsky," or "Gide."

During balmy prewar days the tendency was to consider American civilization immature — strong in science, weak in literature and the arts. Many American novels appeared in Japanese translations as soon as their publication; but few gained anything approaching a universal appeal, with the notable exception of *The Good Earth, Gone With the Wind,* and a handful of others.

In the three years since the surrender, military censorship and the inconvertibility of the Japanese yen have made the translation of works copyrighted in Great Britain and America an extremely complicated process. Last year one publisher brought out *Arch of Triumph*, by Erich Maria Remarque. It was an immediate success, but the issue was soon withdrawn because of an unfortunate mix-up in the publisher's translation privileges.

However, despite the seeming superficiality of the current craze for American culture, a very real search for ideas is going on. The sudden collapse of militarism plunged the social and intellectual life of the nation into confusion. Some people continued to cling to old beliefs; but many, especially the young, can no longer be content with the rationalization that superior material might alone had defeated Japan.

Amidst the many attempts now going on to fathom a way of life dimly perceived to be fuller and more satisfying than the old traditional one, some are bound to be ludicrous, some even dangerous. For instance, a professor in one of the leading Christian universities of Japan explained Puritanism to his students as the main cause of American capitalistic exploitation — because it was a system imposed by a minority on the majority, whereby men were made to enslave themselves in order to surrender their profits to the church. The professor was a Marxist; and, frankly, Marxist teachings are popular in most universities because they seem to be logical, and, like a mirage beckoning to the weary wanderer, appear to offer a solution to the dire muddle Japan finds itself in today.

The answer to this professor's theories is not to shout, "Off with his head!" but to make accessible to students such books as will give the other side of the question;

to make possible the rendering of independent judgement.

The whole trouble with our nation in the past was that we allowed other people to do our thinking for us. Now we must learn to think for ourselves. There is great need for sympathetic understanding of this situation, and especially for presenting us with the raw material from which we are to derive our own conclusions in a positive but unobtrusive way.

Recently Occupation authorities have given permission for the translation and distribution of a number of current American books and magazines. This is a big step in the right direction. For when one gets an idea through books, one has the opportunity of chewing it, of digesting it, and of weighing it in the balance with other beliefs. If, through such experience, one is thoroughly convinced of the validity of that idea, it is founded on a rock. Any amount of searching and groping is worthwhile when it leads to that peak of fulfillment.

— Takashi Oka for *The Christian Science Monitor*, July 8, 1948.

Chapter 7

Principia

By the time I got to Principia, I was 26 years old and had a college diploma from Japan. But I knew that I wanted to have more than just the one year that Principia had initially offered me, so Dr. Alfred Gertsch, the Dean of the Faculty, agreed to take me on as a junior, giving me two full years in Elsah, Illinois. He put me in 27 North (now Brooks North) – Mako Matsukata's old house.

I loved Principia. I was astounded by the spaciousness of the campus, which was larger than anything I had ever experienced in Japan. There were only about 500 students, but the campus was 2,000 acres – just outside of St. Louis, along the bluffs of the Mississippi River. I enjoyed sitting on those bluffs and looking westward across the wheat plains of Missouri and Nebraska towards the Rocky Mountains, and – in my mind's eye – beyond them to the West Coast and the Pacific Ocean. There, on the far side of the vast ocean, was my homeland, Japan.

I arrived at the end of July 1948, and did manual work around campus, cleaning up the dormitories and preparing for the fall. The dorms weren't co-ed then, so when we went into the women's dorms, we always shouted "Man on the floor!"

Despite my scholarship, I had limited funds at Principia, so I continued to work throughout the year – in the campus kitchen and, later, in the library. As I did so, I remembered some of the stories my mother had told me about Mr. Yosuke Matsuoka (Foreign Minister and Ambassador to the League of Nations in the 1930's) – how he had worked his way through college in Oregon, washing dishes, etc. But that thought was not enough for me to overcome the smells of the dish-drying process. After a month or so in the college kitchen, I found more congenial work as a telephone operator, first at night, then sometimes during the day. It was a great way to discover who was dating whom. Once, I fell asleep and was woken up by a bunch of girls who were worried as to why their calls weren't getting through.

Although Principia was a tiny college, it had a student body from all over the United States, so I got to know people from a variety of backgrounds. This was still a period when there were veterans returning from military service, on the GI Bill. Many of my classmates had had some pretty remarkable experiences during the war – fighting in Germany, or studying in Denmark or France. They all seemed so mature, compared to me.

I also had older Japanese friends who had attended Principia. Emi Abiko was the first Japanese student at the college, and I knew her husband Toshio and their whole family. During the war, the Abikos had stayed in Karuizawa for a while, before moving into the Matsukatas' fortress-like storehouse in Gumma.

I loved all four seasons in Elsah. The sprouting green of spring is delightful, as is the golden foliage in September or October. The summer is usually hot and muggy, but not always. Sometimes the breeze is stiff, but often it could be mild and caressing. I walked the campus whenever I got the chance, even in winter when the cold was bracing. Sometimes I walked solo, sometimes with friends like Dick Gillespie or Jim Goodsell. Maybe once or twice with Phyllis or Betty Merrill, to whom I felt close because – although of American parents – they had lived in Tsingtao and Shanghai, China, and they had visited Japan on their voyages to and from the United States. I had occasional dates with Betty, and also – separately – with Phyllis, her older sister. Betty was lively and fun. Phyllis was more subdued, but just as much fun once you got to know her.

I learned to drive from August Janssen, who – although a very good friend – was not such a good teacher (to this day, I don't drive very well). Janssen was from a well-to-do Dutch family in Indonesia, and he had a big, roomy Kaiser. I bought it from him, then eventually sold it for $50 to Paul Carr, who cherished it for many years. One summer night at Principia, August suggested that the two of us go driving, and he took me in his Kaiser to a place that was swarming with fireflies – as if the air in front of us was full of stars. We sat silently for a while and watched the fireflies flickering in the dark.

Some students would go swimming in the Mississippi, but for me its brownish water seemed too dirty. I also knew there were rattlesnakes on the cliffs, but fortunately I never encountered one. However, one of the campus nurses told me about a student that had come to Cox Cottage infirmary with multiple snakebites. A brave, unflappable woman, the nurse had had to suck the venom and spit it out. I played a minor role in that emergency; as switchboard operator, I helped to contact the student's family. The young man was healed after a short stay at the infirmary.

One time late at night, a bunch of my friends and I went swimming nude at a deep pool in a quarry not far from Elsah. As I remember, someone at Rackham (one of the dorms) suggested a swim at night, and students at other houses joined in. We could easily have put swimsuits on, but we didn't – perhaps because there were no women. Although that was my only experience with skinny-dipping, it seemed to have been the custom in small-town America, from which many Principia students came. Lynn Noah told me that, when growing up, he often swam nude and thought nothing of it.

Whereas St. Louis was the cultural center of the region – where we would see the Sadler's Wells ballet or the symphony – Elsah was a picturesque village. But Elsah was also close to the border with Kentucky, and just west of the river lay Missouri, which was basically a southern state, parts of which reminded me of the poverty and hunger of postwar Japan.

* * * * *

Because I had just two years at Principia, I had to cram a great deal into that time. I read Shakespeare, Milton, Emerson, and took a general course on American intellectual history. I had always wanted to study English literature, which, in retrospect, was probably not the best choice, although Principia was a strong liberal arts college. Bob Peel would have recommended Harvard, where he had studied under the famous American historian Perry Miller. Before he graduated, Bob had worked as a teaching fellow and could have stayed on at Harvard, but then Principia offered him a job. As a Christian Scientist, and with a few friends already there, he thought that Elsah might be interesting for him, at least for a few years. I often saw him on campus, and in the summer we would both go to Boston, where I worked as a copyboy at the *Monitor*, and where I continued to hone my journalistic skills, writing freelance articles.

In 1950 as I was about to graduate, Dr. Gertsch suggested that I stay on for a year at Principia to teach English. I had already been accepted for the Asian Studies program at Harvard, but I decided Principia would give me a good teaching experience, so I took the job and delayed Harvard for one year. I became an instructor in freshman English, which, as it turned out, was quite a difficult job.

I felt I had not accumulated enough experience of life to be qualified to teach college freshmen, who were only a few years younger than myself. Many of the students came from the rural communities of Missouri or Kansas, and they would ask me questions about all kinds of things – about relations with the opposite sex, about their friends, about very serious choices in their lives. I tried to answer such questions to the best of my ability and had to dig deep into my own religious faith. I also went back to Mrs. Lee for counsel.

Christian Science affirms the supremacy of good and the nothingness of evil. Yet all sorts of unhappy experiences abound.

So what do you do? Each of those experiences tests your faith. And I found my faith was adequate to keep me in the Church.

There is also controversy among Christian Scientists about whether their children should go to a Christian Science school, or whether they should broaden their horizons by attending a non-denominational school. But I enjoyed the time I spent at Principia. I had grown up in Japan, where Christians are a very small minority, so for me it was a very broadening experience to meet various kinds of people on campus. Some were very good in academics, others in sports, but the one thing they had in common was their religion.

Also during the course of my one-year instructorship at Principia I ceased being afraid of girls. It's strange – when I first went there, the women, who were actually several years younger than me, seemed so mature. They knew so much more than I thought they would know. When I was growing up in Japan, there was very little mixing of the sexes, all the way through age 17. Only in university would men and women attend the same classes, and even then I had relatively few women classmates. However, at Principia – especially in those immediate postwar years – there were more women than men. So my unease had come from simply not being around women. Over the course of that year, when I had all these girls as my students, I overcame my timidity and soon felt that I could more or less be on an equal footing with them.

Indeed, going to America opened up a whole new prospect for making friends, both male and female. I didn't make a huge number of friends, but certainly many more than in Japan, because in Japan there simply weren't enough people of my age who had a similar background to mine. That sense of being in a minority – or even a minority within a minority – remained strong. As a result, I was always more careful than I should have been when meeting new acquaintances, because I didn't want to show too much of what was going on inside me.

As I began to feel more at home in America, I became mentally free in a way I had not before. I felt I had gained something. In a way, that's true of all people who travel and live outside their own back yard. Also, I still had a connection with the Japanese community I had grown up with. Mari Matsukata was teaching nearby at Washington University in St. Louis, and I invited her to come visit me a couple of times. I remember she joined several of my friends and me on a rambunctious hayride.

I've been back to Principia from time to time. The most recent occasion was my 50th reunion, when I saw quite a few classmates. To this day, our sense of shared experiences remains very strong.

Chapter 8

HARVARD

In 1951, I moved to Cambridge, Massachusetts, on a scholarship through the Harvard-Yenching Institute to study the recent histories of China and Japan. Although Harvard in those years had a fairly small department in this field, there were some very good teachers and scholars, including John K. Fairbank, who was the leading authority on China, and who served as my advisor. I took several seminars with Fairbank, focusing on classical Chinese. It was a two to three year course, and I took three years, spending more time on language – I was reasonably fluent by the time I graduated.

The scene of student life was centered around Harvard Square. We would go there for ice cream and cheap lunches, and to the movie houses nearby. An old theater on Brattle Street not only showed movies but also live plays. On Saturdays, I would go with my friend Nancy Young – whom I had known at Principia – to buy groceries at the Haymarket in downtown Boston. That area of the city, near Scollay Square, was a rough part of town then, and it had a burlesque theater called the Old Howard, where we college kids would go from time to time. I remember one show there that ended with the performer totally naked and clinging to the curtain, which whisked her off the stage as it closed.

In those days there were maybe about eighty Japanese students at Harvard. Every now and then we would get together at the Philips Brooks House, a turn-of-the-century mansion that was the community center for the international students. That's where I met a senior named Minoru Makihara, whose English-speaking friends called Ben. This was long before children came along, but many years later Ben's son Jun would marry my daughter Mimi. Mimi and Jun both went to Harvard, and they met at one of the Thursday teas given by John K. Fairbank, who was also their professor.

Ben, like myself, spoke fluent, native-quality English – as did our good friend Tatsuo Arima, who later became the Japanese ambassador to Germany. This meant that we had a somewhat different kind of education from most of the other Japanese at Harvard. We didn't particularly share the same interests, but that fluency created a special bond between us. By the time I met him, Ben was focused on business. He would go on to work for Mitsubishi, as had been more or less preordained for him, because his father had worked for Mitsubishi as the head of their London bureau before the war.

I also knew Henry Kissinger when I was at Harvard. At that time, he was still a teaching assistant to William Yandell Elliott, but he quickly became famous by writing a book called *Nuclear Weapons and Foreign Policy,* in what was a new field then. I knew Kissinger fairly well because of a funny incident. One day he brought me a letter – handwritten in Japanese and obviously by a woman – which he asked me to translate. Kissinger said, "It has nothing to do with *me* – it's all about a *friend."* The woman wrote that she had enjoyed meeting him, and that she was hoping their relationship would continue. While I was reading, Henry kept saying the letter was for some friend of his, and that he had *nothing* to do with it, that he had *no idea* what the relationship was, and so forth. I don't remember whether the young woman was a student or not, but it was an amusing situation.

Over the next twenty-five years or so, our paths continued to cross, as I covered the Vietnam War. Henry became recognized as a celebrity playboy – he liked parties, he liked women, and he liked a certain degree of notoriety. He was skilled at publicity. Behind this reputation, he was able to engage in serious negotiations undeterred. So for journalists, Kissinger was very good copy. He knew exactly how to create the sort of stories that would keep the press hanging on his lips.

* * * * *

I very much enjoyed my years at Harvard, but I didn't study as well as I could have, because my attention was being pulled in another direction. I continued to write freelance articles for *The Christian Science Monitor*, which by then seemed like a natural evolution for me. I was interested in political, economic, and social reporting – not sports, not financial – and in the summer of 1952, I got a chance to attend the political conventions leading to the presidential election. That's what got me hooked on being a reporter.

In 1952, Adlai Stevenson, who was my favorite presidential candidate, ran against Eisenhower. I desperately wanted to attend the conventions, first the Republican and then the Democratic, both of which were in Chicago. But I couldn't get the *Monitor* to send me, because its own senior correspondents were already there. So I found work in Chicago as a translator for the Japanese newspaper *Yomiuri Shimbun*. *Yomiuri* had a reporter in Chicago, but he didn't speak English and had no interest in attending the convention – he told me he preferred to stay in his hotel room and watch it on television. So I got all his passes and went to the conventions and just had a ball.

I was excited to be on the convention floor. I could see just about everything going on – and I didn't have any responsibility of writing a story about it. I got around to wherever I wanted. At the Republican convention I tried to stick close to either Eisenhower or Robert Taft. This was long before Kennedy's assassination and the ensuing heightened security, so I was right behind Eisenhower – I could have touched him on his head if I'd wanted to.

The Taft people were very angry, feeling that Eisenhower more or less stole the nomination because of his war reputation.

Taft had fought through all the grubby details of Republican politics and now had a chance to seize the nomination. But then this war hero Eisenhower showed up. Within the Republican party, Eisenhower belonged to the liberal wing, and he had no real political background. But he had been the commander of Allied forces during the war, dealing with Konrad Adenauer and Charles de Gaulle and other temperamental leaders, and he had a very quick smile. He said things the way people wanted to hear: nothing that was very clear-cut – you could interpret it however you wanted. I know it was a very bitter pill for the Taft people to swallow. Douglas MacArthur was also there, thinking his own moment was coming. MacArthur had already given his famous speech – "Old soldiers never die, they just fade away" – the year before, and with his address there at the 1952 convention, he did, indeed, fade away.

A few weeks after the Republican convention, the Democrats held theirs, also in Chicago. It was the summer holidays, so I stayed in town and continued with jobs translating for Japanese newspapers covering the conventions. Once again, the *Yomiuri* guy just stayed in his hotel. Although television was new – it was still black and white – and probably exciting enough for him, I preferred to be right on the convention floor.

I was a fan of Adlai Stevenson, as I think most college kids with liberal inclinations were. He was an excellent orator – he usually spoke quite informally, and when he did give a more formal speech, he was very convincing. I think Stevenson was one of the most eloquent figures in American public life. I remember that at the convention he showed the soles of his shoes – which had holes in them, illustrating that he had the common touch. He was unlucky in that his opponent was Eisenhower. To some extent, Stevenson ran sacrificially, because he knew that he had no chance of winning.

Joseph McCarthy was a very loud voice in the politics of those years, claiming he had a list of so many names of

Communists and so on. I thought he was an angry speaker. But those who believed what he said very much supported him. Even Taft – who, though he had lost the nomination, was still beloved by the conservative Republicans – tried to rein him in. Then, in 1954, Edward R. Murrow made his famous broadcast exposing McCarthy. I listened to part of it while I was in a car going from New York to Washington. There were three of us crowded into the front seat because we were all trying to hear the radio. Murrow was a hero to me – as well as to many other young people at that time – because he took on McCarthy, which under the circumstances was not easy to do.

* * * * *

When I returned to Harvard in the fall, I wasn't really sure if I would continue to work for the *Monitor*. My professors – both John Fairbank and Ed Reischauer – persuaded me to stay in academia, so I finished my Master's degree in 1954, and started work on a PhD, passing my general exams in History and East Asian Languages. But Reischauer was somewhat more understanding than Fairbank of my wish to go into journalism, so that's what I did.

As I adjusted to the demands of my new career, I realized there was no time for me to work on a doctoral dissertation. I wouldn't get around to finishing that for another fifty years.

Chapter 9

Hiro and the Arc of Asia

In 1954, while I was running around with various Japanese correspondents in New York and Washington, my mother was back in Tokyo giving English lessons to a young woman named Hiro Imai. Perhaps unsettled by the swarms of American GIs still in town, and fearing the influence that a nondescript American might have on his daughter, Hiro's father, Giichi Imai, insisted that she study with an English-speaking Japanese teacher. Via a family friend, he found my mother, whom he approved as Hiro's tutor. My mother, in turn, suggested that I should meet Mr. Imai, because he was a prominent journalist working in New York.

Mr. Imai had been brought in to take charge of North American operations for the *Asahi Shimbun*, one of Japan's top newspapers. I was friends with many of the Japanese journalists in New York, having covered the political conventions together, as well as other events in US-Japanese relations, such as Prime Minister Yoshida's visit to Washington in 1954. They told me that the new bureau chief for the *Asahi Shimbun* was supposed to be very strict. They said he made his staff come to work at 9 a.m., instead of noon, as they had been doing. In fact, there was not much work for Japanese reporters in New York to do in the morning, because of the time difference with Japan. It was only in the early hours of the evening (Eastern Standard Time) that news started coming in. So all the *Asahi* reporters in New York thought that Mr. Imai was unnecessarily harsh, because now they would not only be working in the very busy evening hours – sometimes almost until dawn – but also in the morning. At first he was not very popular. He was considered to be an extra layer of bureaucracy that management had imposed on the journalists. In any case, that was the reputation he had when I met him.

The occasion for the meeting was that my mother was in town. She often took long trips to America, visiting friends from Tulsa to Texas and pretty much all over the US, and when she came to New York, I joined her so she could introduce me to Mr. Imai. He had a spacious office in the *New York Times* building, where *Asahi* had its headquarters, and he lived in Schwab House, a big apartment building on Riverside Drive and 73rd Street, with a view of the Hudson River from the window.

I don't think it was because of any Machiavellian design on my mother's part, but when we got to the Imais' home, Hiro was also there.

I suppose you could say that it was love at first sight, because I was really struck by Hiro in a way I had never felt before. Japanese girls I had known were either very forward or very shy – the well brought-up girls I had known were quite shy. But when I met Hiro, I encountered a person who was totally straightforward. She wasn't overly forward, but she wasn't shy either. We had a very good conversation, and I thought: "Oh... I'd like to know her better." I suggested taking her to the Cloisters. A couple of days later, Hiro and I went to the Cloisters, and that's how our relationship got started.

At that time, Hiro was living in Manhattan with her parents, for whom her presence was quite essential. Her mother didn't really speak English, so Hiro accompanied her for grocery shopping and all the other daily business of living in a city like New York. Being an only daughter, she had her own dream to leave the shelter of the family and go to Vassar, but she never got to do it. Her parents insisted that she stay at home to help her mother. So she stayed in the city and went to Barnard.

Hiro was born in 1932 in Nishinomiya, between Osaka and Kobe. The family followed her father's work as he was assigned to various cities, living in China for a year in 1935 before moving back to Japan. In 1939, the *Asahi Shimbun* sent her father to New

York – this time alone. He stayed there only a few months. Then, thinking that war with the US was eminent, the newspaper sent him to Argentina (which was neutral for the first few years of the war), and he spent the war in Buenos Aires. In a way, Hiro told me, he had a rather easy time of it, because he didn't go through any of the bombings and hunger of the war. Meanwhile, Hiro's school in Mikage was bombed, forcing her teachers to hold classes in various buildings around town. But it wasn't until almost two years after the war had ended that her father found a freighter that would bring him back to Japan. So she didn't see him at all for those eight years. When he finally returned, they didn't recognize each other.

After the war, *Asahi* shifted its headquarters from Osaka to Tokyo, and at the end of 1947, Hiro and her family moved to Tokyo, where her father served as the Foreign Editor. Because he spoke English, he had the duty of dealing with all the American Occupation censors and supervisors – at which he bristled. Hiro attended the prestigious high school of St. Maur's, and then took her first two years of college at Tokyo Women's University. It was during these years that she began taking English lessons from my mother.

The lessons were held at my parents' house, which was designed – like my grandparents' house – in a mix of Western and traditional Japanese styles. Hiro said it was my mother who introduced her to American customs. She also introduced Hiro to Christian Science in Tokyo, but Hiro, being rather non-religious, didn't cotton to it.

When her father was assigned to the *Asahi* bureau in New York, the family moved again, arriving in the city in November 1953. Hiro began classes at Barnard in February 1954. Having been an English literature major in Tokyo, she wanted to switch to art history at Barnard – but her father insisted that she had to finish what she'd started. So she stayed with literature. The family lived at Schwab House, just down the river from her college, and on weekends I'd come down from Boston to see her. I had a friend who lived up on 110th Street, and I would stay with him before catching the train back to work on Monday.

In June 1955, Hiro invited me to her graduation ball. I would have accepted right away, but the timing presented something of a crisis. I had joined the *Monitor's* staff on June 1, 1954, and within a year I had a letter from Erwin Canham, the *Monitor's* Chief Editor, formally appointing me to be the Asia Editor. It was a terrific opportunity, but, at that time, the only Asian country I had ever seen was Japan. So, upon receiving Canham's letter, I quickly planned a six month trip across Asia. The trip coincided precisely with Hiro's graduation ball.

Although we were dating, we had only known each other a relatively brief time. I was not necessarily committed to her, and she was not committed to me. I knew I had a budding friendship with Hiro, and at the same time I had this budding career. So at that point I thought the career came first. I told her that, unfortunately, I couldn't go.

* * * * *

Before I became the *Monitor's* Asia Editor, I was reporting on international politics as much as I could and also writing book reviews. Now with the responsibility of covering all Asian news – from Tokyo to Istanbul – I felt I really had to see these places in order to have any sense of actuality about them. So I planned to make a circuit through Asia – starting with two months in Japan, then continuing west through Hong Kong, Taipei, Saigon, Rangoon, Calcutta, Bombay, New Dehli, Karachi, and Istanbul. I called these cities the Arc of Asia, because they were in the non-Communist countries where Americans were allowed to travel. The *Monitor* was not paying anything for my travel expenses, just my salary, which was quite low – it was something like $52 a week. As a copyboy I had made $39 a week, so I didn't really get much of a raise. But my father was happy that I had decided to become a journalist, and he agreed to support my trip through Asia.

Beginning in July 1955, seven years after arriving in America, I made my first trip back to Japan. I wanted to see my father and mother, as well as to bring my knowledge of Japan up to date, so I stayed through August. Many of the Western-style houses in Tokyo had been more or less forcibly rented out to American officials and businessmen, and our Tokyo house was no exception. A pleasant family called the Janows were installed in our house, as part of the Occupation, while I stayed with my parents in Karuizawa. A friend of my father's, Mr. Tani, who was with the Foreign Ministry in Japan, gave me introductions to all the Japanese Ambassadors in the countries that I went on to visit. I would usually meet the Foreign Minister, and often I met the Prime Minister, as well.

In August, I traveled to Okinawa, which at that point had transformed into a sort of American colony, even though the Occupation had officially "ended" in 1952. They used the US dollar as the local currency. From Okinawa, I went to Taiwan, where I wrote about a successful land reform program. But Taiwan was also the first place in Asia where I saw people with bare feet everywhere I went. I remember seeing water buffalo ambling along the relatively narrow roads, amid a cacophony of bicycles and motorcycles. By September, I had made it to Hong Kong, which at that time was still a British colony and valuable as a window into China.

In Vietnam, I found plenty to write about. The First Indochina War had just ended the year before, with the defeat of the French, and the Geneva Accord of 1954 separating the loyalists from the Communists at the 17th parallel. The Communists who were in the south should have gone north, but didn't, and the nationalists who had been in the north were trying to go south – and the 17th parallel had just become the new frontier. All that sorting out was still going on when I got there. I immediately began writing about Ngo Dinh Diem, who had recently returned from exile and had quickly consolidated power. Dr. Phan Quang Dan, a political opposition leader in Saigon, and whom I had originally met at Harvard, helped me with introductions.

I visited followers of the Cao Dai religion, whose holy city is Tay Ninh, northwest of Saigon. A syncretic religion, Cao Dai was started in 1926 by a Vietnamese intellectual who was trying to marry western and eastern religions. They had bishops and archbishops, like the Catholics, but they also had women who served in these roles. I visited their Holy See temple in Tay Ninh, a colorful place built like a Gothic cathedral, but with eastern imagery, such as the two storks of Chinese iconography. Victor Hugo is one of their saints.

Because they had fairly large groups of believers throughout the south, I was able to visit some Cao Dai centers on my trip through the Mekong Delta and discussed not only their religion but their attitudes towards the French and what they expected for the future. Cao Dai, of all the various religions of Vietnam, was not really anti-French. Other more patriotic religions adamantly opposed the French presence, appropriating the figure of Ho Chi Minh into their worship. By contrast, another religion called Hoa Hao was Buddhist in origin. However, both the Cao Dai and the Hoa Hao had their own armies, which made them attractive to all the movements in Vietnam, whether pro-French or pro-Communist. But Ho Chi Minh was a rather difficult figure for these religions and political movements to digest, because he was first of all a nationalist, and yet also a Communist. I found that the Cao Daists tended to be more anti-Communist, but they were not a united movement; the bulk of them were somewhere in between. So it was a complicated picture.

I visited Thailand, Rangoon (Yangon, the former capital of Burma, now Myanmar), spent all of twenty minutes at Angkor

Wat, and then went to India – Calcutta, Delhi, and Bombay. I interviewed Nehru and was struck by how handsome he was, with his signature red rose in his boutonnière. Then I hopscotched across India, stopping in Bhilal, in Rourkela to see a couple of steel mills, and Bhakra, a dam that the Americans were helping to build near the Himalayas. The Americans were giving financial help and also sending engineers who had worked on the Boulder Dam in the US.

The *Monitor* had a correspondent in Bombay named Sharokh Sabavala, who was a Tamil and a polished graduate of Oxford. Sharokh introduced me to various people, including the Parsees, the community of his own heritage. The Parsees had a custom called "sky burial." When a Parsee died, they would take the body to what they called the Towers of Silence. At the top of a hill was a big stone structure where they would cut up the body and leave it exposed for the birds, which would eat the body clean, leaving only the bones. I saw a Tower of Silence in Bombay, and I overheard stories about ladies who were having a tea party some distance away, when all of a sudden – plop – a bird dropped a human eye into their teacup.

From Bombay I went to Karachi and Peshawar, which was still part of the Northwest Frontier Province. A month later, I ended the trip in Istanbul. I love Istanbul – it has all the amenities of a modern European city, as well as the exotic byways, including the old Hippodrome, where the Romans had their chariot races, and endless nooks and crannies to get lost in. I completed my trip around the world to New York, via London.

Today, many of these cities have become quite westernized, if not entirely cosmopolitan – you can see all the American movies in Bombay that you can see in the States. But in 1955, each of these places felt very distinct from the others – and certainly distinct from the West. For a young reporter, my trip was a fascinating and eye-opening experience.

* * * * *

I came back to New York just before Christmas of 1955. I went to the Yajimas' home in Port Washington, where Hiro was staying for the holidays. She and I met again, in front of a roaring fire at the Yajimas, and that's when I decided that Hiro was the one I wanted to marry. It turned out that she also wanted to marry me.

Soon after seeing in the new year, I asked our old family friend Miye Matsukata – who by then had her own jewelry store in Boston's Copley Plaza – to design an engagement ring for us.

Hiro and I got married on September 8, 1956. I later found out – rather incredulously – that Haru and Ed Reischauer had been married on the exact same day. Even later, I discovered that a fellow journalist named Ronald Stead, who worked for the *Monitor* as a British war correspondent based in Singapore, was also married on that same day.

We were married in the Madison Avenue Presbyterian Church in midtown Manhattan. It was a large church with a small chapel next to it and a separate reception hall a few doors away. A couple of weeks before the wedding, I went to the church and met the pastor, the Rev. Victor Baer, and told him the wedding would be a simple and traditional Protestant ceremony. Hiro had her good friend Nicola Bailey as her maid of honor, and I had Kiichi Yajima as my best man. My ushers were Jack Curtis and Rod Nordell, the book editor of the *Monitor*.

Although we were the first people in our families to be married in the United States, Hiro and I didn't exactly settle down there. I soon found out that my job would prevent me from settling down anywhere for long.

Dear Otosama, February 9, 1958

It was a great surprise to receive the Asahi Evening News and to see an article by Kang Hsiao in it. Hiroko says you liked it; but frankly I must confess I do not feel at ease about any of the articles I have written about India or Ceylon. To write about a country after a visit of eight or nine days is difficult, unless one is already thoroughly acquainted with the country. I realize that a journalist does not always has the time to do a thorough job and that he must often do the best he can within a limited period of time. I tried to cover as much ground and to see as many people as I could during the period of my stay; but I realize that I still have quite far to go before I can master the business of being a journalist.

Above: Excerpt from a letter to my father-in-law (*otosama*).

Chapter 10

Hong Kong and Saigon

Gordon Walker died on May 31,1959, soon after returning to Tokyo from an expedition to the offshore islands of Quemoy and Matsu. He was in his early forties.

There's a stereotype that real gung-ho U.S. war correspondents are a hard-drinking, chain-smoking lot who do whatever they can to get a story. The description fits Gordon Walker perfectly. I suppose that somewhere in the back of his mind he still had some sense of the Christian Science in which he had been brought up, but he was not particularly devout. He loved the good life – he wined and dined and had many girlfriends. But Gordon, with his thick Boston accent, was first and foremost a journalist. He was very prolific, writing over 1,500 articles for the *Monitor* in 19 years, and he served as the *Monitor's* Chief Far Eastern correspondent. Gordon had a profound influence on my work: he taught me how to write and judge a good story.

Other journalists whom I tried to emulate were Erwin Canham and Saville Davis. Erwin was the person who hired me, and he had worked for the *Monitor* during its early traumatic days of internal dispute, seeing the paper through to a steadier course and a better reputation. His successor was Saville Davis, to whom I was also very close. Saville was deeply interested in Japan, China, and the larger politics of Asia.

Gordon Walker's death meant that I was to succeed him as the Chief East Asia Correspondent. Gordon had transferred his headquarters from Boston to Hong Kong in 1956, so the new job also meant that Hiro and I would have to move to Hong Kong.

* * * * *

Before we left, our first child was born. Megumi (meaning "grace" in Japanese – we always called her Mimi) was born in Boston on July 12, 1959. We wanted her to be born in the US, so she would be a US citizen – in fact, she became a US citizen before either Hiro or I did. At the time, we were still living on Falmouth Street, in Church housing, above a couple of ladies who were always complaining that we made too much noise. Happy to escape their complaints, we moved to Hong Kong.

On the way, we spent some time in Japan so the grandparents could see Mimi. But we didn't stay very long at all – Hiro and I wanted to bring up our children independently from our parents, and we didn't want to live in a city where either of them were. We wanted to be on our own. That's why I had chosen Hong Kong, instead of operating the East Asia bureau from Tokyo. I moved around doing stories hither and yon, but always came back to Hong Kong, as did most of my journalistic colleagues. We traveled around to the somewhat unsavory parts of Asia, but kept our families safe in Hong Kong.

We rented a rather large flat in a six-story apartment complex owned by Mr. and Mrs. Siuning Mok. Doris, the wife, had six mothers-in-law, four of whom lived on the top floor. Every morning, Doris and her husband would make the rounds, giving their daily greetings to all the mothers. Across the hall from us lived an American couple, Inger and Bob McCabe. She was a freelance photographer, and he worked for *Newsweek*, and they became our close friends.

As the East Asia correspondent, my first two years in Hong Kong were rather hectic. Everyone was trying to find out what was going on inside China, and to that degree Hong Kong served as a good listening post. Since most of the Beijing air traffic went through Hong Kong, we journalists would try to interview politicians and intellectuals en route at the airport. But for most of 1960, bigger events in the region kept me on an airplane myself.

I had tried to get back to Boston to take my US citizenship test, knowing that it would be easier for me as a US citizen to follow the major political press conferences around the world. Instead, I flew to Seoul, where Syngman Rhee was toppled by the people's revolution in April. A few days later, I barely had time to write about the CIA's U-2 spy plane that had been shot down over Russia. In June, I was back in South Korea, covering Eisenhower's trip through Seoul, and then through the Philippines. Ike's visit to Tokyo had been cancelled suddenly because of the protests over the US-Japan Security Treaty. The student protests on the streets of Tokyo – and the violent police response – succeeded in toppling Premier Nobusuke Kishi and lasted for several months. Further shocking the Japanese public was the October assassination of the Japanese Socialist leader, Inejiro Asanuma, by a knife-wielding 17 year old nationalist – live on national television. Meanwhile, in Formosa (Taiwan), Generalissimo Chiang Kai-shek was still hoping to invade the Chinese mainland, successfully arresting and imprisoning his political opponents on the island. And in November in Saigon, an abortive revolt against Ngo Dinh Diem resulted in the arrest and torture of Dr. Phan Quang Dan, who had helped me in my travels there five years before.

I spent the first few months of 1961 in Laos – the headline of my first article there read "Laos: Little War, Big Implications." For some of us, the reality that the Cold War would focus on this relatively small conflict – "lilliputian," as I called it then – was quite clear.

It was in Laos that I had a close encounter with a somewhat smaller tragedy. I was in a tiny plane at the edge of an airfield, waiting to take off, when a large Russian-made plane flew very low over us and crash-landed off the runway in a paddy field. People were jumping out of the plane and running through the paddy fields, and within minutes the plane caught fire and exploded. It was a disaster on a very human scale – I could see each person who had been on the plane, and I knew that some were still trapped inside. Unlike the firebombing of Tokyo or other events whose scale defies human comprehension, I could process this one – it was all there in front of me. I got out of my plane and tried to help however I could.

* * * * *

> ***How is Peking faring?***
>
> To understand what may be going on inside Communist China it is important to differentiate clearly between what the West knows, or thinks it knows with some degree of assurance, and what it can only infer. The West knows that from 1959 Communist China has suffered three successive years of poor harvests…
>
> – Takashi Oka for *The Christian Science Monitor*. August 15, 1962.

Over a million refugees had fled to Hong Kong by the time I wrote this article in 1962. Chairman Mao's disastrous Great Leap Forward – which forced peasants to give up their land to state-run collective farms – combined with years of drought, led to a humanitarian crisis. In April and May of that year alone, 70,000 Chinese, mostly from the south, crossed into Hong Kong. There were two main points of entry into Hong Kong from China – one was by car, the other by train – and at both of them the British border guards were just overwhelmed.

During this enormous flow of refugees, my neighbor Inger McCabe and I went out to the New Territories, which were on the mainland but part of the British crown colony of Hong Kong.

We took Inger's turquoise Volkswagen Bug and crossed by ferry over to Kowloon (meaning "Nine Dragons"), where the train to Beijing starts. Once we got beyond Kowloon to the New Territories, we could see green fields and rice paddies all the way to the border with China, where two enormous flags – the Union Jack and the five-starred Red Flag of China – flew opposite each other.

That was also where we could see dozens and dozens of Chinese children who were trying to get to Hong Kong. They were mostly from nearby villages, but some had probably traveled much further, and they were stuck there, hiding from the police. We saw a couple of boys, about 8 or 10 years old, hiding behind a clump of bushes. Inger and I picked them up and put them in the back of her car. She had a lot of things in the back seat, and the kids were small – so they were safely stashed away. We drove them, hidden in the rumble-seat, back to Inger's house in Hong Kong.

The boys' names were Puisam and Bingsam. Inger, being very good at publicity, made and distributed flyers appealing to her friends in the Hong Kong community to support her – and they did. People sent money, and she was able to put the boys in proper schools. Eventually Puisam and Bingsam were educated in the US and did quite well. Hiro and Inger and I kept in touch with them ever since.

In the fall of 1962, Hiro and I found time to take a vacation. We left Mimi with a friend in Hong Kong and traveled to Paris, London, Florence, and around Europe for three weeks. We would still retreat to Karuizawa every other year or so, in the summer. But these were frenetic years for a newsman in Southeast Asia.

```
                        124 Pokfulam Road
                        Hong Kong

                        January 8, 1962

Dear Otosama,

        When I left Tokyo in November 1960, I never expected to
spend so many months-- over a year, in fact -- away from Japan.
But although last year I spent on the average one out of every
three months away from Hong Kong, each of my trips took me
south, except for one short visit to Taiwan.

        I must confess, though, that I am grateful to be a foreign
correspondent. It is difficult for Hiroko, I know, to have me
away so often; but as for me, it is only two years since I left
the home office in Boston and I feel there is a vast amount of
experience and knowledge which I need to acquire. Working for a
small paper like the Monitor has advantages and disadvantages.
The disadvantage is that I lack the staff and budget that a
large bureau would have. The advantage is that I am completely
free to do as I want, the only limitation usually being a
budgetary one. I have had a very indulgent editor, who very
seldom tells me WHAT to do -- though if he is dissatisfied with
something I have done, he immediately informs me in no uncertain
terms.
```

Above: An excerpt from a letter to my father-in-law.

I had been flying back and forth between Hong Kong and Saigon so much that I felt as if I only saw my family at the airport. By November 1963, Hiro was pregnant with our second child and due very soon. Then, on November 2, Ngo Dinh Diem was assassinated. I raced back to Saigon, trying to cover a rapidly shifting series of historical events, and tried to wrap up enough of my work in time to get back to Hiro.

But I was a day late. Our friend Inger, who was also pregnant, drove Hiro to the hospital. Although Inger was due a month later, she looked more pregnant than Hiro, and when they walked in the nurses tried to attend to Inger instead of Hiro. Despite the confusion, our second child, Sakuya (Saya), was born in Hong Kong on November 14, 1963.

In Japanese, *saku* means "to blossom," and *ya* is like an exclamation point – "oh the flower is blooming." But *sakuya* also means "last night." Hiro had discussed the name with her mother and told her of our plans to name the baby Sakuya (after her father's mentor's daughter), but when I sent a telegram to our relatives in Japan that said "Sakuya born," they must have forgotten that discussion, thinking instead that the baby was born yesterday. They wrote back: "Boy or girl?"

We lived in a quiet and desirable part of town, away from the hustle and bustle of Hong Kong harbor, which was always full of ships, from small ferries to the US Navy. But from where we were on Pokfulam Road, right next to the Queen Mary hospital on the back side of Victoria Island, things were calm – even with all the mothers-in-law above us. The building faced west, so we always had spectacular sunsets.

At home we spoke English. I wanted the children to do this, and Hiro went along with me. If we had spent more time in Japan, I'd have made more of an effort to teach them Japanese, but we were only in Karuizawa for a few months of the year. Mimi was four years old and attending a British kindergarten. On the way to her school, we would see the Union Jack, to which she would say: "Hello, flag." After we had passed it, she'd say, "Bye bye, flag." Saya's birthday coincided with that of Prince Charles – which had a slightly more poignant meaning for us while we were living in what was then still a Crown colony.

By late 1963, the Vietnam war was just beginning, but already it seemed that there was nothing else in the news but Vietnam, day after day. I occasionally made a short trip to Cambodia, which was going through its own revolution under Pol Pot, but mostly I stayed in Vietnam.

I had a friend in Washington who worked as an adviser to President Kennedy, and he would give me updates about which particular news stories Kennedy was following. One day, he told me that the president had read one of my stories. In the article, I wrote that I had been with the South Vietnamese forces, chasing the Viet-Cong across a huge expanse of paddy fields, but we lost them before we even got halfway across. My friend said Kennedy had happened to read that – then turned to Walt Rostow and asked whether the US couldn't do something to help the government side so that the Viet Cong couldn't get away so easily. I don't think my story necessarily changed anything in US foreign policy.

On November 23, I was back in Hong Kong with Hiro, Mimi, and a three-week-old Saya. I remember getting a telephone call about 4 o'clock in the morning from Earl Foell in Boston saying that Kennedy had been assassinated.

At that moment, the bigger story – at least locally – was that Ngo Dinh Diem had been assassinated. Three weeks earlier, both he and his brother Nhu had been killed by their own generals in a military coup.

*****

In 1964, I received a two-year fellowship from the Institute for Current World Affairs to cover the war in Vietnam. The fellowship was similar to a Fulbright, which meant that I finally had the means to bring Hiro and the girls to Saigon with me. John Hughes, my friend and *Monitor* colleague, moved into our apartment in Hong Kong as we moved out. We had been assured that Saigon was still safe at the time – but on the first night we arrived there we were welcomed by a big explosion at the US military base.

We had to quickly adapt to the challenges of living in Saigon. We moved into a ground-floor apartment that had been previously owned by a general's concubine – which meant that it came with a telephone. Just as we settled in, the landlord removed the phone. We had hired a trio of servants to help with the kids – a cook, a babysitter, and a housekeeper – but within a week, we learned that the babysitter had tuberculosis, so we had to fire her. The other two quit in solidarity, but eventually we found more help. Also, we had to purify our water every day, a process that meant boiling and filtering the water in a stone pot.

While we were in Saigon, Saya had her first birthday and learned to walk. Mimi went to a French kindergarten nearby – I remember her singing songs in French. Many journalists and diplomats sent their children to French schools because it was such a consistent system – from Bangkok to Seoul or Saigon, you could find a school in the same French system, so your child wouldn't lose any time in transfers.

The fellowship required me to write an informal but publishable letter to the organization once a month about what was going on in Vietnam – uprisings, coups, the life of the people. These letters were then edited into a series of in-depth analyses. But the fellowship also allowed me to continue reporting for the *Monitor*.

While in Hong Kong, I didn't have much of a staff – two professional translators and a couple of assistants who were Chinese college students – and in Saigon I had even less. Still, I could manage because I spoke French and was moderately fluent in Vietnamese. The pace of the reporting was also manageable – the stories didn't have to be up-to-the-minute, the way they are today. Instead, the pace was more like writing for a magazine.

My friend Bui Diem introduced us to Saigon, taking us to his favorite pho restaurants and showing us the more romantic parts of the city. He was a great mathematician but also a political scholar, and he later became the South Vietnamese ambassador to the US under Thieu.

* * * * *

The biggest problem in Vietnam for the US was that, if there was any single person who could be the national leader of Vietnam, it was Ho Chi Minh. "Uncle Ho," as he was universally known, was popular not only with the Communists but also with the general populace, because he was anti-French – and, later, anti-American – and therefore a respectable nationalist. Bao Dai may have been the Emperor, but he could never play that nationalist role. Other countries in Asia had a communist presence that was kept in check by a strong nationalist leader, such as Nehru in India, or Sukarno, the unquestioned leader of Indonesia. Ho Chi Minh embodied both causes at once. The Americans, out of desperation to find anybody who could compete with the Viet Minh, came up with Ngo Dinh Diem and quickly turned on their public relations machine.

However, Diem was a prickly character. He knew that it would damage his standing to be tied to the coat strings of the Americans, so he quickly dissociated himself from them, trying to make himself seen as a nationalist leader. Diem was a traditional, judicious, Mandarin-type bureaucrat who spoke in platitudes, while his brother, Ngo Dinh Nhu, was his chief advisor and a more active, scholarly type. But Nhu's wife, the famous Madame Nhu, was a real *dame fatale*. In many ways she was corrupt, and she tried to play the nationalist card and put herself and Diem forward as competitors to Ho Chi Minh, who by then was quite elderly. But Diem lacked the persona to challenge the Communists. The Viet Cong may have massacred people and committed other terrible acts, yet they had seized the flag of nationalism before anyone else could do so.

Tri Quang, a Buddhist monk, helped precipitate the crisis of 1963, by leading a protest movement against Diem and his brother Nhu. Tri Quang took refuge in the American embassy, and was granted asylum by Henry Cabot Lodge, who was then U.S. ambassador. The embassy was deeply embarrassed by these events – but what could it do? If it turned Tri Quang out, the embassy would be forever identified with the dictatorship.

Meanwhile, other Buddhist monks were staging very public protests in Saigon and in their stronghold, the temples of Central Vietnam, by setting themselves afire. A monk would sit down in one of the most prominent crossroads in Saigon, pour gasoline over himself, and light it. He would remain praying for a long time, sitting upright in the lotus position, until eventually his body toppled over. Madame Nhu sarcastically – and very publicly – called these fiery suicides a "barbecue," and added "Let them burn, and we shall clap our hands."

Madame Nhu often invited journalists to interview her at one of the floating restaurants moored in the Saigon River, where it meets the Rue Catinat. I remember one time a fellow journalist and I were competing to secure an interview with her. When you're a journalist in a competitive situation, you do all kinds of things to get someone to remember your name, so he sent her a dozen red roses for her birthday. Madame Nhu did, in fact, remember his name. Eventually, I did my own interview with this colorful, arrogant lady. She was friendly enough. Saigon was so dependent on American financial support that its leaders had to be very careful with the international press.

Of course, Madame Nhu was never the type of first lady who would bring the country together. From the beginning, she was controversial and *sui generis*. A devoutly Catholic woman in a position of great power, she had passed morality laws under Diem's rule, for which she was widely mocked as a hypocrite. I don't want to defend her actions, but, in the whole murky business of Vietnam at that time, there were many hypocrites. Vietnam is a Confucian society, so a lot of people criticized her because she was a woman in a prominent role in politics. Still, between the self-immolating monks and Madame Nhu's response, the situation seemed almost medieval.

The self-immolation of the Buddhist monks was a big crisis that Kennedy faced in Vietnam. I think the Cuban missile crisis was also very much on the minds of the American officials. Whatever their rationale, the decision to support the generals and the monks against Diem played directly into the hands of Ho Chi Minh. In the coup of 1963, General Duong Van Minh, then head of the army, ordered the arrest of Diem and his brother.

The two were put in a military vehicle that was supposedly going to take them to prison, but when the vehicle arrived, both brothers were dead.

Dual Task for Regime: The War and Democracy

South Vietnam faces a new and uncertain dawn.

Hope is the keynote in the wake of the dramatic armed-forces coup that ended the oppressive nine-year rule of President Ngo Dinh Diem.

As for the United States, it has disclaimed all responsibility for the coup. There is a general feeling Washington may have to walk circumspectly in Saigon. Up to the last minute there seems to have been a serious disagreement between military and civilian Americans over the support to be accorded to the now-fallen Ngo regime.

It is felt the United States could make no greater mistake than to place overemphasis on stability in a situation where long-pent-up national emotions are bound to come to the surface."

— Takashi Oka for *The Christian Science Monitor,* November 4, 1963. Saigon.

The Vietnamese army didn't want to take responsibility, although clearly somebody inside the army had killed them. At the time we journalists assumed that General Duong Van Minh had given the order, since he was in charge of the military. I interviewed General Minh a few days after Diem's death. He was a big guy and quite popular, but very cryptic.

> "Don't call me excellency," the big, broad-faced soldier said with a smile. "I'm a general, and I stay a general."
>
> We were meeting the chairman of South Vietnam's military revolutionary council in a comfortable, arm-chaired corner of his enormous office on the second floor of the Joint General Staff Building near Tan Son Nhut Airport.
>
> Since the chairman, Maj. Gen. Duong Van Minh, fulfills the functions of chief of state, a journalist colleague had just addressed him as "your excellency" only to get a riposte typical of the general's informality.
>
> Tall and big boned, General Minh talks with an air of grandfatherly benevolence, though he is an all-round athlete still in his 40's. He listens intently to questions as they are put, then answers thoughtfully or with humor, as the occasion demands. He can also be cryptic, as when I asked about the composition of the revolutionary military council.
>
> "We have the maximum," he said in reply to a question about how many generals were on it.
>
> Relations with the United States are

excellent, General Minh said. "We share the same purpose — to beat the Communists."

— Takashi Oka for *The Christian Science Monitor*, November 13, 1963. Saigon.

Diem's assassination was followed by a series of coups led by a succession of generals. The American government, thinking that Vietnam needed a strong military regime, supposedly supported the coups – or at least the first one. But the country had just seen nine years of repressive rule under Diem, so what followed was a period of instability.

I knew two men in the CIA while I was in Saigon. We journalists would get whatever information we could from them, and just as often they gleaned what they could from us, in a seemingly endless effort to sort out rumors from facts. For instance, we learned how the CIA were supplying local tribesmen in the jungle with bows and arrows to fight the Viet Cong. At one point I even accompanied a CIA friend to the South Vietnamese military headquarters in Saigon, where he was meeting the newly empowered generals. Being a Japanese journalist (with an American passport) who spoke English, French, and a bit of Vietnamese, I was considered a neutral-enough party to witness their proceedings. Of course, I was trying to get a scoop – I wanted the Americans to say that they were, in fact, supporting the generals – which the US had never officially said. The official line was that the South Vietnamese generals had moved against Diem, while the Americans had no involvement whatsoever. No one really believed this story, and I knew that the generals would not have acted unless they had been absolutely certain of American support before, during, and after their coup. So I tried to get the Americans to say so, on the record – but, again, they remained annoyingly vague in their comments.

After Diem's assassination, Ho Chi Minh reportedly stated: "I can scarcely believe the Americans would be so stupid." The North Vietnamese Politburo added: "The coup d'état on 1 November 1963 will not be the last." That was true. In less than three months, Minh was overthrown by General Nguyen Khanh in a second coup. Khanh lasted maybe about nine months. Anybody who promised to bring stability had the support of the Americans, but the Americans couldn't be sure whether anyone could actually do that. So there was coup after coup.

* * * * *

In 1964, President Johnson escalated the war by sending a large force of Americans into South Vietnam. But the instigating factor was a very confusing – if not outright suspicious – naval clash between the Vietnamese and the Americans in the Gulf of Tonkin.

> The USS Maddox's spirited defense Sunday against attacking North Vietnamese torpedo boats dramatizes the United States Seventh Fleet's role in the Indochina fighting. But North Vietnam's purpose and motivation remain obscure.
>
> The Maddox, a 2,200-ton destroyer, was apparently authorized to take decisive action against an unprovoked attack in international waters but not to pursue the attackers when they were disabled and started withdrawing.
>
> Pacific Fleet headquarters in Honolulu announced that two of the three torpedo boats were damaged and fled at reduced speed, while one was so heavily damaged

that it apparently could not move.

In New York, Secretary of State Dean Rusk told reporters, "the other side got a sting out of this. If they do it again they'll get another sting."

But in a speech on the same day he rejected the idea of massive military retaliation as a means of obtaining free-world goals. "Military orgy is not the rational path to a decent world order of free men," he said.

What is not clear as this dispatch is being written is whether the Sunday naval action presages new aggressive Communist policy of attack against American ships and other installations.

Observers here believe that, despite Peking and Hanoi's belligerent tone, this is unlikely, because neither country is strong in the two areas where the United States can bring overwhelming power to bear — the sea and the air.

— Takashi Oka for *The Christian Science Monitor*, August 4, 1964. Hong Kong.

Hanoi Offers Its Version

While Peking's response to the Vietnam crisis is awaited throughout Asia, North Vietnam is projecting its own version of the events.

North Vietnam has admitted Sunday's attack by its patrol boats on a United States warship but has denounced the report of a second attack Tuesday as "sheer fabrication."

Hanoi asserted that the American warship had intruded into North Vietnamese territorial waters to intimidate North Vietnamese fisherman.

"Our patrol ships took action to defend our territorial waters and fishermen," the statement said, "and chased the enemy ships out of our waters. This is what happened on the afternoon of Aug. 2."

In regard to the Tuesday attack, which provoked President Johnson's ordering of retaliatory action, the official North Vietnamese news service issued a brief "authorized statement" Wednesday denouncing the report of the attack as "sheer fabrication by United States imperialists aimed at further aggravating the situation in Southeast Asia."

— Takashi Oka for *The Christian Science Monitor*, August 6, 1964. Hong Kong.

U.S. Heartens Asian Allies

Washington's immediate firm response to North Vietnamese provocations in the Gulf of Tonkin has heartened American allies in Southeast Asia.
To South Vietnam, bombing of North

Vietnamese naval installations by American planes Wednesday came as a much needed morale booster.

The bombing, in President Johnson's words, represented "limited" action and will not necessarily be repeated.

The key word in Mr. Johnson's vocabulary was "limited." A not often noticed but prominent word in the Communist vocabulary is "protracted."

— Takashi Oka for *The Christian Science Monitor*, August 7, 1964. Hong Kong.

Peking, Hanoi: Next Step?

The United States is still far from achieving in Southeast Asia the same explicit understanding it has secured from the Soviet Union in Europe regarding what would or would not be considered as cause for war.

The Gulf of Tonkin was an important first step in defining this hitherto hazy area.

— Takashi Oka for *The Christian Science Monitor*, August 10, 1964. Hong Kong.

After Tonkin: Hanoi-Peking Moves Studied For Clues to Southeast Asia Stance

The turquoise-colored waters of the Gulf of Tonkin appear to have regained their calm, at least for the moment. But in the

> wake of the recent brink-of-war incidents, Western analysts here are still asking why.
>
> Why did North Vietnamese torpedo boats twice attack United States warships?
>
> — Takashi Oka for *The Christian Science Monitor*, August 18, 1964. Hong Kong.

On August 4, hours after the alleged second attack on the US Navy, President Johnson made a televised address to the American public, asking approval of the Tonkin Resolution, which allowed him "to take all necessary means" in retaliating. This was also only three months before the presidential elections. But the main concern at that time - and of most American voters - was that Johnson had *committed* the United States to military action in Vietnam, and that he had done so in a way that presidents had not done before. This was almost a declaration of war. In fact the Gulf of Tonkin Resolution, enacted only six days later, was passed by Congress, but without a formal declaration of war. "We still seek no wider war," Johnson said in his televised address. As to whether I or other correspondents believed that, it's hard for me to say - because we now know the aftermath. But in the moment, we certainly felt that this was unusual - it was something no American president had done since WWII.

Years later, an investigation by the Senate Foreign Relations Committee showed that the August 4 attack had not, in fact, happened.

*****

By 1965, Saigon was too risky a place for American civilians. One time we had organized a party for the new prime minister - I forget now exactly which one - but that very day there was another coup, and none of our guests could come. We had to distribute the party food to friends and neighbors.

I remember having Thanksgiving dinner at the US embassy with General Maxwell Taylor and a table full of US marines. I had known General Taylor and his wife Lydia in Tokyo. His wife was a Christian Scientist and had been my Sunday school teacher for a brief while, and I knew her sons John and Tommy. At the dinner, General Taylor, who was fluent in Japanese, introduced me as his wife's Sunday school pupil, which was a bit embarrassing for me. The rest of the military guests were as stiff as we were in the presence of this famous general.

Ultimately, the city became completely unsafe for us. We were still living there when the Viet Cong began throwing bombs down the aisles of movie theaters in town. So I got my family out of Vietnam, and most journalists did the same. We went to Japan for a while and then came back to Hong Kong, which I made my family base once more. Hiro was not at all enthusiastic about being back in Hong Kong – she had never really liked it. She found it a boring place to be, but it was also safe and, again, away from her family. So Hiro and the girls stayed there, and I would commute to Saigon every six weeks or so. I would gather my stories in Vietnam, and then I would write them after I got back to Hong Kong or Tokyo. At the time, I was writing rather long once-a-month reports, so I would usually stay about ten days to write my stories, then go back to Saigon.

It was not so easy to find accommodations in Saigon at that time, because there were so many reporters coming through town. I moved into a fourth-floor apartment at 39 Le Loi, where the *Monitor* housed a succession of journalists. The apartment consisted of a large single room above a garage, with a kitchen in one corner and a bath right next to it.

In those days, every journalist was trying to get into North Vietnam, and had great difficulty doing so. There was a so-called Neutral Nations Commission made up of the Poles, the French, and the Indians. Commission members could travel between

Hanoi and Saigon, so whenever one of them returned from Hanoi, we would try to get stories out of him.

A Casual Visit With the Viet Cong

The pale young man in black peasant garb and Ho Chi Minh rubber sandals talked in earnest, quiet tones. Nine others, also in black, crowded into the palm-leaf hut, listened intently.

A kerosene lamp lighted up their tanned faces, the rough-hewn table at which the leader sat, the split bamboo beds, the tamped-earth floor.

"We will fight to the last drop to chase out the Americans and to reunify our country," he said. "As long as the Americans are here, reunification is impossible."

Over in the corner sat an older man, in open-necked city shirt and trousers. He was a traveler from Saigon, stranded by nightfall in this hamlet deep in the forests. The next morning he would catch a city-bound bus at the crack of dawn. But in the meantime, he was a silent spectator at a Viet Cong propaganda session.

The traveler is a good friend of mine. I have known him a long time, and have absolute confidence in his reliability and courage. With his permission, I am retelling his story in words as close to the original as possible.

> My friend had not reached this particular hamlet by chance. He had waited for some time to see how the Viet Cong live, and whether their motivation and discipline was still as good as some people said.
>
> He came away convinced that, at least in this one hamlet some 60 miles from Saigon, the Viet Cong has established a presence the effectiveness of which does not depend solely on armed force.
>
> — Takashi Oka for *The Christian Science Monitor*, March 2, 1966.

I couldn't interview the Communists myself or I'd probably be taken prisoner. My source was a Vietnamese named Tran Huu Loc, who spoke French and was very well connected to the locals and to the Catholic cathedral. He was a retired district chief, a bureaucrat who went into journalism, and we took a couple of trips together. He was an observant Catholic, and to some extent sympathetic to the Vietnamese Communists.

Later, Tran worked for Elizabeth Pond, my successor at the *Monitor*'s bureau in Saigon. When Vietnam collapsed and the Communists marched in, Tran fled through the Mekong Delta, and managed to get on a boat which was headed out to sea. There, he was picked up by the Americans, who had sent out warships to rescue refugees. Tran was brought to the Philippines, and then eventually to the US, where he and his family ended up, after several trying months.

Tran was neither for the Communists nor for the generals. He obviously had sympathy for the Viet Cong, but he was disillusioned by the brutality of the Communists, not just towards enemies, but towards the so-called neutralists, who were by inclination pro-Communist. The Communists wanted total allegiance, otherwise they considered you an enemy. I had another good friend, Tran van Tuyen, who was also a neutralist. He was taken captive by the Viet Cong and eventually died in prison. And in 1970, Elizabeth Pond was also captured, in Cambodia. She was released after a month in prison.

For me, the war was a troubling experience, where I ended up witnessing a lot more fighting than I had as a soldier in the Japanese army. A military contact would call me at 4:30 in the morning and ask if I wanted to go out with a particular military unit that was going to strike the Communists somewhere. I wanted to understand what was going on, so along with the other reporters, I would go out and cover the strike. Sometimes, however, we would venture out and there wouldn't be a strike, and we would end up waiting around all day.

Once you got out of Saigon into the Mekong Delta, the land was flat and filled with village after village. The Communists had infiltrated many of them – the Viet Cong ruled the country at night, and the South Vietnamese generals ruled during the day. We would accompany the military into a village, and there'd be a fight, and inevitably people would be killed. But the fighting was on a more or less intimate scale. We'd see eight to ten bodies, all in black pajamas, laid out for the army brass to inspect.

A friend of mine, Johnny Ellsworth, would say, "Well, it's the only place where you can have napalm for breakfast." You could smell the napalm and taste it. It's basically gasoline, and it seemed to have spilled onto everything, including our feet. We were in such close proximity to the fighting because that's just the way the war in Vietnam was. We would board a helicopter in Saigon, and twenty minutes later we were in the thick of the action. It was surreal and sometimes sickening to travel from humdrum city life to witnessing war and sudden death.

Usually we traveled with three or four helicopters, hovering above the jungle. Then we would come to the place where actual fighting was going on, and the army would clear a place for the helicopters to land. As soon as we went down, we had to rush for the first hole we could find, otherwise we would be in an exposed place in the middle of the jungle.

When we did come under fire, it was not like the western front in Europe, where there were masses of artillery and soldiers banging away at enemy lines. That kind of thing didn't happen. A lot of it was really almost like taking potshots. The Viet Cong were guerrillas who were good at running and hiding – then they'd take a hit at you. Sometimes they had already gone, but sometimes they were still around – it was almost impossible to foretell what we might be getting into. Once in a while there was a really nasty eruption of gunfire, but mostly it was just a series of guerrilla skirmishes. We spent a lot of time walking single-file down jungle trails to where we heard the Viet Cong might be. Usually by the time that we had heard about their appearance, they were gone.

The jungle was beautiful – lush green, nicely covered. The sun was searing, so we wanted to be under the cover of the trees. Sometimes a snake lay lazily on a nearby branch, but usually the wildlife was fleeing – we'd see a rabbit hopping away, or a frog. Once I saw a hawk circling overhead, and then it came whooshing down and picked up a rabbit in its claws and took off.

What we were most afraid of were the booby traps along the side of the road. When we walked with the soldiers, we were told to avoid the sides of roads, because that's where the Viet Cong would plant a bomb or a cluster of poisoned bamboo spears, which they would cover loosely with dirt. We were cautious, but sometimes caution wasn't enough.

I remember one early episode in Saigon, when several journalists had just come from the Congo. They were saying, "Oh, this is nothing compared to where we just were." It's puzzling how journalists are always comparing conflicts.

One of the most vivid images was one I didn't see myself.

A friend of mine had just returned from a day out with the army, and he was telling me how they had brought these bodies back in a helicopter. He said they were just throwing them out from the helicopter, and people on the ground were catching them. He said he hardly had a sense that they were real people, who had really died. They were just bodies.

* * * * *

The war went on until 1975, but I was in South Vietnam only through the late summer of 1966. I continued to report on Vietnam through 1968 and the big Tet offensive. By then, the war was all-consuming.

During the Vietnam years, I was traveling around all the time, and I must say it was hard on Hiro. She liked neither Saigon nor Hong Kong – and although she liked Japan, she didn't want to be with her parents. The best thing for Hiro and me and our kids would have been to be together, in the same place at the same time. But we couldn't do it. There was a community of people in somewhat similar situations – other journalists, diplomats, military advisers, mostly Americans, but also French, Russians, and Japanese, who brought their families with them.

One day when we were still in Hong Kong, I heard people talking outside our apartment door. They were women from the American Embassy. Suddenly one of them burst out crying. She had been told that her husband was dead. He was Jerry Rose, my very good friend and our next door neighbor. Jerry had been killed in an airplane crash in Vietnam. Hiro and I tried to take care of his widow, who had a daughter and a son. When Jerry was killed he was working for the anti-Communist Vietnamese government. Jerry's death was a big shock. A number of friends of mine were killed, but Jerry's death hit very close to home – quite literally, they lived next door. They and Hiro and I were close friends.

After some time, we went to Tokyo, and I spent one summer there writing Vietnam stories from material I had already accumulated. We returned to Karuizawa, where Hiro liked the cool weather, and where we all felt at home.

Then I got word that I had a new post – Moscow. I was still trying to finish a backlog of stories on Vietnam, and for the next six months I was writing on both Moscow and Vietnam. We moved to the Soviet Union in the early fall of 1966.

Within seven years – from 1959 to 1966 – our family lived in five different cities in five different countries: Boston, Hong Kong, Saigon, Tokyo, and Moscow. In his memoir *Paper Boy to Pulitzer*, my friend and future editor John Hughes described the nature of the job: "Correspondents would usually spend three years on assignment, and then come home." But, in my case, the Vietnam war changed that kind of regularity. I had mixed feelings – I wanted to cover the war, but I also wanted to be with my family. Hiro, meanwhile, didn't know what might happen to me from day to day, which was a tough situation. Also, I had misgivings about living and working behind the Iron Curtain.

But, in the end, Moscow proved to be a good assignment.

Chapter 11

Moscow

Compared with the previous few years in Saigon, Moscow was quiet. The days of the colorful Nikita Krushchev had been replaced by a series of bureaucrats – Nikolai Podgorny was in office when I arrived – and the local news was relatively sedate. There was a small media spectacle when George Romney, the silver-haired governor of Michigan, showed up for Christmas. Romney was running for President back in the US, and he made the customary foreign-relations pilgrimage to Moscow. I remember the Russians all thought he was crazy for walking around in the December air without a hat.

Vietnam still dominated the news. That summer, I had begun writing freelance articles for *The New York Times*, publishing my first piece in the *New York Times Magazine* on July 31, 1966. It was called "The Other Regime in South Vietnam," about the Vietcong's shadowy and pervasive grip on the country. Freelancers preferred to write for the *Magazine* because the Sunday articles were longer than the regular newspaper stories, and they also paid better. So the *New York Times* became quite a source of income for me, and it opened up the possibility that I might write for them more in the future.

The other big headline in 1966 was the revolution in China. Still reeling from the previous seven years, the Chinese turned their society totally upside down during the Cultural Revolution. Everything old was bad – the young people were creating a new society. The so-called Red Guards were really just kids, but they suddenly were given power over their elders – humiliating their teachers, going freely into people's homes and taking their things. The party line was that it was not good to have things. So they destroyed private property, burned books, tortured and murdered innocent people, and did pretty much as they pleased.

Not so long ago, I met some older Chinese who were in their teens or twenties then, and they still had a nostalgia for those days. It was an extraordinary period: they could travel anywhere they wanted to by train – even as far as Tibet – without having to pay a thing, and everywhere they went they would meet fellow young people who were infested with the same revolutionary zeal. Because no one from outside China could come in, the young people didn't know much about the rest of the world, so they had nothing to which they could compare themselves.

Russia's reaction to the revolution in China was quite critical:

Moscow Slaps Peking "Revolution"

Mao Tse-tung's "great cultural revolution" is actually anti-Communist and anti-proletarian. And it is certainly not cultural. Such are the inferences Pravda offered its readers.

"The writings of Aeschylus and Shakespeare, Goethe and Balzac, Pushkin and Tolstoy, canvasses by Raphael and Rembrandt, Delacroix and Repin, music by Beethoven and Tchaikovsky, Mozart and Verdi, productions of many geniuses of art and literature have always been and will always be a source of aesthetic pleasure and will always help cultivate the best humanistic qualities in man... The more backward a country is technically, economically, and culturally, the more it needs to draw from the best achievements of other peoples to overcome its backwardsness." The target is obvious.

Reuters reports that [the Pravda] article compared Peking's cultural revolution with actions by that arch villain of Soviet ideology, Trotsky.

— Takashi Oka for *The Christian Science Monitor*, Sept 19, 1966. Moscow.

By November of 1966, the Soviet leaders – speaking through their mouthpiece at *Pravda* – called directly for Mao's overthrow.

* * * * *

We lived at 12/24 Sadovo-Samotechnaya Street, in an apartment complex reserved for foreign correspondents. Members of the foreign community lived in isolation from Russians, and we journalists were also separated from the American diplomats. Everyone – whether Russian or foreigner – was restricted, and each of us was pigeonholed according to occupation and nationality. The Russian surveillance system had a special department called the Administration for Servicing the Diplomatic Corps, which we knew by its Russian initials U.P.D.K., that took care of foreign correspondents. There was nothing much that we could do outside that system. Had we tried, the Russians would surely have expelled us.

Our building had been built by German prisoners of war and was solidly constructed – the walls were so thick that we couldn't hear anyone next door – but it was also infested with mice and cockroaches, which the UPDK denied. There was a courtyard, and our apartment was the first one on the left. Above us lived Henry Kamm, who wrote for *The New York Times*. Henry went on to win the George Polk award in 1969, and a Pulitzer in 1978. His children went to the French school, and his son Tom was close to Mimi's age. Other neighbors included a Japanese family named Nakao, who had a house near us in Karuizawa. Their daughter Mamiko was older than Mimi, but the two of them would wait at the bus stop together. There was also a German diplomat's wife who made portraits of Mimi and Saya.

Saya was 3 then, and she went to the local *detsky sad*, or nursery school. Mimi was 7, and attended the Anglo-American School, which gave courses in English only to a class of kids from America, England, and Africa. But Mimi also took some Russian classes to learn the language. Mimi and Saya were young, so Hiro was quite busy with them. They had a nanny named Sarah Coles who was on her gap year from Cambridge University. Sarah was a Russian major and lived with us at Sadovo-Samotechnaya for that year.

We were friends with the Govrins, who served as Israeli diplomats – until they had to leave the next year when Egypt declared war on Israel. At that time, Russia had a big Jewish population, some three million strong, but the Soviets supported the Arabs in the Six Day War. Although the politics were complicated, the actual fighting on the Sinai Peninsula was a walk in the park for the Israeli military. Diplomatic relations in Moscow were cut off, the Israeli embassy was evacuated, and our friends had to leave.

Bob Daglish and his wife Ina were our good friends throughout our time in Moscow. She was Russian and worked as a translator, and Bob was a British poet, translator, and intellectual. When they were first married, Bob was working as a British diplomat, but he had to leave the embassy because of American suspicions about the international spy network. Kim Philby, the infamous double-agent of British intelligence, had fled to Moscow in 1963, just three years before I got there, and he was living in a kind of exile in the city, because the KGB didn't trust him either. Sometimes our friends would excitedly tell us that they had spotted Philby on the street corner.

There were Russian kids who used to hang over our wall and trade with all the foreigners. Hiro would get stamps and coins from them, and she would give them bubble gum and other Western items that they weren't technically allowed to have.

In Moscow, everything could be bought. Sometimes the currency was actual money, sometimes it was influence, and the black market was very active. If, for instance, a foreign journalist wanted to buy a car, he would have to order it from the UPDK – a process that could take a very long time and usually involved bribes. Instead, you could buy or sell a car on the black market, as long as you had access to US dollars. The Russian workhorse car of that era was called the Volga (after the river) – a sturdy but unimaginative vehicle – and some of my fellow journalists managed to get one through the less official route.

In order to travel within the Soviet Union, we also had to submit a plan to the UPDK and await its approval. It always took a while, but eventually would come through. Because there was not much in the way of breaking news that we journalists could latch onto, I traveled quite a bit as a tourist and brought the family along.

I went to Tashkent, the capital of Uzbekistan, which was the gateway to Bokhara, Samarkand and Khiva. Over the years, Russia had exiled various populations to remote parts of the country – it had shipped its German population off to Vladivostock, and it had sent the Koreans who had been living in Vladivostock off to Central Asia. So there was still a thriving Korean culture around Tashkent. But it was also an area prone to disease and disaster – a large earthquake struck just a few months before I arrived, and when Hiro visited on a later trip, she had to delay her departure because of a cholera epidemic.

Several times we took vacations outside the Soviet Union,

to Finland or London or Paris, and many of the other foreign correspondents did the same. We visited Hungary, Poland, and Austria, and once we took a train from Moscow to Bucharest, where we changed to the Orient Express and continued on to Paris.

* * * * *

A Russian journalist friend of mine said, "All you have to do is read *Pravda* or *Izvestia,* and you'll know everything that's going on – or at least what the authorities want you to know about what's going on." The situation changed somewhat when famous dissidents started writing letters to the press.

By the late 1960s, after Aleksandr Solzhenitsyn had been repeatedly repressed by the authorities, other not so well-known dissidents started writing articles debunking the regime. Andrei Sakharov was a nuclear physicist who wrote a long indictment of the Soviet system. In 1968, his essay "Reflections on Progress, Peaceful Coexistence, and Intellectual Freedom" was published by the underground presses, and he was looking to have it published outside of Russia. A Dutch correspondent of *Het Parool* named Karel van het Reve had obtained Sakharov's original manuscript and was trying to help.

Karel and I, being foreign correspondents in the same closely observed city, knew each other. So he wrote to me and asked if I could get Sakharov's essay out to the American newspapers. He was going to translate it into Dutch and run it in *Het Parool,* but he knew that doing so would not reach the wider audience that the work deserved. So I suggested the *New York Times,* whose Moscow correspondent was my upstairs neighbor, Henry Kamm.

I recommended the *New York Times* – over my own newspaper – because I knew the impact would be greater than if the story had run in the *Monitor.* The *Monitor* didn't have the circulation that the *Times* had. I was also afraid that the *Monitor* might not publish it at all. My reasoning might have been faulty – in the sense that I could have helped my own career had I run the story myself – but I felt it was the right thing to do.

The *Times*, of course, was very pleased to have this exclusive story. Although I was a mechanism through which Sakharov's essay became public, the real hero was Karel van het Reve. He and his wife became the channels for the dissidents. He told me how, for a long number of years, the telephone at home in their apartment was never left unattended – either he or his wife were at home 24 hours a day. They knew the dissidents might not have more than a moment to make a call, usually from a public phone, and when the call did come through, it would require immediate attention.

That Karel managed to get the whole thing out was an early major breakthrough for the dissidents' cause. It told the rest of the world a previously unknown story of what was going on in the Soviet Union, and all the foreign correspondents benefited from this breakthrough. Sakharov went on to win the Nobel Peace Prize in 1975. I was proud to have helped him along the way.

I kept in touch with Karel after he left Moscow and returned to Holland. When we met again in Amsterdam, Karel was working for the Alexander Herzen Foundation, which helped even more dissident writers find an outlet in the Western press. At that time, Karel and his staff were all working for free – they didn't get a salary, or even expenses – but they were completely dedicated to the mission.

Funnel for Soviet Dissent

In an immaculate white stone house overlooking historic Amstel Canal sits a shirt-sleeved professor whom Soviet propaganda has labeled "one of the most energetic agents of the CIA."

The appellation amuses Dr. Karel Van Het Reve, a tall, well-built man with a sly sense of humor and hands that seem more at home painting or scraping the sides of a boat than leafing through the pages of scholarly books on his specialty — modern Russian literature.

"In 20 years' time, I think Russia will be as free a country as Spain is today," the professor said. "The first Soviet edition of 'Doctor Zhivago' should be coming out in 1985 — no, perhaps 1990."

— Takashi Oka for *The Christian Science Monitor*, April 4, 1972. Amsterdam.

Maxim Litvinov, the Bolshevik revolutionary and Soviet diplomat of the 1940s, had a daughter named Tanya who also became a channel for the dissidents. She helped get their manuscripts out to the West, and her son Pavel assisted her. Peredelkino, where many intellectuals had their dachas, was a safer place to meet than in the city. Most of the writers lived in Moscow, but you could never really meet people in secret in the city.

Red purge: Soviets pursue attack on dissidents in the arts

The campaign against dissidents in Soviet literature and art continues. Wednesday, both Literary Gazette and Red Star, organ of the Soviet armed forces, energetically

> promoted this campaign.
> Red Star accused "bourgeois ideologists" of trying to drive a wedge between the Communist Party and the intelligentsia in the Soviet Union. It quoted Nobel-winner Mikhail Sholokhov as saying that he worked according to his heart, but that his heart belonged to the party. "In those words lies the answer to ill-wishers of our motherland, who negate freedom or creative art work under socialism."
>
> — Takashi Oka for *The Christian Science Monitor*, April 26, 1968. Moscow.

Statements like this by *Red Star* and Brezhnev were the obvious part of the Soviet propaganda machine, whose control was hard to overestimate. At other times, these same journals voiced relatively liberal opinions, mentioning dissidents in a not unflattering tone. But this, too, I discovered was part of the more subtle operations of the Soviet press.

One of these more liberal voices belonged to a *Pravda* writer who had gone missing. I had regularly read his articles, and then at some point I realized that I hadn't seen any of his work in print for a while. Several months went by, and I asked others about him – everyone assured me that he was, in fact, still around. Then, one day, I saw his new article in *Pravda*. I met up with him later, and he told me that he had been in Moscow the whole time, collecting his salary from *Pravda*, which was paying him to keep quiet.

Inside the *Pravda* camp were writers who just repeated the official line, and others who were interested in Western ideas and not simply in echoing what they were told. Every trend was there – liberal, conservative, and in between. Depending on the prevailing atmosphere of the party, certain people who might have been considered dangerously liberal were allowed to be a bit more outspoken – or, if they had been entirely silent, at least given a chance to speak. When the official party line changed again, the more liberal people were shut up. *Pravda* was a large organization that could afford to keep its liberal writers on retainer. These liberals were, after all, a small number of people, surrounded by official flunkies and parrots. They were allowed to do safe things, such as translations, to keep their salaries. Then *Pravda* would trot them out when a particular line seemed to be in the public gaze. That was how the Soviet press worked.

```
Dear Otosama,                          December 21, 1967
     Meanwhile our life in Moscow unfolds peacefully and, in
a certain sense, we are enjoying the experience. Of course we
long for Japanese or Chinese food, we long to be able to go
out to a movie or even to a restaurant without having to make all
sorts of advance arrangements, we long to have normal everyday
contacts with congenial Russians-- university professors, writers,
office workers.  But we are much more at home than we were last
year, and Hiro is getting quite expert at shopping in the market
or in Russian stores for unusual items. The other day I happened
to stop in a paper store to buy some notebooks. I noticed a long
line of people and wondered what they were waiting for. It was
toilet paper -- very rough in quality, and manufactured in
Lithuania, one of the Baltic states. Apparently it is only
available from time to time.  Hiro is beginning to buy more food
in Russian stores-- she has a Russian friend who helps her -- and
thus she has brought more variety into our meals. The other day
she proudly came home with some canned mushrooms(the Russians
have delicious mushrooms-- huge and juicy). She found some people
lining up in a store, found they were buying mushrooms, and joined
the line. Pretty soon other Russians came up and asked her, "What
is the line for?" and she told them, "Mushrooms." The peddlers
in the market all know her and call her "Sestra, sestra," meaning,
"Sister." She can even get them to reduce their prices for her.
```

Above: Excerpt from a letter to my father-in-law.

Despite all the restrictions, Moscow still had a lot to offer. From our apartment complex, it was a twenty-minute walk to the Bolshoi ballet, and a shorter walk to the famous puppet theater down the street. We went to the symphony at the Tchaikovsky concert hall, and saw performances of the Moscow Art Theater.

Shostakovich turned sixty in 1966. I was there for the city-wide celebrations, and I got to meet him – we shook hands. As a famous composer, he was not a person you might think of as a dissident, but he and Stravinsky and Prokofiev all fell in and out of favor with the authorities. The Russian authorities were didactic and wanted a bombastic music that glorified the Russian motherland and so forth. But these composers were in the musical avant garde of their respective times, and not interested in delivering what the party wanted. However, I must say I was not really much of an adventurous music-lover.

Prokofiev and his wife Lina were Christian Scientists. We had mutual friends in London, and I met her in Prague. An American of Spanish descent, she was a singer whose real name was Carolina Codina, but she used her stage name, Lina Hubera. The Prokofievs had been in Russia during a difficult period. Lina was arrested in 1948 on false charges of espionage and sentenced to twenty years of hard labor in a prison camp in the Arctic Circle, along with other Russian intellectuals. Prokofiev died in 1953, so by the time I met Lina in Prague she was a widow.

I was in Prague in the spring and summer of 1968. Until then, Prague was the place where Communists and non-Communists could meet – it was an easier city to travel to and from, and there were more international writers there. I found the Czechs to be some of the most intellectually interesting people I had met behind the Iron Curtain.

The spring of free speech

Czechoslovaks are drinking deep draughts from the exhilarating spring of free speech these days. Each day in their newspapers, each evening on television, they participate in the most searching discussion about the ills of the past and their hopes for the future.

Members of the same family take positions

for or against a particular point of view, for even within the broad categories of pro- or anti-reform, pro- or anti-democratization, there are innumerable shades of difference. The mass media, which for so many years has been employed to churn out the same gray party-approved propaganda line, are now exploding with the full-bodied, many-colored tones of unorthodoxy, dissent, and challenge to thinking by rote...

— Takashi Oka for *The Christian Science Monitor*, July 9, 1968. Prague.

We were all amazed by what was going on in Prague, and we were worried that it would be stopped. I remember discussing with Bob Daglish and Ina just before the Soviet crackdown – would the Russians actually come in, or wouldn't they? After all, they had intervened in the Hungarian uprising in 1956. Indeed, Russian tanks did roll in, and at the end of summer the Prague Spring was ruthlessly stamped down. I had left Prague by then and covered the reaction to the invasion from Karuizawa.

1968 was an incredible year, especially for a journalist. In January, the Viet Cong launched the Tet Offensive. That summer, the Soviet invasion of Czechoslovakia sparked demonstrations all over the world. Riots erupted in Chicago and many other American cities after the assassination of Dr. Martin Luther King, Jr., and then again in Chicago at the Democratic National Convention. Student protests broke out all over America and Europe. I remember going to Paris and seeing that the big, lovely trees along the boulevard had been cut down to make barricades – it was like a scene from the history books about the French Revolution.

I was there covering the American-North Vietnamese

peace talks in May 1968, trying to read between the lines of Henry Kissinger's comments to the press. But no one in the streets was paying much attention to Vietnam at that point. Students with red and black banners were leading strikes and riots all over Paris, and the whole city closed down. I couldn't get out – the trains, airplanes, buses, everything in France shut down. The only international airport that was still open was in Geneva. So a small group of us journalists hired a taxi to Switzerland.

A few days later, in June, I was in London when Robert Kennedy was assassinated. The British were just as shocked as I was. When I came back to Moscow, the Soviet press was in full swing, blaming his murder on the violence of capitalist society.

But the student riots weren't confined to Europe and America – there were also riots in Tokyo. I ended up covering those protests as well, but for a different newspaper. In the fall of 1968, after twenty years of writing for the *Monitor*, I went to *The New York Times*, which had hired me to be its Tokyo correspondent.

```
Dear Otosama,                                  August 16, 1968

     I appreciated very much the wise advice you gave me when
I consulted you before going to Karuizawa.  When I left New York,
I told Seymour Topping(Foreign Editor of the Times) that I wanted
a few days to think things over carefully, and that I was
especially anxious to consult with my father-in-law, who was
not only a newspaperman but had known the Times intimately over
a long period of time.  Mr. Topping thought this an excellent idea:
he hoped that I would accept a job with the Times, but
recognized that the step required careful thought.

     What you told me that night crystallized many thoughts that
had been going through my own mind.  I was able to separate the
really important factors from less worthy considerations such as
vanity or personal ambition.  I particularly appreciated the fact
that you took a completely impartial attitude towards the two
proposed jobs open to me, pointing out the good points and the
bad points of each.
```

Above: Excerpt from a letter to my father-in-law.

Chapter 12

Tokyo

From September 1968 until the end of the year, I was in New York City, writing for the Metro Desk of *The New York Times*. Mimi and Saya went to the Dalton School for that semester. Then we went to Japan, reaching Tokyo on Jan 2, 1969, right after New Year's, and I was very busy right away because of the student protests. I remember Saya said the Tokyo students looked like Jesus, because they all had beards.

In Japan, the student movement differed from the anti-war protests in the US and Europe in that the Japanese also delivered an anti-elitist message aimed at the Japanese establishment. What made these protests more extraordinary was that the students leading the charge came from Japan's most elite universities. The medical faculty at Tokyo University and the Marxist intellectuals were out in the streets alongside more populist demonstrators from Nippon University. It was a revolution that represented a coming together of people from very different backgrounds, and no one had ever seen anything quite like it before. Japan is a small country, so the protests created such an uproar that even people who would normally not be interested in that kind of thing were very much drawn in – and on the side of the protesting students.

The protest continued throughout 1969, at one point paralyzing over sixty universities across the country. But the focal point of the fight between students and police was in the compact area of Suidobashi, along the canal that runs through the center of Tokyo (which had been the outer moat of the shogun's castle). Tokyo University turned into a battleground, with the police brandishing long sticks and batons, and the students wielding staves and rocks. Fortunately, Japan is not a gun society, so only a few people died. However, over the course of the year, the demonstrations grew more violent. Protestors began hurling Molotov cocktails – and, in one instance at Kyoto University, sulfuric acid. Later that year, officials at Kyoto University called in riot police to clear out a clocktower that the students had occupied, while at another university outside Tokyo, rival student factions turned on each other and threw three students from a window, killing one. By the year's end, several university directors had committed suicide.

One time, when I was covering the student protest in Hiroshima, I had to flee from the police myself. I was interviewing students on the second floor of a garment shop above a restaurant – both the shop and restaurant had been converted into the students' ad hoc headquarters – when suddenly the police showed up on the street below and started arresting whomever they could find. I was young enough that the police would not have distinguished me from the students, and before I knew it, the students had figured that they would make a break for it. As the police charged up the stairs, we jumped out of the window and fled across the black-tiled rooftops. There were at least thirty of us. We all ran until we felt we were a safe distance away, then slowly climbed down. Other students in Hiroshima continued to fight the police all night.

After a year of continuous protests, the momentum finally declined. The public grew tired of it all, and the demonstrators shifted their focus onto other subjects – such as the new airport at Narita, which the government was planning to share with the American military. Thousands of people protested, but Narita was forty miles from the center of Tokyo and not so easy to get to, so the protests soon dissipated.

* * * * *

Okinawa presented a different story. People from all over

Japan descended on the island to protest the large and ongoing US military presence there.

An island chain that begins south of Kyushu and curves southwest to Taiwan, Okinawa had historically been an independent kingdom. Its people have a distinct culture, with beautiful forms of dance, pottery, and clothing made from banana fiber. The Okinawans speak an old language that is unmistakably a dialect of Japanese, but most people from the main islands do not understand it. And for many years, Okinawans have had a complex about their relationship with Japan.

In feudal times, while the rest of Japan was subordinate to the Tokugawa shogunate, Okinawa had its own king. The king paid tribute to Japan, but Okinawa remained a separate country until 1878, when it finally became a Japanese prefecture. At the end of World War II, when all of Japan was occupied by the United States, the Okinawan islands were given a different status, leaving them in a political limbo, under direct US military rule. When Japan regained independence in 1952, Okinawa was not included in the area returned to Japanese jurisdiction – it remained under American military occupation. Thus, Okinawa owed allegiance to three countries: the United States, Japan, and to itself as a semi-independent territory.

By 1969, Okinawa's status had become a major political issue in Japan, not only because of the B-52 bombers based on the island, but also because of a stockpile of nuclear weapons, which the US kept on Okinawa to deter China and North Korea. American officials insisted that Japan was free of nuclear weapons, but this fiction remained valid only because the US kept its nuclear weapons in Okinawa – which, technically, the Japanese did not control. The US knew that storing nuclear weapons on the main islands of Japan would cause a storm of protests, but on Okinawa the military could do as it pleased.

While I was back in Tokyo, both Okinawans and Japanese

were demanding that Okinawa be returned to Japan, and the protests outside Kadena Air Base increased dramatically after a B-52 crashed near an ammo dump, where nuclear weapons were supposedly stored. In November of 1969, Prime Minister Sato was planning to visit President Nixon in Washington DC to discuss the new US-Japan security treaty, and one of the main points would be the status of Okinawa. Knowing this, I went to the island that summer and wrote a feature for *The New York Times Magazine*, giving the Okinawans as much of a voice as I could.

Okinawa Mon Amour

> In Okinawa the sun is strong, the sea a palette of blues and greens. Spinning along Highway 1 north from Naha toward Nago, away from the fume-choked military traffic of the American base complex in the finger-shaped main island's center, a visitor catches vistas of dazzling sands, of inviting green coves and inlets.
>
> In the fields of sugar cane and sweet potato bordering the highway, wiry, small-boned men and women with broad-brimmed straw hats or carefully knotted towels on their heads are out hoeing their straight furrows or cutting the long, untidy cane by hand….
>
> This is Okinawan Okinawa, an area of farms and forests, with neat, moderately prosperous towns and pockets of hamlets where life goes on almost as rhythmically as before World War II, when all of Okinawa was a quiet, neglected backwater of Japan, the poorest of all the empire's

> 47 prefectures. Northern Okinawa survived the bitter battle between Japanese and American forces at the end of World War II relatively intact; the southern third of the island was devastated.
>
> There is also an American Okinawa, the largest and most intricate complex of bases on one island in the Far East, inextricably interwoven with Okinawan Okinawa...

Only a small minority of Okinawans wanted total independence, because the local economy depended on both the Japanese government and the US military presence. About 75,000 US soldiers were stationed there, and the base employed 50,000 islanders. However, there was surprisingly little interaction between the two communities, with each side going their own separate ways. Fearing economic collapse if the military decided to leave, most Okinawans preferred the security of being an official part of Japan.

> "Nowhere else in Asia," said the outgoing American commander on Okinawa, Lieut. Gen. F. T. Unger, in a speech in Tokyo last January, "does the United States have complete freedom to station, deploy, and support balanced forces equipped with the full range of modern military resources. Only on Okinawa can we station any type of weapons or units. Only from Okinawa can we deploy forces to any threatened area in Asia. Only through Okinawa can we provide unrestricted logistical support to forces committed anywhere in Asia. These freedoms give our forces on Okinawa

a flexibility and responsiveness unmatched anywhere in Asia."

Sixty thousand marines pass through Camp Hansen on the island's east central coast every month on their way to and from Vietnam….

Daily, eight-engined B-52 jet bombers from Kadena Airbase roar down its 11,000-foot runway with bombs for South Vietnam. The black-painted, high-tailed bombers can be clearly seen just inside the wire mesh fence that seals off the huge 5,000-acre airbase from Kadena Village.

Okinawans dislike B-52s because of the noise they make and because they are being used in the Vietnam war, which is as unpopular in the Ryukyus as it is in Japan. Last November, a B-52 loaded with bombs crashed just after take-off in a field not half a block from the Chibana ammunition dump, where nuclear weapons are supposedly stored. The exploding bombs shattered window panes and damaged structures in Kadena Village. More important, the crash awakened widespread fears that the very presence of a military base in an area as crowded as central Okinawa might cause danger to local inhabitants…

During my visit to Okinawa, I saw these eight-engined B-52 bombers. They made ear-shattering noises as they lifted off from the Kadena Air Base just outside of Naha. For local residents – who resented not only the presence of a foreign military, but also the very war it was fighting – it must have been maddening.

In 1970, the security treaty between the US and Japan was up for review, which would determine the extent of the US military sway in Okinawa. Leading up to the treaty, Sato's big slogans in 1969 were "Return Okinawa to Japan" and the "Three Principles of Nuclear No's" – no possession, no production, no introduction. However popular this platform was in Japan, it depended entirely on what the US was willing to concede. My friend and former professor Ed Reischauer had served as the US ambassador to Japan from 1961 to 1966, and had a hand in shaping, both formally and informally, US foreign policy throughout that decade, and specifically in 1969. The US argument was that it wanted to keep what it had, without drawing up a new treaty that could potentially involve the Japanese Diet or the US Congress.

Japanese opinion was divided, from the socialists who opposed nuclear weapons of any kind and who wanted the US to leave, to the right-wing businessmen who just didn't want nuclear weapons on Japanese soil. Either way, Japan as a whole wished to stick with Article 9 of its Constitution, which says that it will never become a nuclear power. Meanwhile, Okinawa operated under neither the Japanese nor the US Constitution.

> The United States came to Okinawa through conquest in World War II. More than 12,000 Americans lost their lives.… On the Japanese side, 65,176 soldiers and 110,052 civilians were killed. The overwhelming majority of civilians were Okinawans, among them schoolboys and schoolgirls pressed into service as construction workers and nurses…
>
> To the extent Okinawans harbor bitterness, they seem to direct it, not against the

Americans, but their own Japanese fellow countrymen, who, they feel, sacrificed Okinawa so that Japan proper might be spared invasion...

"I felt an indescribable loneliness when I returned to Okinawa from Taiwan after the war," Chobyo Yara reminisced recently in his wood-paneled office in Naha. Yara, a chunky, broad-faced, smiling man who looks like any Okinawan grandfather (and, in fact, boasts of five grandchildren), is the first elected Chief Executive of the Ryukyu Islands.

"That green, peaceful Okinawa in which I had grown up had been utterly destroyed. American soldiers, white and black, were everywhere. The Okinawans were living in tents.... Almost all my normal-school classmates were dead. My own oldest daughter, 17 years old, was dead. We had sent her back to Naha from Taiwan [where Yara was teaching high-school physics] for her schooling, and when the Battle of Okinawa began, she and her classmates were drafted as auxiliary nurses. The tragedy of war, the tragedy of defeat, really came home to me at that time. I felt that, whatever the cost, we must create a world in which there would be no more wars." ...

Yara knew what the political score was, and being a socialist pacifist, he welcomed the visiting protestors and the attention they brought to his cause. He was a reversion movement leader, and he was Chief Executive of Okinawa - a position he gained despite US attempts to keep him out.

> To Japanese, American rule over Okinawa represents the last remaining restriction on Japanese sovereignty imposed as a result of defeat in World War II....
>
> The consciousness of having been given second-class treatment for many years, first by the Japanese and now by the Americans, is very strong among Okinawans. "I feel myself to be a Japanese, but the people from Japan proper did not look on Okinawans as real Japanese for a long time," said a young journalist. "They considered us not quite Japanese, and not quite Chinese, sort of half-and-half. Many Okinawans feel they have to prove they are real Japanese, not just to the Americans but to the Japanese also."...
>
> The islands remained poor and were considered a semi colonial outpost of Japan until well into the 20th century. In his best seller, "The Ugly Japanese," Prof. Masahide Ota of the University of the Ryukyus indignantly relates how an Okinawan woman was exhibited at an anthropological exposition in Tokyo as if she were an animal in a zoo, and how in the early 20th century some politicians proposed that Okinawa be attached to Taiwan, then a new Japanese colony, instead of being made a prefecture of Japan.
>
> "The past 100 years have been a clear

> testimony to the fact that the Japanese Government invariably chose to overlook, if not openly discriminate against, Okinawans, whenever it was convenient to do so," [Shinei] Kyan [chairman of the Council for the Reversion of Okinawa Prefecture to the Fatherland] told a gathering of Japanese and American scholars… "And yet… we Okinawans are real Japanese. One million Okinawans and 100 million Japanese have been separated since the war…. Japan is our mother; Okinawa is the child. After years of separation we want to go back to our parent. Even if our parent is cowardly and lacks the courage to take us back, our desire remains the same."
>
> — Takashi Oka for *The New York Times*, April 6, 1969. Naha, Okinawa.

Okinawans loved my article because it gave their side of the story. I'd like to think that it had something of an impact on the American officials who were reviewing the security treaty. Whether it did or not, Prime Minister Sato returned to Naha with a commitment from the US that the islands would revert to Japan –although without a fixed date. Reversion finally happened in 1972, and while it was accompanied by the usual pomp and circumstance, protests against the US military base continued in Tokyo.

In recent years, secret memos have been declassified which show the US's intentions in Okinawa with regard to nuclear weapons and larger military strategy. Reischauer had defended the vague language in the treaty which allowed these weapons to be there on the island. He knew that politically it was impossible for Japan to have nuclear weapons on its own soil. But having them on Okinawa suited the US's purpose of protecting both Japan and Korea, so the policy, however vague, remained intact.

In Tokyo, the Japanese right wing wanted the decision to be an American one, which Japan would have to accept because of its dependence on US protection. All of that was very camouflaged, but clearly there was hesitation on both sides, because both were dealing with public opinion, primarily in Japan, where newspapers generally supported the left. Opposition to nuclear weapons was strong, not just among the Socialists. Even the Communists were divided because they knew the question was really about the US versus the Soviet Union, and Japan was basically on the American side of the Cold War. This was a circle that could never be squared.

The Okinawan controversy doesn't change my opinion of Ed Reischauer. Had he not been the ambassador, he would probably have been against a reversion without an explicit statement that there were no nukes on Okinawa. However, it is US policy to never acknowledge whether Washington does or does not have nuclear weapons in any specific part of the world, so if Reischauer didn't agree with that policy, he could have quit. But, he was making these decisions in 1965, when there was a lot of uncertainty in Asia, particularly in Vietnam (two years after Diem's assassination) and in China (between the Great Leap Forward and the Cultural Revolution). While it's true that a majority of Japanese would rather not have American nuclear warheads stored nearby, a majority of Japanese were also afraid of China. At that time, China was developing a blue-water navy and testing its boundaries by venturing towards Japan.

In 1981, several years after he had left the embassy, Reischauer finally admitted that the US had moved nuclear weapons in and out of Japanese ports. In doing so, the former ambassador addressed the elephant in the room, and some Japanese foreign ministry officials said that he was off his rocker, that he was not recognizing reality. But the reality was that both sides had carefully constructed a fiction and had insisted on it for a number of years. The truth was that most people who were interested in this matter knew that the nukes were there, and I think we all knew that at some point everything would have to come out in the open. The Japanese had preferred that the situation remain unclear, and until the Reischauer bombshell, the Americans had obliged.

The Reischauer Shock

Prof. Edwin O. Reischauer appears to have ripped the veil off 20 years of lying by successive Japanese governments and of complaisance by American governments.

It appears that Mr. Reischauer, the United States's foremost scholar on Japan and American ambassador in Tokyo from 1961 to 1966, has decided that the time has come to call a spade a spade. The repercussions have shaken Prime Minister Zenko Suzuki's cabinet and have even caused the high-flying Tokyo stock market to take a tumble. Market analysts sagely talk of the "Reischauer shock" and whether prices can recover before the end of the month.

The immediate effect of the Harvard scholar's remarks in press interviews May 18 has been on domestic politics in Japan. But a kind of shaking-out process has been going on in Japan's relations with the US as well — a process bound to be complicated by Mr. Reischauer's comments.

Are Japan and the US really allies, or

> are they just friends? What is Japan's proper defense role? How can frictions over trade be prevented from spilling into the defense security area, and vice versa?
>
> A lightly armed, non-nuclear Japan depends on a security treaty with the US for its defense. The treaty obligates the US to defend in case of attack. It does not obligate Japan to defend the US unless the attack comes in Japanese land, sea, or air space.
>
> It is not a mutual defense treaty, in the way that the North Atlantic alliance is a mutual defense treaty. Hence the question, "Is Japan really an ally?" The answer seems to be "yes, in a political and economic sense, no in a strictly military sense." But this has never been clearly defined…
>
> — Takashi Oka for *The Christian Science Monitor*, May 27, 1981.

Ed was open with me about the subject, although he kept his remarks off the record. I know he was personally opposed to nuclear weapons, but he felt constrained by foreign policy concerns, which he contextualizes in his autobiography *My Life Between Japan and America*. After his government service, Ed went back to Harvard and continued teaching as a university professor. He refused the position of Master of Eliot House (one of the most prestigious jobs a Harvard scholar can have), and focused on his scholarly work.

* * * * *

The Japanese were glad that I, rather than an American, covered Okinawa. The *Times* had two correspondents in Tokyo – I was the bureau chief, and Phil Shabecoff was the other full-time correspondent. The *Times* staff was certainly bigger than that of the *Monitor*, but on the writing side it was just the two of us. Shabecoff had been with the *Times* longer than me – he had been their correspondent in Germany, and although he spoke German, he didn't speak Japanese. So the division of labor was that I covered the Japanese news, and he covered the stories related to the Far East in general. While he traveled to Indonesia, Taiwan, and elsewhere, I (for the most part) got to work at home – which, by then, suited me quite well, I must say.

Tokyo is where I was born and where I grew up, so in that sense I was back home. It was still a very expensive place then – and always had been, because space is so limited – and it was crowded. Having just come from Moscow, my family and I felt how loud and busy Tokyo was. I reported to work at the *Asahi Shimbun* building downtown where the *Times* had its offices. This meant that sometimes I could catch a ride to work with Hiro's father, who had a car service that would take him to his *Asahi* office. Hiro wasn't keen on living in the same city as her parents again, but she managed somehow, and our kids got to see both sets of grandparents. It was the first time that we all lived in the same city. The girls got to know Japan and to speak Japanese.

This was also the first time that I, an English-speaking Japanese writing for an American paper, had been assigned to Japan. Among other things, it meant I had to learn to speak proper Japanese again – as I had done when I was translating for the *Yomiuri Shimbun* at the 1952 conventions.

It was a very interesting experience to be in Japan again, covering what was going on politically and socially. Tokyo was the center of Japanese culture – the theater was there, the museums, the old castle. The Ginza was like Fifth Avenue, where all the most fashionable shops were. Trends that later spread across the country came from Tokyo – or if not, it was Tokyo that made a trend fashionable.

The *Times* is a much busier place than the *Monitor*. It publishes a newspaper every day of the year, while the *Monitor* only ran five days a week. The *Times* is never on holiday, so I wrote articles even on Christmas Day and other days that I was accustomed to having off. But the *Times* had the prestige of being read by a much larger audience than I had ever experienced before.

As bureau chief, if I wanted to do a feature – like the one on Okinawa – I could focus on that. I could also plan a series of stories across different parts of Japan so that, over time, the whole country was more or less covered. I was my own boss, in that sense.

There was so much going on. In 1969, North Korea shot down a US reconnaissance plane. Being so close to Japan, anything the leader Kim Il Sung did was of great interest to the Japanese. The Philippines was also in turmoil. In 1970, I flew to Manila to cover the protests against President Marcos's second term in office – riots would continue there for years. In April, a Japanese airplane was hijacked and flown to Seoul. As a reporter, you have to be on the spot because things can get very active all of a sudden. So I hung around Seoul for several days with a number of correspondents, waiting for the hostages' release.

The war was still going on in Vietnam, and there was heavy American bombing in Cambodia. I was in Phnom Penh for about a month – this was a few months after Sihanouk had been ousted in a coup in March. Cambodia was entering a civil war, and although it was dangerous, journalists could still go in and out of the country. There wasn't as much killing going on as there would be later, when the Khmer Rouge started murdering large numbers of people. My focus was still on the American and South Vietnamese strategy on the border. At that particular time, Cambodia was a strangely quiet part of the war, despite the bombing. Cambodia and Laos were also two of the places where, in those days, you could legally smoke opium. So a number of correspondents tried it. I thought it tasted and smelled like chocolate.

The year 1971 was the time of "ping pong diplomacy." The US and China had agreed to have ping pong matches, which became a political story, leading up to 1972, when Nixon visited China. I interviewed the US Ping Pong team captain:

Table Tennis Captain — Jack Howard

...Mr. Howard said that he was "surprised and delighted" when the Chinese issued their invitation and felt that it represented a "whole new start for diplomacy between the United States and China."...

His face looked customarily serious as he admitted that he expected his players to be trounced by the high-school age Chinese, "with scores of 21 for them to less than 10 for us."...

— Takashi Oka for *The New York Times*, April 10, 1971. Nagoya.

Later that year I interviewed the Emperor. He was preparing his first-ever trip to America, and I secured an individual interview with him in one of the palace's reception rooms. I also interviewed the crown prince and one of the imperial grandsons. At nine pages in print, my story was one of the biggest features that I wrote for *The New York Times*

Magazine.

The Emperor didn't say a great deal, but he was friendly. I sensed that his body was not well coordinated. He had a nervous tic – a noticeable, but not conspicuous, movement of his head – that seemed to come on when he was around people with whom he had to be on his guard. He was going to the US and to Europe – it would be his first time in Europe since 1921. The 1921 trip was the first time that he had ever had money in his pocket – his aides had always paid for everything before.

Now, in 1971, Japan was experiencing its first economic boom in manufacturing, the yen was floating, and there was tension between the US and Japan. I remember that the Emperor went to Disneyland.

The Emperor Who Meets the President Today

…Hirohito is 5 feet, 5 inches tall, weighs 143 pounds, wears rimless glasses and sports a wispy mustache, now turning gray. His clothes tend to be baggy. "He would happily wear a suit until it fell to pieces," says one chamberlain, "if the Empress didn't watch out for him." The Emperor walks with somewhat jerky movements, as if he were not quite sure of his footing. This is not, court officials hasten to say, because there is anything wrong with his feet or his nervous system, but because he cannot be bothered about little details like getting the right prescription for his glasses. When the optometrist asks, "How well can you see with this lens, Sire," he answers, "Fine." The optometrist changes the lens, then asks, "And how about this one?" "Fine," answers the

Emperor again. After a while, most doctors give up in despair.

If Hirohito looks like the proverbial absent-minded professor, his one absorbing passion is a subject equally professorial: marine biology, particularly the study of the polyps and jellyfish known as hydrozoa. He has published 11 books on the subject, and sometimes spends three days a week in his laboratory on the palace grounds….

During breakfast, the Emperor watches a television "home drama" — Japanese-style soap opera — and discusses with the Empress the dramas, newscasts, commentaries or concerts they will view on TV in the evening. He does not enjoy Western music, which the Empress loves, but he often goes along with her desires. TV dramas, especially those that concern the lives of ordinary contemporary folk, give the imperial couple an invaluable opportunity to enter the Japanese homes and hear the unembellished speech of everyday people. The Emperor takes literally a good deal of what he sees, applauding the "good guys" and denouncing the "bad."…

—Takashi Oka for *The New York Times*, September 26, 1971. Tokyo.

*****

Japan was not much in the American news then, but I

knew that anything related to New York would get big play in the paper. So I reviewed the major cultural events of Tokyo.

Hair was the first show (that I knew of) in Japan where the cast was totally naked. The police had threatened to arrest people, but in the end they didn't. This was in 1969, the same time as the student protests, and also the same time as the Women's Liberation Front – who had the letters W-O-L-F on their helmets.

Japan Hails Dawning of Age of 'Hair'

They were all up there on the tilted circular stage doing their thing in the finale of "Hair" here last night.

Sedate gentlemen in coats and ties and high school girls in navy blue blouses and long skirts mingled with the bead-wearing and long-haired, the miniskirted or pantalooned. The members of the audience — some crying, some embracing the performers, some curious or bashful — were drawn from their seats not merely by the outstretched inviting arms of the cast but by some urge many found difficult to explain even to themselves.

The Japanese version of "Hair," the American tribal love-rock musical, has been playing to crowded houses twice daily at the thousand-seat Toyoko Theater here since it opened Friday….

Prince Mikasa, brother of the Emperor, termed the show "very philosophical," adding: "I understood one third very well. I feel I will be able to understand another third if I sleep on it overnight.

But the last third probably will forever remain a closed book to me."

— Takashi Oka for *The New York Times*, December 9, 1969. Tokyo.

I also wrote about a musical version of *Gone With the Wind* – I don't think it had nudity.

'Scarlett,' Musical, And Star Cheered By Tokyo Audience

A star was born — or rather reborn — at the Imperial Theater here tonight when Sakura Jinguji received an ovation for her performance in the title role of "Scarlett," a new musical based on "Gone With the Wind," the Margaret Mitchell novel….

It opened tonight before a distinguished audience including Yukio Mishima, the author….

— Takashi Oka for *The New York Times*, Jan 3, 1970.

By then Mishima was rich and certainly famous. He was a fine novelist, whose works tried to marry traditional Japanese ideals with Western modernism. His first book, *Confessions of a Mask*, made him famous at a young age.

Leonard Bernstein met with Mishima when he came to Japan to conduct the New York Philharmonic on a multi-city tour. I interviewed Bernstein and his Japanese assistant, Ozawa, who was also a well-known conductor. They were impressed because the audience was so large and relatively young.

Bernstein, in Tokyo, Assays Japanese Character

To Leonard Bernstein, the Japanese are a people who have wrapped themselves in layer after layer of "rules, courtesies, honorifics, and bowing" as protection against "an inner violence."

"I sense there's some kind of volcano inside a Japanese person, which is controlled by rules of behavior, of courtesy, humility and so forth, learned through the centuries," Mr. Bernstein said in an interview at his hotel here yesterday.

Wearing a blue and white yukata (cotton kimono) with a red silk neckpiece, Mr. Bernstein said he had just arisen — it was 2 P.M. — after a long day and night of receptions, entertainment, and conversations, the most memorable of which was with the author Yukio Mishima....

Mr. [Seiji] Ozawa, a longtime protégé of Mr. Bernstein's, agreed about the "Japanese volcano" in a separate interview. This season he will conduct the San Francisco Symphony and make guest appearances with the Philharmonic.

"I sense it in myself," Mr. Ozawa said. "The Japanese are really a very passionate people. Japanese arts are quiet — on the surface."

Mr. Bernstein feels that Japan's "inner force" can be put to creative use if channeled properly. "Or maybe," he said, "in future it can spread itself out, can level out the emotions, if the rules change and it does not have to be contained in such rigid packages."

Part of his discussion with Mr. Mishima dealt with this subject, the maestro said….

— Takashi Oka for *The New York Times*, September 10, 1970. Tokyo.

After Mishima, Japanese literature was considered a part of world literature, and before him, it had been an exotic outlier. Mishima marked the boundary between the two periods. Up to that point, Japanese writers who had been translated into English mostly wrote in traditional Japanese style – somewhat wordy and not always coming immediately to the point. But Mishima was right in tune with the modern novelists of the day. His novels were about modern Japan – the Japanese who knew Western literature and ideas, but who were also thoroughly Japanese. That was what made him popular in Japan. And because of his Western sensitivity, the Americans and Europeans could see in him something they couldn't find in traditional Japanese novelists.

Nobel Prize Stirs Interest in Japanese Literature

The winning of the Nobel Prize in literature by Yasunari Kawabata, who

> since Tanizaki's death three years ago has been the unquestioned dean of working Japanese writers, has stimulated new interest here in a literature once considered esoteric and remote….
>
> Prof. Donald Keene of Columbia University, one of the foremost Western experts on modern Japanese literature, ranks Kobo Abe with Yukio Mishima, one year his junior, as the two most creative writers of their generation, representing entirely different tendencies….
>
> Writing in Japan can be a lucrative business. Mr. Mishima's novels regularly sell more than 100,000 copies before moving into paperback editions….
>
> — Takashi Oka for *The New York Times*, Oct 29, 1968.

Kawabata had said that he thought Mishima would be the next winner of the Nobel Prize. Foreign Minister Kiichi Aichi – who had advised Mishima at Tokyo University to become a full-time novelist – was a fan.

Mishima was also an actor, director, and model. He was married – but he was also gay. And perhaps most bizarrely, he was a Japanese nationalist. He founded his "Shield Society," *Tatenokai*, a corps of several dozen young male university students, who were his followers and who practiced bodybuilding and martial arts. He was a physical exercise fanatic. He used to lead his group up to a military training grounds near symbolic Mt. Fuji and practice military exercises. Although Mishima had absorbed and interpreted a great deal of Western thinking, he was, from the beginning, a nationalist. He intensely studied the history of Japan, and he was completely at home in the samurai culture of honor and suicide.

I felt there was something too performance-like about the whole thing. His group's exercises were not directly connected to the student protests that been going on for the previous year, although Mishima did sympathize with some of those students. He was more interested in the aesthetics of his cadre – he designed and created the uniforms that his followers wore, with a double row of gold buttons down the front.

Philip Shabecoff and I interviewed him in 1970. Mishima wanted to be known internationally as a writer of standing, and he wanted to talk directly to American newspaper correspondents, rather than going through an interpreter. So, at the interview, Mishima got interested in Shabecoff and tended to talk to him more than he did to me, regarding me as a technical person – the interpreter for the American journalist. It took a bit of time for him to recognize that I, in fact, was the main correspondent for *The New York Times*, and that I was acting as interpreter for my junior colleague. After an awkward beginning, Mishima settled down, and we established a close relationship. He was one of the most interesting people I ever interviewed.

Everyone in Japan Has Heard of Him

..."Ah, you want to know about Mishima," Yasunari Kawabata said with a little laugh. "He is not my disciple, you know, although people sometimes say so.
"Well, then, Mishima has extraordinary talent, and it is not just a Japanese talent but a talent of world scale. It is the kind of genius that comes along perhaps once every 300 years.

"This new work — 'Spring Snow' and the

other volumes — is his best book so far. It used to be said that 'Kinka-kuji' — 'The Temple of the Golden Pavilion' — was his masterpiece. But this new one is greater. Mishima is really going at it with his whole heart now. He has a tremendous gift of words, and it has never been richer than in this new book. I don't know how it will be in translation, but in Japanese it is a masterpiece.

"Before I received the Nobel Prize I said that Mishima would get it. He is one of the most comprehensible of Japanese authors to the Western mind. I regard the prize as having been awarded not so much to me as to Japan. As far as talent goes, Mishima is far superior to me."…

A Western friend recalled having been invited to Mishima's house for dinner; late in the evening, Mishima offered to show the friend his collection of swords. "The swords were beautiful and razor-sharp," the Westerner said. "Mishima took one of them and demonstrated the procedure for hara-kiri — he later made a movie about hara-kiri, you know."

"Then he said he would show me how a samurai used to help a friend commit hara-kiri. He told me to kneel down on the mat. I could feel that sharp edge of the sword almost touching the back of my neck. I was terrified, but didn't dare move. We had been drinking a lot all night."

"Fortunately, Mishima never loses control. But he had a wicked grin on his face after it was over."...

Some of Mishima's friends express concern that he is burning himself out with his extraneous — that is, nonwriting — activities. But Mishima scoffs at such fears and says he knows exactly what he is doing....

— Philip Shabecoff for *The New York Times*, August 2, 1970. Tokyo.

In November 1970, I was planning to go to Karuizawa with Hiro and the kids for the Thanksgiving holiday. Our luggage was packed and lined up in the front hallway at home, and I was just about to leave the office to meet them, when the ticker tape came in. Something was happening with Yukio Mishima.

Renowned Author Raids Tokyo Military, Ends Life

Yukio Mishima and Aide Die by Hara-Kiri — 6 Hurt in Attack

Yukio Mishima, one of Japan's most highly regarded novelists, committed suicide in traditional hara-kiri fashion today after leading a raid by a group of right-wingers on a headquarters of Japan's Self-Defense Forces here....

They asked for an interview with the commander, Lieut. Gen. Kanetoshi Mashida. The general consented to see them in his office, where after a half hour of conversation Mr. Mishima drew his sword while his four companions tied General Mashida to his chair as a hostage. Staff aides, hearing a commotion, rushed into the office but were met with drawn swords and ejected….

Mr. Mishima went to the balcony of the three-story white building about noon and harangued a crowd of about 1,200 members of the Self-Defense Force who had gathered in the plaza below.

He told them that the police, suppressing widespread demonstrations by radical leftists students on Oct. 21 had deprived the Defense Forces of an opportunity to intervene to restore law and order and to change the Constitution.

He accused the Self-Defense Forces of having failed to achieve anything during their 20 years of existence and said, according to persons who were present, that unless the servicemen themselves took action, it would be impossible to change the Constitution and restore the prewar Japanese state, based on rule by the Emperor.

As he spoke, servicemen shouted at him to come down and exclaimed: "We can't act in common with fellows like you."

After a talk of about 15 minutes, Mr. Mishima gave three shouts of "Banzai!" for the Emperor and went inside….

> "They didn't seem to hear me too well."...
>
> — Takashi Oka for *The New York Times*, November 25, 1970. Tokyo.

The situation developed throughout the day. I had a cherubic young American assistant from Ohio named Barry Shlachter who spoke Japanese - not wonderfully, but he did speak it - and I sent him to the site, where things were happening on the other side of a locked door. We were right on deadline in New York, so I had an open telephone line to New York, and another line with Barry, who was just outside the room where Mishima was holding this Japanese general captive.

There was a window of only a few more hours before we could get the story into that day's paper, and Barry couldn't go in the room because the door was locked. However, there was a transom over the frosted glass doors, and if he jumped he could briefly look down on the proceedings. So we were all listening to him jump up and down and relay fragments of a picture. He continued in this vein, telling me what was going on over one phone, while I had New York on the other phone. There was a sequence of him relaying what he was seeing, and then the rest of us asking "And then?" And then Barry told us, "Now I see two heads rolling on the floor!"

That was Mishima and his top follower. The information was received with bated breath in New York - I think the whole newsroom was listening.

> ...The general said later: "I kept telling him, let us hold our lives precious, and, this is unlike you. But he paid me no attention. Then I felt him squatting down. I heard a shout and saw he had plunged a dagger into his abdomen."

> Mr. Mishima cut a straight line across his abdomen, while a student, Masakatsu Morita, slashed off his head with a Japanese sword. This is part of the ritual practice of hara-kiri, in which the man to die asks his best friend to stand behind him and deliver the coup de grace.
>
> Mr. Morita then took the same dagger and stabbed himself while a second student performed the ritual beheading. The three surviving students placed the severed heads neatly on the bloodstained carpet and came out of the room, looking dazed, bringing General Mashida, who was still bound, with them.
>
> — Takashi Oka for *The New York Times*, November 26, 1970. Tokyo.

It was a very bloody affair, so I'm pleased, in a way, that I wasn't right there. The coverage went on all afternoon and into early evening – the general was released, and the other three students surrendered. Meanwhile Hiro and the girls were waiting for me to come pick them up to go to Karuizawa. But our whole Thanksgiving holiday had been sacrificed.

Thousands of people showed up for Mishima's funeral, and there was a brief fear that a rightist insurrection was forming, but most of his followers and fans were simply stunned and confused.

Mishima: A Man Torn Between Two Worlds

> The morning before he killed himself, Yukio Mishima reportedly handed to his publishers in Tokyo the final chapter of

the fourth volume of a tetralogy titled "The Sea of Fertility." Perhaps the title helps explain why this 45-year-old writer, who enjoyed fame, wealth and critical acclaim, took his own life. The title refers to the moon's Sea of Fertility — a dry, cold, sterile place. That "sea" was Mr. Mishima's metaphor for the world and perhaps for Japan, which was for him the world….

In the course of a long conversation with this reporter last spring, Mr. Mishima said that he worked so hard on body building because he intended to die before he was 50 and wanted to have a good looking corpse. He laughed, but then added, "I am half-serious, you know."…

"We always have been an inward-looking people," a Japanese newspaperman said here during a conversation about Mishima today. "I thought recently that, at last, we were starting to be international in outlook, that we would be open to the world once and for all.

"But now Mishima has done this and I think Japan will always be turning back into itself."

— Philip Shabecoff for *The New York Times*, 11/26/1970. Tokyo.

    I think Mishima wanted to leave a record of a beautiful nationalist suicide. He was definitely a performance artist, but he was also a real scholar, and I think his profound understanding of

Japanese literature and art tended to be obscured by his flamboyance.

Symbol of a Japanese Dilemma

Yukio Mishima, his brother said, was a man who "always wanted to exist but never could."

Mishima's claim to a permanent place in Japanese and world literature rests upon his bold juxtaposition of the delicate imagery, the haunting nuances of classical Japanese literature, with a disconcerting and frequently chilling realism, founded on his being a child of his times, thoroughly grounded in Western literature and mentally equipped to travel in the logical, reasoned thought patterns of the West.

He did not always follow these patterns; often he did not want to do so. But it was impossible for him altogether to avoid them. Indeed, his personal tragedy may have been his instinctive recognition that he could not strain out the Western elements in his life and thinking from those elements he considered quintessentially Japanese — not merely the chrysanthemum, as he used to say, but the sword...

He saw a Japan absorbing fast and furiously what it perceived to be the technocratically superior culture of the West, while clinging desperately to what it called its traditional soul, but which it found more and more difficult to articulate convincingly to itself, let alone to outsiders.

— Takashi Oka for *The Christian Science Monitor*, November 19, 1974. London.

*****

I had continued writing freelance for the *Monitor* while I was working for *The New York Times*. Then in 1970, my friend John Hughes became the *Monitor's* Managing Editor. I had known him ever since he had started with the *Monitor* in Boston, and since then he had won the Pulitzer Prize, in 1967, for his coverage of Indonesia. Now he wanted to put together his own team, so he asked a number of people who had left the *Monitor* to come back. Earl Foell, who had gone to the *LA Times*, was one, and I was another. Hughes offered me the job of Paris correspondent.

He knew that I wanted to go to Paris. I didn't have much of a chance of going there with *The New York Times*, and I also found the pace at the *Monitor* was more to my taste than that of the *Times*. Hiro was happy too about going to Paris. Mimi and Saya knew some French, having studied it very early when we were in Saigon. So after a busy three years in Tokyo, we moved again.

Chapter 13

Paris

We lived at 112 bis Avenue de Suffren, a residential area on the Left Bank, off the Cambronne metro stop and just across the street from the UNESCO. Hiro and I were happy to be back in Europe, and the kids were also pleased. Saya went to grade school right near the Eiffel Tower, and she and I were both fond of a delicious chocolate shop on the corner.

By 1972, the *Monitor* had a slightly larger budget than when I'd left Moscow, but it was still a much smaller operation than my previous office in Tokyo. In France, the *Monitor* was a tenant of the British paper *The Daily Telegraph*, and we had a rather large suite of rooms on Rue de Castiglione, across from the Tuileries, in the touristy and history-laden center of Paris.

With a smaller paper came more responsibilities, and I had to write more of the major stories. I was writing fewer articles about art and culture, as I had done with *The New York Times* (although I did get to interview the great Romanian playwright Eugene Ionesco), and more about politics and finance.

Lettre de Noel: Paris Glitters

These closing days of 1971 see the Champs Elysées — to many the most beautiful avenue in the world — turned into a glimmering fairyland with Christmas lights shimmering in every tree.

The shoppers hurrying along the crowded sidewalks, past the animated display windows of the department stores, are buying more — and more expensive —

presents than ever this year.

France, it seems, has enjoyed another good year, marked by political stability and a high economic growth rate — the highest in Western Europe, as a matter of fact. President Pompidou, image of the solid, conservative, astute, bourgeois, non-Parisian Frenchman, rides a not towering but comfortable wave of popularity.

Furthermore, it looks as though France will come out of the world monetary crisis in better shape than almost any other country.

— Takashi Oka for *The Christian Science Monitor*, Dec. 23, 1971. Paris.

After all the riots and great upheaval of 1968-69, the normal life of the city started to revive. Near the Seine, the beautiful tall poplars that the protestors had cut down to make barricades had not regrown, but they had been replaced. Meanwhile, Pompidou had a grandfatherly presence – he was portly and benevolent-looking, and a very shrewd man. After the tumult of '68, he was a soothing figure because he radiated authority.

In 1972, Pompidou made a trip to Niger and Chad in sub-Saharan Africa, where he visited a couple of cities in the middle of the desert, north of the Niger River. I followed him there – it was my first trip to Africa.

We began in the northern part of the desert, where there wasn't so much to see, beyond the atomic installations and uranium mines. But we met with the camel-riding Tuareg tribesmen, whose fair skin stood out – their people, the Berbers, were descendants of the Vandals of Roman days. I continued on to Ft. Lamy, the capital of Chad, close to the border of Cameroon. We visited a few villages, but the only major city was the capital, where the French had their infrastructure.

The situation in Chad was typical of the post-colonial struggles facing many African countries then – religious fighting, guerrilla war, and pockets of strong resentment towards the French. In Cameroon, which was split between British and French control, I found people to be cordial towards the French. There was village life, including a huge, jovial chief with thirty-four wives (I think I met them all – once I shook hands with one of them, I had to shake hands with all of them). By the end of the trip, my main impression was of the dryness of the region. It was a landlocked desert, and it made you realize how important water is.

In most of the French colonies very few people were actually from France or descended from the French. But in Algeria there were about a million. Algeria was legally considered a part of France. Whereas Morocco and Tunisia were protectorates, Algeria was supposed to be a part of metropolitan France. The presence of 1 million French citizens in Algeria was an emotionally difficult subject, and it made the Algerian War a very traumatic experience for both the French and the Algerians.

Torture degrades

Are there ever any circumstances which justify the use of torture?

It is a cruel question to put to a nation which still cannot shake off memories of four years of Nazi occupation, nor of bitter wars fought in Indo-China and Algeria.

> And yet, the question will not let the French go. First there was Gen. Jacques Massu's book, "The True Battle of Algiers," which candidly admitted that the French Army had used torture to extract information from Algerian terrorists. The book was a best-seller.
>
> The Algerian War ended 10 years ago. It is the price of milk, which went up 9 centimes per liter April 1, or the traffic jams on the roads leading out of Paris, that bother most citizens today. At the same time, people do live with their memories, and today's 10-year perspective on the Algerian war seems to provide an opportunity for a degree of introspective self-examination on problems like torture, which put into question the whole proud system of values that the French, along with their neighbors, call Christian and European.
>
> — Takashi Oka for *The Christian Science Monitor*, April 7, 1972. Paris.

After the war, 900,000 French Algerians fled to Europe in just a few months, and they were very loud and insistent about their rights as Frenchmen. By the early 1970s, France was also full of people who had come from Morocco, Tunisia, Martinique, Reunion, Vietnam, West Africa, Italy, Spain, and Portugal.

France — breeding ground for racism?

> Clumps of people — old and young, black, brown, and white, bearded and smooth shaven — stood around, moving from

speaker to speaker as their fancy dictated, often participating in the discussion themselves. They had spilled out from the Labor Exchange, where for most of the evening they had heard a galaxy of labor leaders and fellow workers denounce racism in France.

The meeting was one more manifestation of French concern over outbreaks of racial violence in a society which used to take pride in its hospitality to all strangers, be they black, white, or brown.

There are approximately 3 1/2 million workers in France, of whom a third are from France's former North African possessions of Morocco, Algeria, and Tunisia.

— Takashi Oka for *The Christian Science Monitor*, October 15, 1973. Paris.

* * * * *

In the early 1970s, most of Europe and the US was experiencing an economic crisis, complicated by the ongoing war in Vietnam and the oil embargo. The US dollar kept going down relative to gold, so Nixon changed his monetary policy to allow "floating" currencies. In 1973, I covered the summit with Nixon and Pompidou on the bleak and foggy island of Iceland, which was a convenient halfway place for the two.

This was also around the time that Britain was joining the Common Market, and the European Economic Community was expanding to include the United Kingdom, Norway, Denmark, and Ireland. At the time of the EEC's founding, Britain had not been interested, because the British valued their informal role as the intermediary between the Americans and Europe. Among Europeans, there were suspicions that Britain would play the role of a Trojan horse for Washington. But eventually those tensions eased, and the British joined the EEC in 1973.

> ***Queen's visit to France celebrates end of political frigidity***
>
> The Queen and her husband, the Duke of Edinburgh will be lodged at the Grand Trianon in Versailles, where the British embassy is said to have rejected Louis XVI's bedroom for the Queen as being "too large." She will go to the races at Longchamps, as did her great-grandfather Edward VII.
>
> And, coup of coups, she will leave France aboard the royal yacht Britannia at Rouen, thus walking the pavements of the city where France's greatest hero, St. Joan of Arc, was burned at the stake by once perfidious Albion…
>
> — Takashi Oka for *The Christian Science Monitor*, May 15, 1972. Paris.

At the reception, several officials and other journalists stood in a circle to meet the royal couple. The Queen went around one way, shaking hands with everyone, and Prince Philip went around the other way, and they met in the middle. I got to shake hands with the Queen, but not with Prince Philip.

* * * * *

In Japan, the yen was strong – for a decade, the country's economy had grown faster than any other in the world. Taking note of the recent expansion of the EEC, Prime Minister Tanaka wanted Japan to join the club. So he visited France – the first visit by a Japanese prime minister in eleven years.

The last time a Japanese prime minister had come to France, General de Gaulle was reported to have referred to him as "that transistor salesman." De Gaulle's epithet became famous. It was the way the Europeans looked on the Japanese – they were famous for their electronics and not for much else. There was very little cultural exchange. Tanaka was keen on breaking this deadlock and getting Japan into the EEC, and if he couldn't get EEC membership, then he at least wanted agreement on Japan's position in the global economy.

```
The French promised him the "Mona Lisa."
The West Germans are putting him up in a
castle on the Rhine. And the British —
well, the British never do things by
halves.

Prime Minister Edward Heath met him
personally at Heathrow Airport and
arranged for the top golfer in the
Cabinet, Secretary of State for Northern
Ireland William Whitelaw, to take him
around the Royal St. George's at Sandwich.

For Kakuei Tanaka, Prime Minister of
Japan, and for his countrymen, all this
attention is at the same time flattering
and sobering.

Flattering because it shows — as if any
reminder were still needed — that Japan
has "arrived." Sobering because it
```

> symbolizes the expectations, still largely unfulfilled, that Westerners voice about the role Japan is to play in this multipolar world.
>
> In more ways than one, Mr. Tanaka is the quintessential Japanese. His very name is as common as Smith or Jones. Mr. Tanaka has always been known, affectionately or disparagingly, with admiration or with disdain, as Kaku San.
>
> He perspires readily. His voice is a growl. He is ill at ease with foreigners, and he went through the exquisite banquets offered him by the French at the Elysee and Quai d'Orsay as ordeals to be endured...
>
> — Takashi Oka for *The Christian Science Monitor*, October 1, 1973. London.

Tanaka was known for being unapologetically Japanese. He hadn't been overseas much, he didn't like Western food, and he felt at home only in Japan. He wore suits because, by that time, most politicians were doing so – but he much preferred to relax in a kimono. For him, a Western shower didn't take the place of a good, hot Japanese bath. Tanaka always preferred Japanese food, saying that Western food smelled of butter. Tanaka didn't like buttery things.

*****

In early October 1973, Egypt and Syria, backed by several other Arab nations, launched a surprise attack against Israel on Yom Kippur, when most Israeli forces were at home or in prayers.

Once Israel regrouped, it responded with a vengeance. But at first it seemed a victory for the Arab nations, because the attack was a surprise, and because this time the Egyptians fought better than they had in 1967. In contrast, this war looked like it would last more than six days. I hopped on a plane and reported from several locations, including the Golan Heights and Suez.

> Here on Israel's northern front, the ancient Roman road from Palestine to Damascus bustles with trucks, armored vehicles, and an occasional clanking, soldiers with stubbled chins flashing the V-sign or leaning down to shout the telephone numbers of their families or girlfriends to passing journalists.
>
> Vapor trails left by SAM missiles hang in the cloudless sky, and from time to time enemy shells kick up pillars of black volcanic dust close enough for the journalists to dive instinctively for cover.
>
> At the front or behind the lines, Israelis seem to have a strong sense that the existence of their nation is at stake. "Of course I want to live in peace with the Arabs," said a long-haired lieutenant who had rushed back from London to be called back into service. "But at this moment, can you see any alternative for me except to fight?"
>
> A graduate student at the University of Jerusalem, he hopes to get back to his doctoral dissertation when peace comes. He can see why the Arabs feel as they do, he

> said, and he understands that what they want to do is wage a war of attrition. He compliments them on their improved fighting capabilities. "In 1967," he says, "Israel was full of stories of how the Egyptians fled from us in Sinai, kicking off their shoes so as to run faster. This time — no shoes."
>
> — Takashi Oka for *The Christian Science Monitor*, Oct 16, 1973. Somewhere in Syria.

"No shoes" – that was a quote I remember. As for the byline "Somewhere in Syria," I was based at the headquarters of the Israeli army in Tel Aviv, which was where they published their communiques, and also where I had communication with the outside. The journalists were all there at army headquarters, working under military censorship. We couldn't always get our stories out immediately – everything we wrote had to go through a censor first. But we could choose which front we wanted to go to – Egypt in the south or Syria in the north.

Once we reached the front, I found the experience similar to Vietnam: someone would tell us to be ready the next morning at 4:30 – they wouldn't say where they're going or what they're doing. We'd just have to be ready.

Each press group, however large, would have Israeli officers who would tell us where we could go. The officers had all been drafted quite suddenly once the war started, and they all had civilian occupations. The one with us was a dentist. Nonetheless, we were covering an actual war, so we journalists were essentially on our own. We had to find cover if a bomb came in – although we were on a big, flat plain, and there really was no cover. In Syria, I remember I had to jump into a ditch to protect myself from the mortars and the bombs whistling overhead.

> The control center of a SAM 3 missile battery sits atop a hillock overlooking the road from Ismailia to Suez, its tower smashed in two as if by a giant slicer.
>
> Here and there on the pebbly plain, strands of copper wire glint in the sun. An Israeli escort officer calls out to journalists to beware of mines. Then he decides that the wires do not lead to booby traps, but must have been spilled by some Egyptian soldiers in their haste to escape.
>
> The journalists are like children, climbing over the control tower, peering into its innards, trying to make out inscriptions in Russian and in English, photographing everything in sight, shooing away other journalists whose presence would spoil the authenticity of their photographs...
>
> — Takashi Oka for *The Christian Science Monitor*, Oct. 29, 1973. Suez, Egypt.

The war cost Israelis more than their entire defense budget, and the US gave Israel over $2 billion to pay for it. Immediately after the ceasefire, OPEC proclaimed an oil embargo, which became the next big news story. I wrote several articles about the oil and energy crisis throughout the year, including a four-part series of lengthy articles called "The World's Struggle for Resources."

Appetite of the Wealthy

> Mammoth Japanese tankers form an almost continuous line between home ports and the Persian Gulf, carrying the oil without which the thrum of machines would die down and city lights would grow dim. Japan depends on imports for 99.7 percent of its oil — and oil in turn supplies 74.9 percent of Japan's energy needs.
>
> The pace is incredible. "Ours is a bicycle economy," says Kogoro Uemura, retiring president of the powerful Federation of Economic Organization. "The minute we stop pedaling, we all fall off."
>
> — Takashi Oka for *The Christian Science Monitor*, June 19, 1974. Tokyo.

In Japan, wages were going up 30 percent, but inflation was going up 24 percent. It was an explosion, but it was also like the woman Scheherazade in *One Thousand and One Arabian Nights*. She knows the king will kill her unless she tells him an enthralling story, and she puts off her death by telling a new story every night.

For Europeans it was an especially disorienting period. The oil-producing countries of the Middle East had become powerful in a way that was different from earlier categories of power. Europe was looking at Arabs, whom it had more or less ignored or trampled over for years, in a different light. Arabs were showing how important they were to the West, and that they couldn't be pushed around.

> Dear Otosama, Dec. 22, 1973
>
> We do live in a most fascinating period, it seems to me. I was in England on a public relations lecture for the Monitor when I was suddenly told to go to Israel, and since then I have been travelling most of the time. The whole energy crisis into which we have been plunged seems far overdue -- all the industrialized countries knew energy was going to run short, but so long as cheap Middle Eastern oil continued, everyone wanted to take advantage of it. I am certain not only that Japan will survive, but that she will do well, because the Japanese have a capacity for working hard and for working well together that is unexcelled by any other people. My only concern is that, while Japan does well in adversity -- better than in prosperity, it seems to me -- in the process of dealing with this new challenge the Japanese people may again become inward-looking and less open to the world than they have learned to be. I don't think Japan is afraid of poverty -- Japanese people know very well how they have to behave when they are poor. But I hope people will not lose a certain generosity of spirit, a greatness of heart without which existence will necessarily seem mean and drab. We all have to rethink what are the fundamentals and get rid of frills and luxuries, but among these fundamentals richness of spirit is I think a most important element.
>
> Here in Europe also people are rethinking their lives, trying to sift out what is important and fundamental from what is trivial. There are countries like England which seem to be going through very difficult times. Then there is France, which on the whole is still quite smug and feeling fairly secure, both in terms of jobs and of supplies. To make a united Europe out of many disparate countries seems even more difficult today than two years ago -- but it has to be done.

Above: Excerpt from a letter to my father-in-law.

Throughout 1972, Henry Kissinger and his North Vietnamese counterpart, Le Duc Tho, held secret talks in and around Paris as the principal negotiators trying to end the Vietnam War. They would disappear for a while, and then somebody would find them in a villa in some suburb outside of town, and we reporters would chase after them.

Secrecy still wraps Kissinger-Tho talks

...There is some question as to why it has been necessary for the two so frequently to change their meeting places. The whole Kissinger-Tho series of encounters has come to resemble a traveling circus, with eagle-eyed photographers trailing both negotiators' official escorts to see what the next site might be...

— Takashi Oka for *The Christian Science Monitor,* Dec 7, 1972. Paris.

By December 1972, the secret negotiations had led to an agreement between the US and North Vietnam - although they didn't tell South Vietnamese President Thieu what the new agreement would be until they had finished the negotiations. Thieu was furious. However, the North had made a big concession, at least on paper, which was that the Saigon government could remain in power. Previously, the North had never recognized the South Vietnamese government as legitimate, claiming that they were puppets of the Americans.

But Thieu didn't want to accept the terms of the Peace Accords. For ordinary people in South Vietnam, the facts on the ground were that the Communists governed by night, and the South Vietnamese military governed only by day. People living in South Vietnam had to pay allegiance and taxes to both Saigon and Hanoi. Thieu wanted to change this and have all of South Vietnam for himself, and he opposed anything short of that. So he threatened to stop talking to the North unless Nixon could demonstrate that the US would continue to provide aid to South Vietnam. That was when Nixon ordered heavy bombings - Operation Linebacker II, or "The Christmas Bombings" - in North Vietnam, basically to demonstrate that he meant what he said. That in turn, got Thieu to agree to the terms, and the Paris Peace Accords were officially signed in January 1973.

It was a complicated signing agreement. The two adversaries held a separate ceremony several days after Kissinger and Tho had signed their agreement, which was basically identical to the one that they had drawn up three months before.

Western powers wanted the agreement to work. The Americans by then were thoroughly tired of the war – already three years had passed since the protests at Kent State. Inevitably, there was great pressure to make a public announcement. The Hotel Majestic, where the signings took place, was an old-fashioned building with glittering conference halls. Within, the North and South Vietnamese even argued about what kind of table to sit at – should it be a rectangle, where the two sides could face each other, or a circle, which the US wanted. In the end, they used a round table.

From a signing into the unknown

```
The real shape of the fitful peace that
came to Vietnam Sunday remains to be
worked out between the two principals
involved, Saigon and the Communist-led
National Liberation Front. The visible
signs are mixed. On the ground in South
Vietnam, fierce fighting was reported
hours after the cease-fire came into
effect
```

— Takashi Oka for *The Christian Science Monitor*, Jan 29, 1973. Paris.

The Peace Accords had little effect, because the facts on the ground had not changed. As the North Vietnamese never tired of saying, "Facts speak louder than words."

In December 1973, Kissinger and Le Duc Tho won the Nobel Peace Prize. I wasn't surprised, because the Nobel, like most awards, is a political affair. But I did think it was unusual to give it to the two adversaries. Tho refused to accept it at first, because the war was still going on – although he changed his mind in 1975.

Kissinger reassures an uneasy Europe

President Nixon, meanwhile, prepares to meet Soviet leader Brezhnev again, but this time amid the air of uncertainty that hangs over Washington in the wake of Watergate...

— Takashi Oka for *The Christian Science Monitor,* June 12, 1973. Paris.

Nixon's attempts to cover up, among other things, the secret bombing campaign in Cambodia led to the wire-tapping of US government officials, which led to the Watergate scandal. I think the atmosphere of those days was such that, as a journalist writing about Nixon, you had to assume you were being wire-tapped.

The war continued until 1975, when the North crossed the 17th parallel and Hanoi's regular troops occupied Saigon.

For a while there was considerable guerrilla activity by the South Vietnamese, many of whom were North Vietnamese anti-Communist Catholics who had strong motivations for fighting. But the bulk of them – 700,000 or so – had already become refugees in the South. Madame Nguyen Thi Binh, of the National Liberation Front, was representing them. She was from Ben Tre, a rich southern province, whose governor I knew. His name was Pham Ngoc Thao. He was a Communist who, although originally an appointee of Diem, had helped overthrow Diem in

1963. Thao himself was also assassinated after several more attempted coups. Ben Tre had been the province in which a large military ambush had taken place in 1959 – which some people cite as the start of the Vietnam War.

> "The words once spoken here resonated around the world. People who have never heard of Ben Tre know the phrase, uttered by an American major to Associated Press correspondent Peter Arnett, as together they surveyed the post-Tet devastation: 'It became necessary to destroy the town in order to save it.'"

* * * * *

In early 1974, Pompidou kept disappearing without explanation. I asked his public relations secretary, but he said that Pompidou was not ill, and added that he ate a lot of salt. He said if Pompidou was sick he would not eat salt. That was his argument. The major French hospital, Gralle, where all the famous people went, denied that he was in the hospital, but that is in fact where he was. Pompidou died in office April 1974.

* * * * *

We enjoyed our years in Paris. We were right in the middle of the city and loved to visit the museums and *hôtels particulier*. I walked by the lavish hotels every day to work – the Ritz, the Continental, the Meurice. On the right bank, the Rue de Rivoli goes down to the Place de la Concorde, and on the left, the two boulevards full of people, Saint-Germain and Saint-Michel, go down to the Seine. The Marais was where the fashionable people lived, though there were parts of it that were decaying. The Champs-Élysées was the most elegant part of town, but if you went up towards the Red Light district, where women danced the can-can, there were lots of good little restaurants. Of course, the food was excellent almost everywhere we went.

In some ways it might have been better to have stayed in Paris, and in some ways I wish we had. But I was the one who wanted to jump around so much – I suppose I had just gotten used to a peripatetic existence.

By August 1974, we had moved to London.

Chapter 14

London

The 1970s in London were an interesting period for us. We lived on the west side of London in Earl's Court, which, at that time, was the edge of gentrification. The more posh area of Kensington High Street was nearby, but our flat was on Earl's Court Road, which was a neighborhood of immigrants, mostly Australian. It was close to St. Paul's Girls' School, where Saya spent most of her high school years. Mimi also went to St. Paul's, but only for a couple of years before going to Harvard. I remember Saya had a paper route while we were there, dropping off newspapers at 7 a.m., and collecting presents from her clients at Christmas time.

Hiro was painting then. She had started out in Paris with a classical teacher, then she had a more abstract teacher in London, named Marian Kratochwil. Marian had been a student of the Scottish painter Dame Ethel Walker, and he ended up with many of her paintings, which he gradually sold off. We bought one of hers and several of his. Hiro studied with Marian at least once a week for five years. She would paint at our house in the living room, or at friends' houses, or at Marian's studio, where he had about eight students. She painted with oils, but got more interested in watercolors (which didn't smell quite as harsh), and she experimented with various things, including calligraphy. Then I also got interested in Marian because he was a Polish refugee who told fascinating stories about wartime. It was also in these years that we went to our first art auction, at Christie's in London.

During our London years, I went on a lecture circuit, speaking on current events to Christian Science audiences. There was a series of meetings in London and Paris, as well as in York,

Newcastle, Edinburgh, Gloucester, and Brighton. These meetings were organized by the local Christian Science churches, and various reporters for the *Monitor* were asked to give talks on their area of expertise. In spite of my background on East Asia, I lectured on the thorny situation between Israel and Palestine.

One meeting was held in the small but lively city of Bonn, which at that time was the capital of Germany. For a long time people wondered if the divided Berlin could ever again be the capital. It seemed as if the division of Europe would be permanent, because the Russians were solidly in control of Eastern Europe, and they were not about to give it up. All through that period of the Cold War, West Berlin remained an isolated island in the midst of a Communist sea.

* * * * *

I was the *Monitor's* chief European correspondent, based in London, which meant I covered all of Europe from Greece to Norway. I ended up in Norway more than once because NATO held meetings there – way up in the Arctic Circle in the spring and summer, when the sun never sets.

Norway was in the news then because of a controversial new pipeline connecting Britain to the North Sea oil reserves. Buried deep under one of the most turbulent seas in the world, the oil was difficult to obtain and to transport, and very soon there were a couple of big accidents – an explosion and a spill.

I covered these events in a series of articles about the world's resources, renewable energy, and other environmental issues. One series, titled "Managing Our Planet," expressed some of the frustration at that time towards America, where people still drove their gas-guzzling cars even after the oil crisis. That series took me around the world again, from Bangladesh to Iran, where the Shah was still in power (I interviewed him at another time in Paris). I went to Tehran, Isfahan, and Persepolis, the capital under Alexander the Great, then back to Japan and on to London.

I also wrote about the efforts to end animal testing in commercial and medical labs, as well as the anti-whaling campaign, which became a fraught issue between Japan and the West.

> **Friends of whales fish for compromise acceptable to all**
>
> To the Japanese, the whale is a fish — not a mammal. The ideograph that stands for whale contains an element signifying fish.
>
> There are "protect whale" groups in Japan, where environmental protest groups are almost as active as in Europe and America. But somehow there does not seem to be the strong emotional bias in favor of the whale that exists in the West.
>
> "After all, we never heard of Jonah," said one Japanese delegate...
>
> — Takashi Oka for *The Christian Science Monitor*, June 26, 1975. London.

I also went to Rome to cover the Food and Agriculture Administration of the UN summit about the world food crisis. The biggest difficulty there was the apathy that most northern countries had towards those with less resources - the divide between northern and southern Europe was as visible then as it is now. This was also during the years of expanding the European Economic Community (EEC), on the premise of unifying Europe, which, of course, people have tried to do since Charlemagne. Kissinger delivered the keynote address in Rome - he was in

Europe quite a lot in those years. At one point he went to Wales, where he was met by protestors decrying the situation in Cyprus, the Chilean coup, and a list of other controversies that followed him around.

Another environmental concern involved the Concorde. Everybody was talking about this airplane – which was the first supersonic commercial jet, with speeds up to Mach 2 – and its distinctive shape, with a sleek, sloped nose. As a passenger on a publicity campaign, I didn't feel that it was particularly fast because it was so comfortable and quiet, but it had a large speedometer displayed so we would all know when we passed the sound barrier. All the seats, of course, were first class.

* * * * *

I was in Lisbon, covering the first anniversary of the Carnation Revolution, when Saigon fell – or was liberated, depending on one's point of view. As I thought back on the years spent reporting from Saigon, I was glad to be in Lisbon, where the parades, hammer and sickle banners, and shouting all had a peaceful, festive atmosphere.

* * * * *

Back in London, the IRA was bombing restaurants, hotels, and pubs in the heart of the city, as well as elsewhere in the UK. I was impressed by how Londoners kept going to their restaurants, shops, and theaters, wanting their usual life to go on. As "the Troubles" continued, I spent a lot of time traveling back and forth between independent Ireland and Northern Ireland, and I reported from the embattled city of Belfast.

What life has become in Belfast

"Uncle Jack, where's the searcher?" asked the four-year-old from Belfast on his first visit to a London store.

Normal life in Northern Ireland means being frisked at entrances to stores, restaurants, hotels, and office buildings. It means listening to radio news bulletins about bombings or other terrorist incidents, so as to know what parts of town or what streets to avoid.

It is easy for an outsider to propose solutions, but the lesson of the past seven years, as Secretary of State for Northern Ireland Merlyn Rees tirelessly repeats, is that a permanent solution can only come from within the Northern Irish community itself.

Currently Northern Ireland is under direct British rule, which looks as if it will continue for at least two to three years, because the British will not withdraw until the two communities, Protestant and Roman Catholic, reach an agreement on how to share power...

— Takashi Oka for *The Christian Science Monitor*, Aug 27, 1976. Belfast.

For me, Northern Ireland was a particularly delicate area. Ulster is the Protestant English stronghold in Ireland, and so there was a Christian Science Church in Belfast. Local Christian Scientists were very much on the Protestant side of the fight, and they objected to any stories that, to their mind, glorified the Roman Catholics. I don't think my articles glorified either side. But people from all over the world – but mostly from England – wrote very meticulous letters to me at the *Monitor*, to make sure I upheld the Protestant side. Some of them didn't like the fact that I was Japanese – that I wasn't English enough to write about this issue, or to be the *Monitor's* London correspondent in the first place.

Meanwhile, there was a very bitter and very real dispute going on, which I had to cover. In one incident, a famous British politician was killed – Parliament member Airey Neave, who was assassinated just outside the Palace at Westminster.

Killing of Neave casts shadow on British campaign

Britain's general election campaign begins this week under the chilling shadow of a political assassination.

Members of Parliament of all political parties who mourned the March 30 car-bomb killing of their Tory colleague Airey Neave by suspected Irish terrorists know that there is little they can do physically to protect themselves from similar attempts.

Like the shopkeepers of Northern Ireland who put up "business as usual" signs as soon as they have swept up the debris from the previous night's bombing, politicians feel they cannot allow terror to cut them off from open daily contacts with the voters.

— Takashi Oka for *The Christian Science Monitor*, Apr 2, 1979. London.

I was glad to be working for the *Monitor* and for my friend John Hughes, who was still the editor then. He started out in journalism when he was 16 in South Africa, and he was a responsible newsman. There's a tension between the most sensational news you can get for that particular day, and the underlying trends, which may not be so visible, but which are important in the long run. You have to have antenna for both to be successful. I think Hughes made the *Monitor* much more relevant in terms of world news than it had been before.

*****

My years with the *Monitor* in London coincided with the rise of Margaret Thatcher. She became the head of the Conservative party in 1974 and Prime Minister in 1979. For that five-year period, she was the Opposition leader against the Labour Party (led by Harold Wilson, then James Callaghan), which struggled to deal with continual crises, from union strikes to the violence in Northern Ireland.

Mrs. Thatcher first rose to power within the Conservative party against Edward Heath. By 1974, many people thought Heath belonged to the past. Margaret Thatcher was a new figure – a crisp, bright, and assertive woman. She had gone to Oxford on a scholarship and graduated with a chemistry degree. But she also proudly asserted that she always made breakfast for her husband, no matter how busy her day was.

Heath was dismissive of this young upstart. Conservative party members insisted on an open fight for the leadership, and Mrs. Thatcher won. The conservative establishment was stunned.

Margaret Thatcher: the woman who could become Britain's next Prime Minister

"Pure stainless steel" is how one colleague describes the woman who would become Prime Minister, in the event of a Conservative Party comeback at the next elections…

— Takashi Oka for *The Christian Science Monitor*, Apr 17, 1975. Sheffield, England.

It wasn't my perspicacity as a political journalist to predict, four years in advance, that she would become Prime Minister, it was just the general atmosphere. British conservatives liked her crisp, decisive views, and even some of the Labourites were impressed by her "workers not shirkers" message. Meanwhile, the Labour party was divided between its own left and right wings about many issues, especially joining the EEC. So Thatcher swept in as an uncompromising leader.

I had a solo interview with her, and we got into a big argument over France's status in NATO. For many years, France, under socialist administrations, was not cooperating with the European military, so France withdrew from the military part, and remained a member of the political alliance. But Mrs. Thatcher kept saying to me that France was not a member of NATO at all. I tried to explain the distinction, but she kept insisting and saying "France is not a member of NATO." And I said, "Excuse me, but it is a member of the political alliance, it just doesn't participate in the military side of the alliance." She just wouldn't hear it. You can't really argue with her – she's the Prime Minister. So she just kept her opinion and I kept mine.

* * * * *

The winter of 1979 saw the culmination of protests and strikes against years of economic hardship in the UK. Continental Europe was not in very good shape either, but England was worse. British workers were looking at the Belgians, who did the same work but for almost twice the wage. By February of 1979, over 1.5 million British public workers were on strike. It was a strange period because the British are usually so orderly, but for those weeks the streets were littered with garbage. You could see it – and smell it – everywhere, including our own neighborhood.

Britons' patience with strikes wears thin

In London's Golden Square, behind fashionable Regent Street, a gardener lovingly tends his neatly trimmed rosebushes, surrounded by an Everest-high pile of black plastic rubbish bags. A cleaner from one of the smart offices surrounding the square drags over a roll of carpeting to add to the base of the towering pyramid.

With hundreds of schools closed, more than a thousand hospitals reduced to emergency operations only, and wage demands spreading on numerous fronts, the hard-pressed Labor government, with traditionally close ties to the unions, is facing an increasingly embittered public...

— Takashi Oka for *The Christian Science Monitor*, Feb 8, 1979. London.

Around the same time, Scotland and, to some extent, Wales were making a push for independence. Meanwhile, the Northern Ireland conflict continued on. But all these events tended to strengthen and toughen Thatcher. To her, everything was black and white. After Neave's assassination, Thatcher appealed to the British sense of stability and tradition, and in May she won the general election. While everyone was talking about how she would be the first woman to become prime minister, she pointed out that she would be the first prime minister to have a science degree.

Margaret Thatcher

> Far more than any other Conservative politician of the postwar period, Mrs. Thatcher has within her the temperament of an Old Testament prophet.
>
> She really does believe that the socialist state becomes a pharaoh holding her countrymen in bondage. She really does feel there is "no hope for Britain, no change for perpetual decline," unless taxes are cut…
>
> — Takashi Oka for *The Christian Science Monitor*, May 1, 1979. London.

Margaret Thatcher was a very confrontational person. She absolutely refused to compromise with the striking labor unions. She also refused to compromise on the issue of Scottish independence. Scotland and Wales wanted to be inside the EU but separate from England. Instead she wanted Britain to be more strongly allied with the US than with continental Europe. Consequently, she was popular among the American right, and she and Reagan became conservative icons.

The labor strikes of that period also affected British newspapers. Some were shut down temporarily, and *The Times* shut down for nearly a year. The *Monitor*, being a smaller paper and funded by the church, kept publishing throughout. But this was also during the shift away from the traditional methods of printing, towards new computerized systems. The newspapers' offices suddenly became just like any other office - the interactions between linotypists, writers, and printers was changing, and the smell of ink had gone.

* * * * *

In 1977, I was president of the Association of American Correspondents in London. One of the big perks was being invited to the Queen's garden parties at Buckingham Palace - I went there a number of times. I would get a fancy invitation card, which I had to present at the entrance. My office received four, which I gave to the staff and secretaries, who were very happy to meet the Queen.

Strolling at the Queen's tea party

Although plummy upper-crust accents predominate amidst the floral hats and the tightly furled umbrellas, the atmosphere is one of a fairly decorous family gathering.

The Queen herself, and the members of the royal family who proceed down their respective lanes to the royal tea tent, contribute to the sense of family togetherness. Despite the stiff protocol that keeps her military attendants walking backward ahead of her to make sure she has sufficient space, the Queen puts her guests at ease as she stops here and there to chat, either spontaneously or with pre-selected guests.

The day is perfect — a soft, blue summer sky, with enough breeze to keep the sun cool even as it casts a mellow light on the yellow facade of Buckingham Palace. On this garden side, facing a vista of trees and a small lake, the palace looks more like a stately country mansion than it does from the front, where ambassadors still drive up in horse-drawn carriages to present their credentials and tourists gape from beyond the railings at the daily ritual of the changing of the guard.

And what happens when it rains?

"Oh," said a palace attendant, "the Queen just holds up her umbrella and carries on. The parties are never cancelled, unless the ground gets so soggy the ladies' shoes start sinking in."

— Takashi Oka for *The Christian Science Monitor*, July 27, 1978. London.

I was a member of two press clubs – the Foreign Press Association and a separate club for American correspondents, the AACL, of which I was president for a year. The clubs were a way to meet people and ask for a press conference by a particular political leader, specifically tailored to our interests. I also joined the Reform Club, which is one of the grand old clubs in an elegant building on Pall Mall, where we held receptions for various politicians, including Mrs. Thatcher. As a journalist, the more you saw these people, the easier it was to chat with them.

* * * * *

In 1975, I interviewed David Attenborough for the first time. I really enjoyed him. He made for an easy interviewee, because no matter what subject came up, he had an opinion about it – and a pretty interesting one, too. He had been in charge of programming at the BBC, but he liked to go out and move around, rather than sit in an office.

Attenborough: BBC's man about the world

"Ever since the 16th century," he said, "Western man has overrun the world and imposed on every part of it his own model of organizing the West. Extraordinarily enough, it has never occurred to any of us until the last 50 years that we could be wrong, and it's only now that we are beginning to realize there are very serious shortcomings in our own society."

"Now the essence of homo sapiens has been — speaking as a biologist — that he is enormously versatile, that he has been able to adapt, to change his buildings, to change his family structure, to change his community organization to suit every known living space in the world."

"But we are progressively losing that, so that there are very few examples left of other ways of living, other ways of being human."

"It would be silly for me to try to argue that just because a society is simple, or they don't wear clothes, or they don't have rights, or it's primitive — that it's better than ours. I'm not arguing any such thing. What I am saying is that in the first place, people have a right to live the way they want to, and it behooves us to allow them to do so, and secondly that as human beings we all face very similar problems. We face similar problems about death, or growing old, or bringing up children, or how to be happy or unhappy, and amongst all these [tribal] societies, they all have certain answers, some of which maybe could help us to get new perspectives on our own problems."

— Takashi Oka for *The Christian Science Monitor*, Oct 10, 1975. London.

Attenborough and I talked at length about the social function of art, both in relation to the tribal societies he was studying and to our own. It was a topic that I picked up again that year when I interviewed the American artist Charles Eames.

American takes the bicentennial to Europe

Eames is shocked by the extent to which Americans of today "let specialization compartmentalize us."

For instance, if there is an aesthetic problem to be solved, "people say, that's fine arts." But streets and sidewalks, the soup you are fed in restaurants, the bread you eat — all these come within the scope of aesthetics, Mr. Eames says. "Even ceremony."

That led, in turn, to his comment on the lost art of celebration. "A real celebration comes out of adversity," Mr. Eames maintains. "Our last real one came out of the depression, and culturally the United States has lived off it ever since."

De Kooning, Jackson Pollock, Dorothea Lang, Tennessee Williams, Ben Shawn, Charles Eames himself — all were drawn through the WPA (Works Progress Administration) into a network of exploding ideas that embraced the U.S.

"You could feel the functioning of a network take off," says Mr. Eames. "I don't think you can recover it now. We've lost the vocabulary."

Not entirely, however. The agony of Watergate, combined with Vietnam and the economic crisis — perhaps out of these elements of adversity could come a new celebration of the American dream. What does Mr. Eames think?

"That's the great hope," he rejoined. "In a way this is happening already."

And for the British, for whom the independence of the U.S. can never have quite the same meaning it has across the Atlantic, Mr. Eames also has words of comfort.

"When a daughter leaves the family to start a new life," he said, "the trauma of that separation can be like a battle, or a war. But nobody thinks of it as the daughter's victory, or the mother's defeat. Four, six, ten years go by, and everyone comes together to celebrate the setting up of the new household."

— Takashi Oka for *The Christian Science Monitor*, Oct 15, 1975. London.

My own daughters were leaving the parental nest during these years. Mimi left for Harvard in 1977, and Saya went to boarding school at Milton Academy in Massachusetts in 1979.

* * * * *

By the late 1970s, the "great imperial family" of Britain had been shrinking for decades, while more members of the extended family had steadily moved to the inner cities of the British Isles. Originally, if a person was a citizen of a Commonwealth country, he or she could come into England without restrictions. Then the British made it more difficult for non-Britons to enter. Many people came through North Africa and got as far as France, but were stuck at the Channel. The port towns of Calais, Dieppe, and Cherbourg were full of people who would spend years waiting for an opportunity to sneak across.

Those who did make it to Britain found themselves a part of huge immigrant populations – Indian and Pakistani were the largest, but there were also smaller communitites from Sri Lanka and the West Indies.

Margaret Thatcher capitalized on the sentiment that these immigrants posed a cultural threat to the traditional British identity. I found that peculiar. The British had a very insular, almost tribal, conception of "their people," even from the Scots and the Irish. Over time, racial prejudices grew more pronounced, and anti-immigration protests were held across the UK, and tensions festered for years before exploding into riots in 1981.

I interviewed people across the UK who were from these various communities – from Guyanan policemen in Peckham, to Barbadian community-relations workers in Wellingborough and elsewhere. No matter where in England I went, the immigrant population was often impoverished.

Britain's race rumblings

More and more Britons seem to be exercised about the presence in their midst of approximately 1.8 million Asian and West Indian immigrants and their British-born children. Britain's population of either West Indian or Indo-Pakistani origin forms less than 4 percent of the country's total population. But it tends to be concentrated in inner-city or suburban ghettos in London, the Midlands, and the industrial cities of the north.

The opposition Conservative Party picked up an 11-point lead over Labourites after party leader Margaret Thatcher's much-quoted remarks on non-white immigration.

Labourites have angrily retorted that Mrs. Thatcher was "making racial hatred respectable."

— Takashi Oka for *The Christian Science Monitor*, March 6, 1978. London.

In the midst of all the protests and occasional outbursts of violence, I was generally impressed by the way British authorities policed their cities. The British police didn't carry guns. If an extreme situation required firearms, such as a standoff with IRA militants, then they would call in an Army division. Otherwise, they had only a stick and helmet. French and other European police carried arms, and of course the Americans. But that was the kind of society Britain was.

Keeping the Queen's Peace

"If I had to carry arms as a part of my normal equipment, I would resign." said police constable Peter Smith. "I think it's totally unnecessary."

In 18 years on the Metropolitan Police Force, Mr. Smith has used his truncheon only once — during the so-called St. Pancras bread riots when police were ordered to charge the rioters.

"In the day that we give up the truncheon for firearms, the day of the British police as we know it will be gone forever."

— Takashi Oka for *The Christian Science Monitor*, Dec 15, 1977. London.

For one story, I spent a night riding in a patrol car with the police. We ended up on a car chase, racing around in the dead of night - and yet the police wouldn't put their siren on, because they were conscious of the general public and always tried to keep the night quiet. So they just gave short little bursts on the horn. After the story ran, I took my new friends to dinner. They brought their wives, and Hiro came, too, and we had a nice dinner at the old Post Office Cafe.

* * * * *

In March 1978, the former Prime Minister of Italy, Aldo Moro, was kidnapped by a terrorist group called the Red Brigades. He was killed by his captors, but the story kept me in Italy for a month. I traveled from Rome to Umbria and Tuscany and down to Naples, and wrote an article comparing the city of Florence to Detroit. Both cities were decaying, and the Florentine mayor flew to Detroit to see it himself. Florence had always had tourism, but in the end it also got a lot of help from the government to rebuild. Detroit had cars, but then the cars left.

Another big story was the Lockheed scandal. Lockheed had bribed various governments to buy its planes, and the scandal involved many prominent figures, including Prince Bernhard of the Netherlands and Japan's Prime Minister Tanaka, who was ousted because of his role. Tanaka had been all set for a long stay as Prime Minister, but it was discovered that he had taken over $3 million in bribes. He was arrested in 1976, and was on trial for almost seven years – Japanese trials take a notoriously long time. During the early stages, the newspapers were full of stories about Tanaka's life behind bars, including his new diet of prison food.

* * * * *

In 1979, I had my heart set on becoming the State Department correspondent in Washington DC. We'd been in London for five years, and I had always wanted to be stationed in DC, but then China opened up.

No American journalist had been allowed into China for decades. Then in 1979, China and the US signed an agreement for an exchange of correspondents, and I had the opportunity to go. It was a last-minute opportunity, so I asked the family what I should do. Hiro and the children discussed it, and they said that they wanted to go to China. This surprised me, because I thought that Mimi and Saya would prefer Washington, but they all wanted to go to China. The girls were growing up and going off to college and boarding school then, but they would have the chance to visit us in Beijing in the summers.

It was the summer of 1979, and we didn't know how long it would take for the visas to come through, so we moved back to Japan. During that period of limbo, I did stories on South Korea, Thailand, Afghanistan, and Laos. Japan's economy was still booming. Ohira had just run a successful campaign for prime minister. He was one of the few Japanese prime ministers who was a Protestant Christian, but he was only in office a short while. In July 1980, Ohira suddenly fell into a coma and died.

In the summer of 1979, I covered President Carter's visit to Japan, including a town hall meeting in Shimoda, where he answered every question, no matter how difficult. He didn't dodge the tough ones. That summer saw the Tokyo summit of Western leaders, where the energy crisis was still the focus. Those yearly summits forced the Japanese to be more forthcoming in global relations.

I followed President Carter to South Korea, which was about to go through a major transition. I interviewed Kim Dae Jung, the South Korean opposition leader, who was under house arrest. After Kim had fared well in the 1971 election against President Park, Park had the Korean CIA kidnap Kim from his Tokyo hotel and bring him back to Seoul. Then he changed the constitution, effectively banning direct elections. It was a dangerous time, but we journalists could still go – for a while anyway. South Korea had been through a spate of these kinds of changes – free at one moment, then clamped down by the government the next.

I also interviewed a South Korean dissident whom I had met about twenty years earlier. Our first encounter was when Seoul opened up after Syngman Rhee, and "David," as I called him, had survived the shootings and hangings that followed the student protests.

South Korean dissidents: one generation later

David and his friends spoke in guarded tones as they met me in coffee parlors and pungent Korean restaurants they had introduced me to earlier. The new government had embarked on an austerity program. Imported coffee being no longer available, we were served bitter ginseng and pine-nut tea. Some of David's student acquaintances had gone to work for the newly created Korean Central Intelligence Agency. Other friends had been arrested by the same agency. No one was quite sure who was to be trusted.

Seoul was almost unrecognizably changed. Twenty-story skyscrapers raised their heads where clusters of sloping tile-roofed Korean houses had been. Men with A-frames were rare, and so were shoeshine boys. A Korean shoeshine is still the most mirror-bright in the world, but at 70 cents a shine, it costs ten times what it did in the early 1960s.

David took me to a succession of Korean eateries, sometimes with his family, sometimes with his friends. Once, in the best Korean kalbi (charcoal-grilled ribs

> of beef) restaurant in the East Gate market, we each had 12 cloves of garlic — one for each piece of kalbi wrapped in a lettuce leaf. On previous visits I almost always paid the bill; this time, David insisted on doing the honors. He does not yet have a car, but otherwise he has fulfilled most of his material ambitions: his own apartment, refrigerator, television set, and piano (he still finds a stereo too expensive). His wife takes piano and swimming lessons.
>
> So I was surprised when, out of the blue as we were sipping frothy white soybean soup in a popular snack bar, David asked me how he could emigrate to the United States...
>
> — Takashi Oka for *The Christian Science Monitor,* Aug 24, 1979. Seoul.

Two months later, I was back in Seoul covering Park's assassination. He was killed by his own CIA chief.

* * * * *

After about six months, the visas finally came through. Hiro and I got to China just before Thanksgiving of 1979. Earlier that summer, I came through Boston and had a nice lunch at the house of Earl Foell, who by then was the *Monitor's* editor. At that time we knew we were going to China, and Hiro said to Earl: "Don't keep us there too long."

We ended up staying in China for five years, which was long enough.

Chapter 15

Beijing

The most exciting part about moving to China was that it was unknown. It was not just the city of Beijing (then still called Peking by most Westerners) but the whole country that was new to us. So there was a lot we had to learn.

According to the original agreement, there was to be an equal number of journalists exchanged between the US and China. But because of how strictly China controlled the number of its newspapers, there were far more American news organizations that wanted to come to China. By the time we finally arrived at the Qianmen Hotel in Beijing, there were about eighty American and European journalists in the group.

When Hiro and I got to Beijing, the Chinese Information Ministry was still in the process of building sufficient housing for all the Western correspondents. They said they would be finished in the spring. In the meantime we all had to wait at the Qianmen until proper housing became available, lined up in order of our applications. The agencies – AP, Reuters, and UPI – and *The New York Times* were in the first batch, and the *Monitor* was later on. That process took us a couple of years – which meant that Hiro and I lived in the Qianmen Hotel for the next two years, along with many other journalists.

Bruce Dunning from CBS called our group "the Qianmen Commune," because we all lived in the hotel together. We had our meals together, every day, as if we were in a boarding house. A few journalists stayed at the Beijing Hotel, which was like the Waldorf Astoria of China, although the prices between the Beijing and the Qianmen were not so different in those days. When Earl Foell came to visit (by then he was editor of the *Monitor*), he stayed at the Beijing Hotel. By contrast, we found out later that our hotel had at one point had served as a detention center for prisoners.

Some correspondents had been training for years for this opportunity, while others knew very little about China. I had studied Chinese history at Harvard and spoke some Chinese, so I managed okay. But, in a way, nobody had a particular advantage, because China was new to all of us, and we were treated equally by the Chinese authorities. They would address us every day as one group, and we would frequently make group trips to a village or a neighborhood where an "event" was orchestrated by the Chinese authorities. Everything we did was hedged with restrictions. There was nothing we could do that the Chinese authorities would not immediately know about. We were in Beijing on assignment, and yet, to the Chinese authorities, we were all Western spies coming to snoop on them.

Hiro and I could pass as Chinese, to some degree. Our clothes and everything else would have given us away, so we bundled up in Chinese clothing when we went outside. I could pass for Chinese in appearance, but when I spoke, my accent gave away my disguise. Hiro also passed as an "overseas Chinese," because many Chinese had relatives in other parts of Asia. She would meet people on the bus stop or somewhere and see if they would want to speak Japanese or English. One couple did, and they advised her how to dress more appropriately, so she bought a Chinese jacket. Then they told her she should walk slowly. They invited her to their house, and eventually she introduced me. We met some young couples and artists and writers in that way, and became friends with them. But we later found out, in talking with one of our contacts, that despite our precautions, the Chinese authorities knew exactly where we were at all times.

We had an office in the Qianmen Hotel with a translator and a driver. But the hotel staff always took a nap right after lunch – they said they had "the right to take a nap for two hours" on a bed in the office. Lunch was at noon, and they didn't have to come back to work until 2:30, so they would sleep. That was their rest period, and it was quite sacred – we couldn't get them to change it. Generally a lot of Chinese would take breaks from 12 p.m. - 2 p.m., and nothing much would happen during that period. Such was the state of affairs when we got to China, and probably had been since the end of the Cultural Revolution. When we came back home after lunch, we had to tiptoe while they snored. Eventually some of our fellow correspondents wrote about the custom in the newspapers, which shamed them into stopping, but naps like that went on for at least the first six months of our stay.

I found Beijing in some ways an easier place to live than Moscow. The two cities were similar in that they were both under monolithic Communist regimes. But while in Russia it was difficult to get supplies of foreign goods, it was easier in China. There were even more English language bookstores in Beijing than in Moscow (of course, Russia had been a Communist country for thirty years longer than China). When we were in Russia, fresh lettuce had to be imported by train from Helsinki, which was the closest free-world city. In Beijing, supplies of certain items were somewhat limited, but as time went on that situation improved. Some of the journalists would shop at the airport, where they could stock up on cigarettes and candy. Groceries in Beijing came from government-run stores, which would have certain foods in bulk. But sometimes they just didn't have items – like fruit. You learned to grab what you could and do the best you could with it.

China's Everyman has to scramble for basics

```
Some children in Peking are forced to
attend  classes  under  the  trees  because
their    schools    do    not    have    enough
```

classrooms. In an industrial district of Wuhan, a worker who wants to buy pork ribs for stewing must get up at 3 or 4 a.m. and stand in a queue until 7.

These are some of the problems workers and their families face in rapidly growing industrial districts where the amenities of living have fallen far behind the expansion of housing.

Chaoyang, in Peking, has a population of more than 880,000, with over 500 factories and a worker population of 350,000. But it has only two small cinemas and one workers' club.

A hall of culture built by the Central Ministry of Culture in 1958 was destroyed during the Cultural Revolution. Nine months ago, city authorities decided to build a large theater, but nothing has happened….

— Takashi Oka for *The Christian Science Monitor*, Nov 14, 1979. Peking.

For Western journalists, it was an exciting year. The smallest changes in Chinese life were newsworthy. There were millions of bicycles and not many cars, so when the first private cars appeared they caused a sensation. Hiro and I remember the first time we saw a Chinese girl wearing lipstick, or when a woman wore a stylish dress for the first time. And then we saw a dog in Beijing – someone's own pet on a leash. Until then, dogs were food. Eventually these changes translated into larger steps, like the privatization of land and the dismantling of the commune system.

Also in that first year, we met Sidney Rittenberg and his wife Wang Yulin. Sidney was a journalist and linguist who had translated for Mao, and who had been imprisoned twice for several years on charges of espionage. When we met him, he had recently been released from his second imprisonment, and we invited them to Qianmen. It was there that Yulin recognized a wing of our hotel as the place where she had once been detained.

Dissent is a divisive issue for Peking leaders

An intense debate apparently is going on within the establishment here over the extent to which dissent should be tolerated in a communist society.

On Nov. 11, Public Security forces broke up a crowd queuing to buy copies of the Wei Jingsheng trial transcript at Peking's Xidan "democracy wall." They seized the transcripts, scuffled with the crowd, and arrested several people.

Mr. Wei, currently China's best-known dissident, has been sentenced to 15 years for alleged sale of military secrets and counter-revolutionary activities.

Since the handwritten poster version of the transcript has been on the wall for weeks, the lesson local intellectuals draw from the incident is that the authorities will continue to tolerate the wall itself, but not the sale of printed matter they consider "poisonous."

Li Qing, editor of the April 5 Forum, a magazine that printed the transcript, has also been arrested and is said to be under investigation regarding how he managed to obtain a tape of the Wei trial.

The Nov. 13 article [in People's Daily] reports a speech by Li Bai Hua at the recent writers' congress in Peking. Mr. Li is an Army writer who was branded a rightist 20 years ago and was forced to remain silent until the fall of the "gang of four," headed by Chairman Mao's widow, [Jiang Qing], in October, 1976.

Mr. Li not only criticizes the dark years of the Cultural Revolution, but also says that even today there are writers who do not dare keep diaries and young authors who cannot be published in any of the established magazines. He refers to the execution of Zhang Zhixin (Miss Chang Chih-hsin) in the mid 1970s and calls her a "martyr whose blood awakens more and more people."
(Miss Jiang was a party member who was sentenced to death for daring to criticize the "gang of four" — some say even Chairman Mao himself — at party meetings)

Finally, he pins his hope on the young and says, "Have courage. Without courage there will be no breakthrough, and without a breakthrough there will be no literature."

— Takashi Oka for *The Christian Science Monitor,* Nov 20, 1979. Peking.

Wei Jingsheng was the first conspicuous dissident who wrote openly on Democracy Wall, which was a brick wall at the intersection of Chang-an Boulevard and Xidan, in the center of Beijing. People started putting up posters on this stretch of wall and making speeches, and it became a gathering place. But if too many people showed up, the police would either arrest them or scare them away, so they had to be discreet. Whether at night or during the day, something was always going on there. Since Wei Jingsheng's writings were banned, you could read them on the wall, but you had to copy them yourself.

From their viewpoint, the Chinese authorities were experimenting. They wanted to ease their controls somewhat, but there was no agreement as to what the final restrictions should be. You couldn't openly criticize the Communist government, but you could criticize individual leaders if you could show that they were corrupt, or in some way breaking the law. But you couldn't do it on the basis of freedom of speech. Everything you said had to be justified in Communist terms. This was similar to the old Confucian precept that individual character is held in higher regard than the law. So if someone breaks the public's trust because of a flaw in their character, then it becomes possible to criticize them.

Hiro and I had a good friend, Liu Nienling, who was a Chinese American writer who had published fiction and essays in several well-known literary magazines around China. We had known her in the late 1950s, at the Harvard-Yenching Institute, where she and Hiro both worked in the library deciphering Chinese characters. Nienling and Hiro had children around the same time in 1959. When we moved to China, Nienling was frequently visiting Shanghai. I would see her when I reported from there, and she would come to see us in Beijing. Being a writer herself, she introduced us to a circle of literary people, both men and women.

The most famous of those writers was Wang Meng. He was a national figure, one of the first modern Chinese writers to become well-known in the West. He was not a declared dissident, but in a way he was exploring the outer limits of a published writer's freedom, sometimes employing fairly penetrating criticism. We also met a poet named Jiang Jie, and I met Li Bai Hua, but not Wei Jingsheng, who was in jail at the time.

We also became acquainted with several painters, such as Yang Yanping and Zeng Shanqing were professors at Tsinghua University. They were a cute couple. She was in college when he was a professor there – she loved his lectures on the arts, and eventually they fell in love and got married. He had been trained as a classic Chinese painter, and she had gone to the Academy of Western Art in Beijing. During the Cultural Revolution she had to paint billboards of Mao's portrait, but Zeng's work was deemed objectionable by the authorities, and he was sent off to the countryside for a couple of years. When we first visited our new friends, they had just two rooms – one room for Zeng's mother and son, and the other room for himself and Yang. There was no space to paint, so they worked on the bed.

Whether in China or in Russia, there were many talented people who were prevented from showing the full scope of their gifts because of censorship – and from isolation from the rest of the world. These artists were hungry for knowledge of Western trends and forms, so we supplied them with art books whenever we could.

Today Zeng and Yang are prominent painters, and we are still friends. They eventually could sell their paintings, and now they have a house with a swimming pool on Long Island. When we first met them, Yang had said she had two great desires: she wanted space to work on her paintings, and she wanted to take a bath every day. Now she can.

* * * * *

Every so often we would get together with a small group of writers and artists for dinner. That was different than in Moscow, where we had also met with dissident writers and intellectuals, but where the food was sort of standard Western fare and not terribly interesting. In Beijing, a traditional Chinese dinner could be huge, and full of different dishes. There was one dish that was called "grass in the summer and worm in the winter," or at least that's what people said. It was somewhat of a rarity, but pretty tasty. Food was important to us, because there wasn't really much else besides eating that we were allowed to do. There were the official restaurants to which we had been referred – one was in a hotel called the Democracy Hotel – but we preferred the local fare.

Even though the Chinese began to have dogs as pets, they still ate them. I never did so – the smell was too strong, as was the association. I think it must be an acquired taste. I had a very good Chinese friend who found it difficult to understand why Westerners would have dogs as pets but not eat them, whereas to him they were delicious to eat but could also be pets. In Hong Kong, the British considered the practice barbaric – and passed laws banning it. You had to go out of the city, to a village in Kowloon, where rich people would go to eat dog.

Snake soup was considered a great delicacy. It didn't come out looking like snake, but more like shredded chicken – although one time I saw a cook take a live snake and, holding it by the head, just strip the skin off with a single, quick gesture, and then put it in the soup. Snake is a winter dish that's supposed to warm the insides of your body.

Morning exotica

A well-traveled friend once told me that breakfasts are among the severest tests of acculturation. You might be able to face sheep's eyes or bear's claws at some exotic banquet. But for breakfast you long for simple toast and marmalade.

I was reminded of this remark years ago, during my first visit to Vietnam. I had gone there wide-eyed from graduate school, determined to "meet the real people," whoever they might be. I had arranged for myself a fabulous tour of the Mekong Delta, dripping with local color. My hosts were members of the Cao Dai sect, whose pantheon included Lao-Tzu and Li Po, Buddha and Victor Hugo.

In a restaurant by the muddy Mekong, as wide as the Mississippi in flood, I had a marvelous Sino-Vietnamese dinner. According to my notes, it included baby oysters, lobster, ducks feet, pork stomach, roast pigeon, various kinds of salad and a crab and mushroom soup flavored with coriander. I learned to say *ngon lam* (delicious) and *no roi* (I've had plenty, thank you), and from the middle of the feast both expressions punctuated my every sentence.

In the morning I was awakened about four o'clock by the sound of a bell. Softly peering into the front room, I saw a Cao Dai priest in white robe and long beard, murmuring prayers, burning incense, and striking a bell in front of the altar common to all Cao Dai households. From all around the courtyard came similar sounds.

In tingling good humor and with a pleasantly anticipatory appetite I sat down with the family for the first meal of the day.

Then suddenly, with the first steaming bowl of congee, heavily flavored with coriander and with bits of meat floating in pools of fat, culture shock hit me. The night before I had found coriander in the crab-and-mushroom soup fragrant and delicious. This morning it was an alien smell. The meats in the congee seemed alien; the vegetables likewise; even the rice gruel, the main element in last night's soup, repelled me. I could not rise from the table without being rude, so I sipped my congee without enthusiasm. When my hosts, out of politeness, asked me what kind of breakfasts I usually had, a wave of homesickness assailed me.

And yet I took pride in my bicultural heritage. Japanese born, of parents who had lived in America, I was equally at home with scrambled eggs and toast, or rice and soybean soup. There had been just one oversight on my parents' part: they had failed to include coriander and fatty meats among my breakfast smells and flavors.

Since then, I have learned to enjoy coffee with iddlies in Madras, and deep-fried stick bread with frothing bean soup on the Taiwan-held island Quemoy. I have acclimatized myself to elaborate Korean breakfasts, featuring perhaps fifteen different dishes and including that spiciest of condiments, kimchi — cucumber and other vegetables pickled in garlic and red pepper. I still think that "meeting real people" should be the highlight of anyone's visit to any country. But I know now that real people include presidents and pedicab drivers, ladies of fashion and housewives, peasants and factory workers and captains of industry, with all the gradations in between.

If breakfasts are tests of one's adaptability to societies where shaking the head may mean yes, or a hailing gesture taken as one of farewell, it may be because breakfasts are generally such simple, unpretentious occasions, where no one dresses up for company, where the day is too fresh to be complicated with ritual and make-believe. A breakfast is an honest meal, and those who enjoy it, wherever they may be, are honest people.

— Takashi Oka for *The Christian Science Monitor,* Apr 15, 1980. Peking.

*****

Things in China were changing quickly in those first few years. One day I saw that the newsmen on TV had switched from wearing the traditional blue "Mao" jacket to a Western suit and tie. There was also a sense of recovered freedom about traditional Chinese art forms like the Peking theater and opera, which had been suppressed during the Cultural Revolution.

Only a few years before, the cultural norms of the country had been dictated by the "Gang of Four," an all-powerful group within the Communist party, led by Mao's wife Jiang Qing. She had been the Chairman's fourth wife and twenty years younger than he. I interviewed the Chinese writer Ding Ling, who had been imprisoned for five years, at the express orders of Jiang Qing. He told me that she had been an actress in early years and that she was bored and felt trapped in her relationship with Mao. She had even tried to stage plays for herself, but Mao had refused. Instead, she and the other three members of the "gang" controlled the artistic tastes of the 800 million citizens of China. As one intellectual told me at the time, there were only eight approved revolutionary plays for the entire country.

After Mao's death in 1976 and the decline of the Revolution, Jiang Qing was labeled a traitor, and by 1980, she was on trial for treason. I was in the audience in the courtroom.

Mao's widow at center stage in China trial

'Gang of four' trial open to restricted audience

A proud, lonely woman stood at the bar to face a battery of 35 judges, many of them once her victims. Jiang Qing, Mao Tse-tung's widow, was brought to trial with nine codefendants Nov. 20 before a special court at No. 1 Zhengyi Lu (Justice Street).

Madame Mao (or Miss Jiang as she is called here) looked composed and conscious that she was the star of the occasion as she entered the crowded courtroom escorted by a bailiff and took her place beside her codefendants. She was dressed simply, in a black Mao suit, her jet black hair combed straight back.

In human terms her story is the story of a would-be Joan of Arc who ended up in the public mind as a witch.

Can she have a fair trial, as the current Chinese leadership promises? "I cannot predict the results," says Ding Ling. "The people have great anger against the 'gang of four.'"

Jiang Qing is said to have shown an actress's facility for remembering names and dates, and her entire defense is said to be based on the contention that whatever she is accused of doing was done on the orders of Chairman Mao himself.

To what extent the authorities, who accuse her of crimes (as distinct from the "mistakes" committed by Mao) will allow the public access (through television and newspapers) to what she has to say for herself, remains to be seen. The trial is open only to 880 selected spectators from all over China.

— Takashi Oka for *The Christian Science Monitor,* Nov 21, 1980. Peking.

I noted that the Chinese referred to her actions as "crimes" and to Mao's actions as "mistakes," because, to the Chinese people, Mao was still a great figure. If they repudiated Mao, they would have to disavow some of the fundamental tenants of Communism. So the official line was that he had been misled by people underneath him, while Jiang Qing was evil from the beginning. She was the scapegoat.

Jiang Qing's defiance in the courtroom reminded me of Marie Antoinette. She had lost all of her power, but her sense of superiority never left her – she looked down on the judges and prosecutors as if they were still her minions. She was not going to beg for mercy.

* * * * *

Even though we were being monitored very closely by the Chinese authorities, Beijing was different from the Soviet Union and its satellites. But I remember one instance that was similar to Moscow. There was a Chinese journalist for the *People's Daily* who was one of the first to speak frankly about the political reality in China. Then he disappeared without a trace, only to resurface some months later.

As a journalist, I knew how far one could go with the authorities, but, like everyone else, I tried to push these limits a little bit. After all, the Communist party couldn't monitor our thoughts. But several of my colleagues, among the crowd of Western journalists in Beijing, did push the limits, and were immediately censored. Graham Earnshaw was a British correspondent (and a great singer) who had several run-ins with the Chinese authorities, as did Tiziano Terzani, an Italian who wrote for *Der Spiegel*. Tiziano got into a number of scrapes – once when he went swimming in the sea, against the express orders of our Communist chaperones. John F. Burns was a Canadian correspondent for the *Toronto Globe and Mail* who showed up a few years later. He left, then came back to China with *The New York Times* around the same time that we were leaving, and he was arrested driving a motorcycle and charged with being a spy.

Frank Ching, who opened the Beijing bureau of *The Wall Street Journal*, wrote a book called *Ancestors: 900 Years in the Life of a Chinese Family*. Over such an enormous span, you see a repeated cycle of repressions and censorship – for instance, against Buddhist monks during the Qing dynasty. So what we were experiencing then was, in a way, a part of this larger cycle.

* * * * *

I spent most of my time in Beijing, but as the political situation continued to change over the years, Hiro and I were able to travel quite a bit by ourselves. We usually had an official guide or translator traveling with us, but not always – sometimes we were allowed to check in with an official after we got to our destination. This was also my first assignment since we'd had children where the children were not with us, since Mimi went to Harvard in 1977, and Saya was in boarding school before going to Berkeley in 1981. So it was just me and Hiro again.

Xi'an (Chang'an) was the former capital of the Tang Empire and a big tourist attraction. We went there and to Chengdu, which is the airlines' connection point for Tibet. Towards the end of our stay in China, we traveled to Lhasa with a group of journalists. The food we were served was somewhat insipid. A few of the correspondents complained, and Hiro got mad at them. She said if they didn't like it they shouldn't have come. What did they expect? The Tibetans didn't have that much themselves to eat. The situation was pretty bad when we arrived in Lhasa, but not terrible. We could see the Tibetans moving around at the central shrine and praying. Some were on their hands and knees, showing their respects – the way to accumulate virtue was by making laps around the temple. But we saw Chinese soldiers, too. When we left Tibet, we were searched all over for any unauthorized written material – they forbade self-published texts written in Chinese. That kind of censorship differed from year to year and even from month to month, and after we left things grew worse for Tibet.

We went to Shanghai, Suzhou, and Yangzhou, with a

translator in tow. One time we were driving by ourselves, when we passed by a Christian church, on a narrow street in some village not too far from Xi'an. It just happened to catch our eye. We stopped and asked the locals about it, and they said there would be a service the next day. So Hiro and I planned to stop by again the following day. But that night, our official guide came to us and, having already gotten wind of our inquiries, warned us not to go. He told us that if we tried to attend the service, then he would certainly be punished. So we didn't go back.

*****

Beijing was cold and dry, with winds swirling in from Mongolia. There was very little rain, so the roads were always dusty. By the time I arrived in 1979, the big commercial and industrial centers – especially Shanghai – already had serious pollution problems. This was one part of the many complex transitions China was trying to navigate at that time, and we could see the change unfolding – the development of industry and finance, literacy and schools, and battles about freedom of speech. On the one hand, the Chinese wanted to absorb all the latest technology. On the other hand, they wanted to filter out whatever was threatening to the Communist regime. They were experimenting – and, in its relations to China, so was the West. The cities were expanding rapidly, and the Chinese were trying to develop Beijing in a more planned way. But the best laid plans of mice and men often go awry.

Peonies and politics of Peking's spring

```
A young friend of mine, a senior in a
provincial university, was recently told
by his girlfriend, also a senior, but at a
university in Peking, that she no longer
```

wished to marry him. The two have known each other since childhood. ''When you graduate this summer,'' the girl told him, ''you are hardly likely to be assigned a job in Peking. As for me, I don't know where I will be assigned either, but there is almost no chance we will be given jobs in the same city."

This girl's parents had to live apart for 21 years, because her father was an engineer, her mother a biologist. Both had roots in Peking, but neither was given appropriate work in the capital. Her father was assigned to an institute in a mid-Yangtze valley city, her mother to a university south of Peking
''I don't want to have that kind of a marriage,'' the girl told her fiance when she broke their longstanding engagement. Yet this is precisely the kind of marriage that many Chinese workers, particularly professional people, must lead. People cannot freely choose their jobs. They must accept jobs assigned to them by the state. Changing jobs requires such a daunting process of red tape that many people simply do not bother.

— Takashi Oka for *The Christian Science Monitor,* May 5, 1982. Peking.

Because of tradition and standards of living, the intellectual elite was concentrated in three large groups - one cluster around Beijing, another around Shanghai, and one around Guangzhou (Canton). But most of the major companies started their people off in the provinces, and these people had to keep traveling around, working their way up, until eventually they might live in one of the big cities. It was bureaucratic and difficult to keep people together, but that was the system. Under Communism, the bureaucracy was organized on what had already existed for at least a thousand years, when the Mongols had established an imperial government.

When Deng Xiaoping came to power, he tried to change this. Having led modern China after Mao and out-maneuvering the Gang of Four, he was – I believe – one of the world's most extraordinary leaders. By 1989, he was stepping down and trying to ensure a smooth transfer of power to his successor. But he was having difficulties with the "old regime" of bureaucracy – military leaders like Marshal Ye, who was in his eighties and who opposed promoting younger men to various levels of the party. The old regime clung to their positions of power – they all had relatives and hangers-on, and just by presuming on that relationship they sometimes managed to keep their power. But Deng and others gradually stripped the substance of power from those positions. The high officials were allowed to keep their official cars, big red limousines modeled on a Cadillac – but their role turned into more of an honorary position. The administrative layer disappeared, and the real power descended to the civil and party bureaucracy. I interviewed several of these generals who were retiring, and after a while they all asked me if I knew how to help them to retire in the United States.

* * * * *

By 1982, I was still covering the major political events in China – including the 1980 visit to Peking by Reagan's running-mate George H. W. Bush – but I also wrote about what was happening in the arts. I reviewed an avant-garde play by the Peking People's Art Theater, which was staged in a banquet hall. The following year, Arthur Miller came to China to direct an all-

Chinese production at the Capital Theater. The play, of course, was his famous critique of American capitalism, *Death of a Salesman*. Miller didn't speak Chinese, and only one member of the cast spoke English – Ying Ruocheng, a founding member of the People's Art Theater who played Willy Loman, and who also interpreted for his director.

China was officially trying to revive its intellectual class in these years, although the focus was mainly on people with technical expertise – scientists, engineers, economists, statisticians, etc. Chinese artists and writers still had to tread carefully.

> ***China invokes great writer's name in crackdown on arts***
>
> China's communist leaders have chosen the centennial of their country's greatest modern writer to call for sharper criticism of writers and artists who have "published gravely erroneous views."
>
> In his day, Lu Xun (1881-1936) fought for freedom of artistic and creative expression against warlords and the Kuomintang government of Chiang Kai-Shek. Author of the bitingly satirical "Diary of a Madman" and "The True Story of Ah QM," Lu Xun looked to the communist to free China from centuries of feudalism and the encroachments of the Western powers and Japan.
>
> Today, using carefully selected quotations from Lu Xun, the party leadership is trying to justify its effort to impose ideological conformity

> on workers in literature, publishing, and journalism. Party chairman Hu Yaobang delivered the party's message Sept. 25 before an audience of 6,000 gathered to honor Lu Xun's memory in the Great Hall of the People.
>
> "While fully affirming the main trends of our literature and art, we must point out that it still has certain unhealthy, negative features which harm the people."
>
> — Takashi Oka for *The Christian Science Monitor*, Sep 29, 1981.

Any reasonable person would criticize the atrocities of the Cultural Revolution. At its height, it was kids running amok – burning books and theaters, humiliating their teachers by forcing them to wear dunce caps and demeaning slogans, and also outright murder. Those people who were kids back then were still around, and some of them were still in power, and they didn't want to be reminded of what they had done. So the authorities saw works by people like Bai Hua – at whom Hu Yaobang was directing his message that day – as a criticism of themselves.

I traveled back to Japan at the end of 1983 to cover Nakasone's reelection, and I made brief trips back to South Korea to cover the ongoing crisis there, but mostly I stayed in Beijing. I covered Reagan's visit to China in 1984, as well as Nakasone's visit that same year. And I continued to interview Chinese dissidents, including Ai Qing, in 1983. Ai Qing had been imprisoned, tortured, and exiled at various points in his life, but he is now regarded as one of the finest Chinese poets of the 20th century – although his son Ai Weiwei is now more famous.

1984, Premier Zhao visited the US, in what many people

saw as a maturing in Chinese-American relations.

> This is no longer the season for Mr. Deng to be photographed wearing a cowboy hat in Texas, but rather for Mr. Zhao to be probing the secrets of California's Silicon Valley. They seem to be convinced that the Western world is about to experience a new industrial revolution, and this time they want to position their country so it can catch and ride this new wave...
>
> — Takashi Oka for *The Christian Science Monitor*, Mar 12, 1984. Peking.

...and that is exactly what happened.

Chapter 16

Tokyo – *Newsweek* and Television

After five years in China, I was invited to help create the first Japanese edition of *Newsweek*. Up to that point, the magazine had only been published in English, and its executives figured that they could reach a larger audience in Japan. So Hiro and I moved back to Tokyo, and I started with *Newsweek* in 1985.

At that time, the Japanese publishing world was organized into monthly and weekly publications. The monthlies were usually serious and had rather long articles, while the weeklies catered to the more sensational and ephemeral. In contrast, we wanted to establish a serious weekly. That had never been done before in Japan, so we reckoned that there would be room for it in the Japanese market.

Katharine Graham, who also owned the *Washington Post*, was the strong and gracious owner of *Newsweek*. Enticed by the idea that *Newsweek* could steal a march on its big rival *Time*, she came to Tokyo and began working with me and a small team. The innovation of the model, as well as the concept of a foreign-language edition, intrigued Graham and kept her involved at the center of the project.

At the beginning of this pioneering process, *Newsweek's* representative Fay Willey wanted the magazine to be as exact a copy of the English language version as could be. Indomitable and self-confident, Fay Willey was also my co-editor and had to vet everything. But she didn't speak or read Japanese, so she had to take on faith what she was told. I tried to allay her fears, but she was still rather suspicious, leading to occasional flareups. But generally we got along, and I think she did trust me.

I was in a position to crisscross between the Japanese and American sides of the project. The American side included Kay

Graham's boy genius Al Smith, who was only about 30 when he became the head of *Newsweek*. He was a big tall guy, prematurely balding, who flew airplanes as a hobby. Kay was always worried that he would crash his plane, but flying was his only chance to get away from her.

On the Japanese side was Keizo Saji, the heir to the Suntory fortune, who had started a publishing venture that was investing in the new edition of *Newsweek*. Also working for me was Tatsuo Naka, whose father was a journalist for the Kyodo news agency, and another bright Japanese clerk named Suitsu.

Having worked for many years as a reporter, I enjoyed seeing the business end of things. It was an interesting time for me, but not without difficulties. Both Saji and Kay were strong-willed. Saji came from the Japanese culture where people are always giving each other presents, and he would give Kay all these rare whiskies, for which the Suntory distillery was famous. Although Kay came from a wealthy family herself, it took her a while to become accustomed to Saji. I remember one time he sang the old western song *Rawhide*, before an audience that included Kay and Al – a masterful performance, brimming with self-confidence.

The Japanese edition of *Newsweek* was launched in 1986 and was a modest success. *Time* and other publications were skeptical that *Newsweek* would be sustainable, but the new weekly created a niche for itself – not very large, but modestly profitable. The boldness of the new concept worked, and we made it a truly international magazine.

My commitment to *Newsweek* was for two years, which I extended for a while after. By 1987, I was back writing for the *Monitor* on a regular basis.

* * * * *

Newsweek had been a new and interesting experience for

me, but I was happy to be back at the *Monitor*, working at my normal pace again, and traveling from time to time. From 1987 to 1989, I made several trips to South Korea, covering the student protests in Seoul and the run-up to the Olympic games.

In 1987, Noboru Takeshita was elected Prime Minister of Japan, and I wrote a three-part series on the departing "charismatic king of Japanese politics" Nakasone and his legacy. I had interviewed Nakasone several times and knew him well. He had been a friend of Reagan and of Thatcher, and he had led Japan through its rich years, creating a huge trade surplus with the US. Although, in October, I had to cover the "Black Monday" stock market plunge, which began in Hong Kong and quickly spread to Japan, Europe and the US.

Around this time, the Christian Science church began to proceed with one of the most ambitious plans in its history – a foray into television.

* * * * *

News in Two Tempos: Con Brio and Serioso

Television news or, if you will, information programming has come to a crossroads. One sign points in the direction of entertainment, complete with ever more breezy hosts and livelier graphics. The other road leads to a more traditional brand of journalism, its emphasis on clear, simple, reliable reporting....

"USA Today: The Television Show"... is determined to provide information in an entertaining manner.... It seems abundantly clear that the show will hew to the

> concept heralded recently by Allen Neuharth, chairman of the Gannett Company, for USA Today, the newspaper: "To satisfy your mind without stimulating or testing it too damned much."
>
> "World Monitor," on the other hand… is attempting nothing less than to provide a whole and balanced picture of the world….
>
> But the sense of substance is unmistakable….
>
> No flashy graphics. No pop music. No aggressively ingratiating hosts. The sheer integrity of "World Monitor" is invigorating.
>
> — John J. O'Connor, *The New York Times*. September 20, 1988.

Hiro and I were still in Japan when the church began laying the groundwork for this multimedia venture, which included radio and would culminate in a 24-hour cable news program called The Monitor Channel. While the expansion into television would roil the church in controversy for many years, it was a project that Hiro and I experienced from afar, removed from the eye of the storm in Boston.

Jack Hoagland was the entrepreneurial figure who launched the TV channel. At the time, he was manager of the Christian Science Publishing Society, which published the *Monitor* and the church's other periodicals. In the 1950s he had been a Sovietologist at the CIA, and he was a Yalie – I remember he was always singing songs from the Whiffenpoofs. In 1986, Jack enlisted Hiro to help him start the television venture in Japan.

At first, Hiro worked as a liaison, introducing the

Monitor's executive staff to Kyoto, but soon she was helping assemble an international conference, via live satellite broadcasts, connecting Boston, Sao Paulo, London, and Tokyo in the spring of 1986. After a couple of weeks of preparation, the *Monitor* was able to connect all the parties working on the other three continents for a live television conference. Impressed by Hiro's business acumen, Jack hired her as the Business Manager for the TV channel in Tokyo. Hiro was very efficient, particularly in managing the relationship with NHK, the Japanese national broadcasting company.

The *Monitor* relied heavily on Hiro for her business connections. At first she worked closely with an independent production company run by Bruce MacDonald and Kyoko Kato. As the *Monitor's* needs grew, Kyoko introduced Hiro to a Mr. Aoki at NHK, who then introduced her to NHK's president, Mr. Shima, who at that time was an all-powerful figure – everyone called him "the emperor (*tenno*) of NHK." Shima gave the green light, and the *Monitor* established a strong relationship with NHK's subsidiary, called NHK Enterprise. Hiro said that one of the reasons that the connection worked so well was that the *Monitor* was a good customer – it was paying a lot.

They spent about a year preparing for regular television broadcasts, with Hiro traveling to the US quite often. She organized the production in Japan from beginning to end – hiring TV producers, cameramen, sound, assistants, securing locations, and negotiating with NHK. Two years later, in 1988, the The Monitor Channel finally launched.

In September 1988, I was on camera for *World Monitor News*, the first broadcast for Monitor TV, with a report on the pro-democracy demonstrations in Burma, live from Tokyo via satellite. That first broadcast also featured a report from Chile about Pinochet by the *Monitor's* expert on Latin America, James Nelson Goodsell, who was a fellow graduate of Principia. The anchor for the show, John Hart, was a pro from NBC. It was broadcast live from the *Monitor's* headquarters in Boston, in partnership with The Discovery Channel.

As the channel continued, we relied on our connections with NHK Enterprise in producing the segments from Japan. We rented a space on NHK's property, and they gave us access to their equipment and facilities. In Tokyo, we had a staff of about thirteen. One of the most important figures in those early days was Sandy Socolow, the savvy CBS senior producer who had worked closely with Walter Cronkite, and who taught me a great deal about television reporting.

The first broadcasts were weekly. I would write the Asian news stories, and Hiro would coordinate most of the logistics, which were quite complicated. When I was writing for the paper, I could be anywhere, but television requires on-the-spot images, from Tokyo to Brazil. So now I had to think in terms of visuals when I wrote. NHK helped us with this too by letting us use their footage.

At first we focused on Japan. We did a story on Tadashi Suzuki, the great Japanese actor who was famous for his training methods. He had a studio theater in Toyama on the Japan Sea. It was much easier to show Suzuki on TV than to try to describe his methods on paper, so we did live interviews. We went on to interview people all over Japan, and eventually farther away – to Mongolia and elsewhere.

In retrospect, I don't know how we managed to do it, because I had no previous TV experience. Hiro has a level head, but she was also relatively new to the television industry. I had faced a camera only a couple of times before. In 1958, I had appeared in a short documentary film for the *Monitor* called *Assignment: Mankind*, and there had been a few other things like that along the way. But it was not something I had been trained to do.

Later, I hosted a series produced by NHK for the Monitor Channel called *The Silk Road,* which ran for several dozen episodes. For that series, they filmed me in a studio in the Peabody Essex Museum in Salem, Massachusetts. I found that television seemed to agree with me, and I had a good time doing it.

* * * * *

In 1992, it became clear that The Monitor Channel could not continue. In March, the editors suddenly got word that all operations related to the Monitor Channel were cancelled. After four years on the air, the television venture was over.

I was surprised at how suddenly it happened. Hiro had said that a few days before the directors announced that they were going to pull the plug, she had arranged a lunch with Hoagland and NHK. She said no one said a word about it then. Hoagland already knew it was finished, but he didn't tell anyone else.

As I mentioned, the expansion into television was controversial within the church, but this memoir is not the place to address that.

After the Monitor Channel shut down, Hiro continued as a business manager, extracting the *Monitor* from the various positions it had gotten into. And I was glad to still have work with the newspaper – I stayed on writing opinion pieces for another five years. By 1992, I had been working for the *Monitor* for forty-four years, and although I could have retired, I was happy doing what I was doing. So I didn't particularly want to retire. I knew Japan, and I was comfortable there. Had they had wanted me to go back to China or Russia, it would have been a different story.

The First Gulf War didn't have a tremendous impact on Japanese society, other than the fact that the US was borrowing money from Japan to pay for it. The bigger events of that time – the collapse of the Soviet Union, Tiananmen Square – had all been covered while I was working for the Monitor TV Channel. In fact, Hiro and I had been on vacation in Indonesia when Tiananmen happened. We were with our good friends Nick and Sheila Platt (Nick was ambassador to the Philippines) and Inger and her second husband Oz Elliott, and there were some anxious moments as we tried to telephone Oz's daughter, who was a journalist stationed in China. We were relieved to hear she was safe.

I traveled to the US frequently in the mid 1990s, covering various topics, including GM's new Saturn car. In my London years, I had visited the Rolls Royce workshop in the rolling farmland of Crewe, England, and here I was in the cornfields of Spring Hill, Tennessee, examining the US effort to imitate the Japanese.

Hiro was taking care of her parents in Tokyo during these years, while I was flying back and forth to the US to visit my Aunt Kiyo, who was living in a retirement home in New Jersey. Aunt Kiyo stayed in New Jersey until she died in 2004 – she lived to be 102. Hiro's father passed away in 1993, and her mother in 1995. Two years later, we moved to Washington DC.

Chapter 17

Washington DC

I had wanted to be the Washington correspondent back in 1979, before we went to China. Now I had the opportunity to live and work there. We had friends in DC, the politics were always interesting, and there were cherry blossoms in the spring. I think the cherry trees in DC are prettier than in Japan because they take very good care of them – they take the old trees out periodically and replace them with new ones.

The articles I wrote for the *Monitor* during these years tended to focus on a global picture, because the daily, petty politics of Japan were not of much interest to the outside world. But it was also around this time that I started writing about a Japanese politician named Ichiro Ozawa. I had worked with him for a while in Japan and knew him quite well. Ozawa was interested in the British electoral system as a model for Japan, which until then had large electoral districts, with two to five people elected from each district. Ozawa preferred the British style, which has smaller districts, with only one representative per district. Eventually he was successful, and today Japan has only one seat per district.

I retired from *The Christian Science Monitor* in 2002, but I continued to contribute articles from time to time.

Then I went to Oxford and began my doctoral studies on the history of Japan. I wrote my thesis on Ozawa's efforts to import the British electoral system. Classes at Oxford were on a schedule of three eight-week terms per year, with holidays in between, and I could audit any classes I wanted. Hiro came too, and we rented a flat on Banbury Road, a five-minute walk from St. Anthony's College. On the weekends, we took trips into London to see plays and go to restaurants, and we made the most of our time there. I got my PhD in 2008.

Since then, I have written an article here and there for the *Monitor*. My most recent piece was on November 17, 2010, about President Obama and the shift in global power over the last half century.

* * * * *

Looking back over my sixty-two years with the *Monitor*, I would say that I attempted to be responsible, according to my own standards of what was right and wrong. Every journalist is bound, to some extent, to the standards of the newspaper for which he or she is writing, and *The Christian Science Monitor's* standard informed my writing. If I was writing about a problem like environmental pollution, then I tried to call attention to what could be done to make it better – a kind of "purposeful reporting" that has been inherent to the *Monitor's* mission since its founding.

There's always been a contradiction in that mission, because the *Monitor* is a newspaper reporting the news of the day, and yet it is a newspaper with a specific viewpoint, which speaks to "purposeful reporting." All of us who worked there knew that we were reporting for a newspaper that had to compete against *The New York Times* and *The Wall Street Journal* and everyone else. But over the years, the way the *Monitor* has tried to compete is by supplying news that is accurate and truthful, and that also expresses a viewpoint consistent with the teachings of Christian Science. Because I am a Christian Scientist, I embraced that viewpoint.

Acknowledgements

I would like to express my deep appreciation to the following friends and former colleagues who helped clarify my thoughts, thus helping me shape and write this memoir: Louisa Campbell, Judith Huenneke, Clayton Jones, Judith Matloff, Daniel Sneider, Barry Shlachter, and Ben Williams.

This memoir is also dedicated to my wife Hiro, whose stalwart support, both moral and logistic, in sickness and in health, has carried me through these many years. And also to the next generation, my children, and grandchildren, Mimi and Jun, Kazuma and Takuma, Saya and Luc, Miyé and Morio, and my brother Akira's children, Jun, Midori and Kimiyo. All of them, while continuing to navigate the world between Japan and America, are extending their lives far beyond, thus fulfilling my mother's legacy to raise global citizens.

Articles Cited from *The Christian Science Monitor*

"Japan's Outcasts – Freedom Now?" 10/22/1979
"Japan – Feudalism's Echo" 10/23/1962
"A Japanese Grandmother" 5/14/1974
"A Time for Women – and Change" 6/23/2006
"A Father's International Flair" 4/30/2009
"My Link to America, My Best Friend" 10/2/2000
"A Bond Between Cultures – Tane Matsukata's Students Learn to Forget Their Differences" 11/4/1982
"Taro's War: Memoir of a Japanese Torn Between Two Worlds" 11/19/1981
"A Meeting that Set the Course of My Life" 9/25/2003
"A Golden Bridge Between Worlds" 10/23/2002
"Letter from Tokyo: Postwar Trends" 7/8/1948
"Laos: Little War, Big Implications" 12/14/1960
"How is Peking Faring?" 8/15/1962
"Dual Task for Regime: The War and Democracy" 11/4/1963
"Minh Stakes Out Saigon's Goals" 11/13/1963
"Seventh Fleet: Role Punctuated" 8/4/1964
"Hanoi Offers Its Version" 8/6/1964
"U.S. Heartens Asian Allies" 8/7/1964
"Peking, Hanoi: Next Step?" 8/10/1964
"After Tonkin: Hanoi-Peking Moves Studied For Clues to Southeast Asia Stance" 8/18/1964
"A Casual Visit With the Viet Cong" 3/2/1966
"Moscow Slaps Peking 'Revolution'" 9/19/1966
"Funnel for Soviet Dissent" 4/4/1972
"Red Purge: Soviets Pursue Attacks on Dissidents in the Arts" 4/26/1968
"The Spring of Free Speech" 7/9/1968
"The Reischauer Shock" 5/27/1981
"Symbol of a Japanese Dilemma" 11/19/1974
"Lettre de Noel: Paris Glitters" 12/23/1971

"Torture Degrades" 4/7/1972
"France – Breeding Ground for Racism?" 10/15/1973
"Queen's Visit to France Celebrates End of Political Frigidity" 5/15/1972
"They Promised Him the Mona Lisa" 10/1/1973
"To Israel, Issue is Survival" 10/16/1973
"First Talks Follow Mideast Cease-fire" 10/29/1973
"Appetite of the Wealthy" 6/19/1974
"Secrecy Still Wraps Kissinger-Tho Talks" 12/7/1972
"From a Signing Into the Unknown" 1/29/1973
"Kissinger Reassures an Uneasy Europe" 6/12/1973
"Friends of Whales Fish for Compromise Acceptable to All" 6/26/1975
"What Life Has Become in Belfast" 8/27/1976
"Killing of Neave Casts Shadow on British Campaign" 4/2/1979
"Margaret Thatcher: The Woman Who Could Become Britain's Next Prime Minister" 4/17/1975
"Britons' Patience With Strikes Wears Thin" 2/8/1979
"Margaret Thatcher" 5/1/1979
"Strolling at the Queen's Tea Party" 7/27/1978
"Attenborough: BBC's Man About the World" 10/10/1975
"American Takes the Bicentennial to Europe" 10/15/1975
"Britain's Race Rumblings" 3/6/1978
"Keeping the Queen's Peace" 12/15/1977
"South Korean Dissidents: One Generation Later" 8/24/1979
"China's Everyman has to Scramble for Basics" 11/14/1979
"Dissent is a Divisive Issue for Peking Leaders" 11/20/1979
"Morning Exotica" 4/15/1980
"Mao's Widow at Center Stage in China Trial" 11/21/1980
"Peonies and Politics of Peking's Spring" 5/5/1982
"China Invokes Great Writer's Name in Crackdown on Arts" 9/29/1981
"Peking Promotes China-US Ties as Vital to Asia Peace" 3/12/1984

Articles cited from *The New York Times*

"Okinawa Mon Amour." Takashi Oka, 4/6/1969
"Table Tennis Captain – Jack Howard." Takashi Oka, 4/10/1971
"The Emperor Who Meets the President Today." Takashi Oka, 9/26/1971
"Japan Hails Dawning of Age of 'Hair.'" Takashi Oka, 12/9/1969
"'Scarlett,' Musical, And Star Cheered By Tokyo Audience." Takashi Oka, 1/3/1970
"Bernstein, in Tokyo, Assays Japanese Character." Takashi Oka, 9/10/1970
"Nobel Prize Stirs Interest in Japanese Literature." Takashi Oka, 10/29/1968
"Everyone in Japan Has Heard of Him." Philip Shabecoff, 8/2/1970
"Renowned Author Raids Military, Ends Life." Takashi Oka, 11/25/1970
"Japan Fears Reaction Abroad to Writer's Suicide." Takashi Oka 11/26/1970
"Mishima: A Man Torn Between Two Worlds." Philip Shabecoff, 11/26/1970
"Review/Television; News in Two Tempos: Con Brio and Serioso." John J. O'Connor, 9/20/1988